D1196560

The Motion Aftereffect

The Motion Aftereffect

A Modern Perspective

edited by
George Mather
Frans Verstraten
Stuart Anstis

A Bradford Book
The MIT Press
Cambridge, Massachusetts
London, England

This book was set in Palatino on the Monotype "Prism Plus" PostScript Imagesetter by Asco Trade Typesetting Ltd., Hong Kong and was printed and bound in the United States of America.

Library of Congress Cataloging-in-Publication Data

The motion aftereffect : a modern perspective / edited by George
  Mather, Frans Verstraten, Stuart Anstis.
     p. cm.
  "A Bradford book."
  Includes bibliographical references and index.
  ISBN 0-262-13343-1 (hardcover : alk. paper)
   1. Motion perception (Vision) 2. Neuropsychology. 3. After-
images. I. Mather, George. II. Verstraten, Frans. III. Anstis,
Stuart
QP493.M68   1998
612.8'4—dc21   97-52191
                                                    CIP

Contents

Preface

This book is concerned with a visual illusion that is without doubt one of the most striking phenomena known to vision science. It is generally known as the motion aftereffect (MAE), and refers to the illusory movement of a physically stationary scene following exposure to visual motion. For example, if one stares for a while at a stationary point while a textured pattern drifts across the field of view (e.g., a rock located in the middle of a waterfall), then for a short while after the movement stops, or after one's gaze is transferred to a stationary pattern (e.g., the scenery surrounding the waterfall), apparent movement is seen in the direction opposite to the previous motion. First reports of the phenomenon are very old, dating back at least two thousand years to the ancient Greeks. Aristotle (1955) noticed the effect after viewing rapidly moving water (in his case a river). An easy way to generate an MAE today is to slowly rotate a straw table mat or patterned plate for a short time (30 seconds should suffice) while gazing steadily at its center. After the mat or plate is stopped suddenly, it will appear to rotate in the opposite direction for a few seconds. Despite the apparent simplicity of the phenomenon, careful and detailed research over many years has revealed a surprising degree of complexity in the underlying mechanisms, and has taught some general and important lessons about how visual information is processed by the brain.

History of Science

We can gain some insight into the long history of scientific research on the MAE from the list of references cited in the three major reviews that have appeared in this century: Wohlgemuth's (1911), Holland's (1965), and this book. The upper plot of figure P.1 shows the number of papers cited in each review as a function of publication year. During the 86 years between the publication of Wohlgemuth's first cited reference (1825) and the publication of his own monograph, only fifty-three cited papers were published. In most years no papers were published at all, and in only 5 years during this period did the number of cited papers published exceed

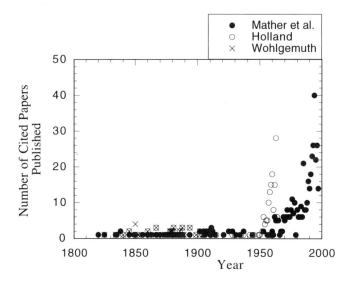

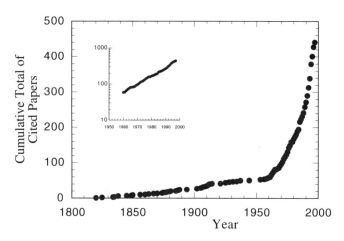

Figure P.1

Publications relating to the motion aftereffect (MAE) over the last 200 years. The upper plot shows the number of papers published per year, as revealed by citations in the three major reviews of MAE research that have appeared this century: Mather et al. (this book); Holland (1965); and Wohlgemuth (1911). The lower graph is a cumulative plot by publication year of papers cited in this book. Up to 1960, the number of publications grew linearly (main plot), but since 1960 growth has been exponential (i.e., linear on log-linear axes; inset plot).

two. The scarcity of published reports may explain why the phenomenon was rediscovered so often during the nineteenth century (another factor undoubtedly was that several reports were in German). Wohlgemuth was ploughing an almost virgin field. Single-handed, he at least doubled our knowledge of the MAE. The low publication rate continued right up to the early 1960s, judging by the papers cited in Holland (1965) and in this book. Since then there has been an explosion of interest in the MAE.

A cumulative plot of references cited in this book by date (lower part of figure P.1) shows that cited publications grew linearly up to about 1960, with an average of just one new paper appearing every 2 years. Since 1960 publications on the MAE have grown exponentially (see inset in lower plot of figure P.1), in keeping with the pattern for scientific publications generally since journals were founded (de Solla Price 1963). The number of MAE-related papers published doubles about every 12 years.

Why was there such an explosion of interest in the MAE only at the start of the 1960s? The foundations of our knowledge about the visual system had been laid many years before. The neuroanatomy of cells in the visual system had been first described at the end of the last century (Ramón y Cajal, 1892). The importance of the visual cortex, and its topographic organization, had been known since early this century (largely from examination of soldiers who suffered head wounds in the Russo-Japanese War; see Glickstein, 1988). However, even in the 1950s, David Hubel (1988) recalls "looking at a microscopic slide of visual cortex, showing the millions of cells packed like eggs in a crate, and wondering what they could all conceivably be doing, and whether one would ever be able to find out" (p.4).

In the late 1950s and early 1960s Hubel and Torsten Wiesel (Hubel and Wiesel, 1959, 1962) were, of course, able to find out just what the cells were doing by measuring their electrical discharges in response to visual stimuli, using microelectrode recording techniques developed by Hartline (1940), Kuffler (1952), and Barlow (1953). We can thus trace the upsurge of interest in the MAE to the birth of modern neuroscience. Once hard information became available on the electrophysiology of individual brain cells, new theories sprang up relating the activity of these cells to perceptual experience. Some of the earliest discoveries were of cells that respond selectively to visual motion (Hubel and Wiesel, 1959). A possible link with the MAE was very soon identified (Sutherland, 1961) and a flood of scientific research ensued, which continues today unabated. The MAE has thus been at the heart of modern neuroscience since its inception. Unfortunately, Holland's (1965) review appeared too early for him to appreciate the impact of the new electrophysiologic data. His monograph contains no references at all to it, or to the new theoretical approach to the MAE.

The modern flow of research is such that half of all the citations in this book are to papers published in the last 12 years. As de Solla Price (1963) points out, this "peculiar immediacy" of science means that "so large a proportion of everything scientific that has ever occurred is happening now, within living memory." Consequently we can justifiably claim that research on the MAE is largely a modern phenomenon and the aim of this book, as its title suggests, is to assess the current state of knowledge in this important area of neuroscience. Its contributors, active researchers in the field from many different laboratories, have themselves played a major role in shaping the modern conception of the MAE.

Before leaving the realm of what might be called "metascience," it is worth noting the bias that figure P.1 shows toward the recent, evident in Holland's (1965) review. Fully half of the papers he cited were written within the 7 years preceding his book. Yet most of those (1958–1965) papers have now fallen by the wayside, and all too few of them have survived to be quoted in this book. The "recency peak" tells us that the overall growth of the literature is even greater than that evident from the number of papers cited in this book. Clearly, many papers have not survived very long in the reference lists. Clinical applications of the MAE were popular in the 1960s (e.g., for the assessment of personality disorders), a trend that was well represented in Holland's review. However, this branch of MAE research has since atrophied, as more specialist clinical tools have emerged.

Each of the chapters in this book concentrates on a specific set of issues relating to the MAE , including experimental paradigms, empirical results, and theoretical explanations.

Scope of the Book

Although the MAE was first mentioned by Aristotle, it was first described in detail only in the 1800s—by Purkinje (1820, 1825) and by Addams (1834). In chapter 1, Nicholas Wade and Frans Verstraten recount early discoveries of the MAE, and give a review of some basic concepts surrounding the effect.

How should we measure the MAE? Wohlgemuth (1911), and many others since, simply measured the duration of the MAE with a stopwatch. More sophisticated methods have now come into play. It would be very convenient to be able to null out the MAE with real motion, but the problem is that the MAE makes a stationary test pattern paradoxically appear to drift without changing its position. Theoretically, this suggests that motion-sensitive channels have adapted, but that position-sensitive channels have not. In practice, any moving test objects do change their position, so do not provide an effective null. One nice solution is to use a mixture of drifting plus twinkling random dots (Newsome and Paré, 1988). The larger the proportion of randomly twinkling dots, the lower the signal-to-noise ratio (SNR). Blake and Hiris (1993) discovered that an observer could null an MAE by adjusting the ratio of drifting to twinkling dots in a test pattern. Allan Pantle provides more details in chapter 2, and discusses the thorny problem of "reactivity" (the act of measuring the MAE with a particular test stimulus itself influences the phenomenon).

When measured using luminance gratings, the MAE, like most after-effects, shows some tuning since it is stronger for some spatial frequencies than for others. This is true both for the adapting and the test spatial frequencies. The consensus seems to be that the MAE is strongest when the test and adapting spatial frequencies are the same, and when these differ by one octave the MAE falls to about half. Yet an MAE can be seen perfectly well when the eyes are closed, so no test structure is necessary! This paradoxical finding suggests that the MAE may have two components, one very short-lived and very broadly tuned for spatial parameters. It provides interocular transfer, so it must involve binocular cells. The other component is long-lived, spatially tuned, and probably monocular, since one can induce opposite MAEs in the two eyes (see Favreau, 1976). As for temporal tuning, an adapting frequency of 5 Hz seems to give the strongest MAEs (Pantle, 1974). "Velocity aftereffects" can be examined by making the test field move in the same or the opposite direction to the adapting motion, instead of using a stationary test field. Usually, test motions equal to or slower than the adapting motion are apparently slowed, while test motions faster than the adapting motion are apparently speeded up. Test motions opposite in direction to the adapting motion are also generally slowed. This pattern of results could be described as "velocity repulsion." The MAE can show the little understood phenomenon of "storage", such that its decay is arrested if the eyes are closed immediately after adaptation. Studies of tuning are reviewed by Peter Thompson in chapter 3. He assesses the extent to which they have shed light on the underlying mechanisms of the MAE.

A favorite teaching demonstration which undergraduates enjoy is to ask them to adapt one eye to a rotating pattern, and then to view a static test pattern with their other eye. Typically they report "interocular transfer" of the MAE, but at about half-strength. Moulden (1980) explained this rather well in terms of pools of monocular and binocular cortical neurons. Studies of the binocular and interocular properties of the MAE, discussed by Moulden, Patterson, and Swanston in chapter 4, reveal the close links between binocular vision and motion perception.

Addams's (1834) waterfall, or the drifting striped gratings used so often in modern research, provide a nice simple motion stimulus. But in the real world, or even in the laboratory, things are not always so simple. What happens when two adapting fields move in different directions, either viewed in alternation or else seen sliding transparently over each other? Can "second-order motion" of texture-defined borders give rise to an MAE? Can attention modulate the MAE? Are the different MAEs generated by static and by dynamic test patterns consistent with a single mechanism? Jody Culham and her many co-authors comprehensively survey these questions, and the implications of the answers, in chapter 5.

A physiologic explanation of the MAE first became possible in the early 1960s when motion-sensitive cells were found in the cortex of cats. In primate brains, motion and direction selectivity are found in the magnocellular stream passing through area V1, and are also found in the middle temporal visual area (MT), otherwise known as V5. Lesions in area V5 can cause motion blindness, as in the woman who could not judge when to stop pouring a cup of tea (Zihl, von Cramon, et al., 1983). It appears that V1 cells may sense local moving contours, while cells in MT put the information together, solving the aperture problem to see moving objects (e.g., Adelson and Movshon 1982). A large number of electrophysiologic and evoked potential studies of motion adaptation are reviewed by Michael Niedeggen and Eugene Wist in chapter 6.

Sutherland (1961) was the first to propose a ratio theory of the MAE, pointing out that the direction in which motion is seen depends upon the ratios of firing of cortical cells sensitive to movement in different directions. Cells that had viewed prolonged motion would fire less readily, so that apparent motion in the opposite direction would be perceived. Instead of attributing the MAE to an imbalance between opposed motions, Mather (1980) proposed that motion sensors tuned to all directions around an imaginary two-dimensional clockface are involved in direction coding, and all contribute to the MAE. In addition, the MAE may involve adaptation at multiple neural sites within the visual system. What is the function or purpose of the MAE? Is it the result of a weakness or design fault in the visual system, or does it have a biological value for the organism? Since the MAE involves a misperception of the world, it would seem maladaptive, so why has it survived? New theories suggest that adaptation is not a weakness but rather a method for ensuring that the visual system maintains proper calibration given its very variable visual diet. All of these theoretical issues are assessed by George Mather and John Harris in chapter 7.

The Motion Aftereffect

Chapter 1

Introduction and Historical Overview

Nicholas J. Wade and Frans A. J. Verstraten

1.1 The Basic Phenomenon

Motion perception is now at the heart of visual science, but it was not always so. In antiquity there was an appreciation of the thresholds of motion: some objects changed their position but did not appear to move (like the sun) and others moved too quickly to be seen (like shooting stars). However, relatively little attention was paid to other aspects of visual motion until the dioptrics of the eye had been adequately described in the seventeenth century. The motion phenomena that were remarked upon prior to that time were those in which there was some conflict between vision of the same objects under different circumstances. Induced motion and the motion aftereffect (MAE) were two such instances.

The MAE refers to the modification of motion perception following prolonged observation of a regularly moving stimulus. Typically, the MAE involves the apparent motion of a stationary stimulus in the opposite direction to a previously observed one, but it can also result in a change in the apparent velocity of a moving stimulus. A more specific definition may be found in chapter 2. The study of the perceptual consequences of prolonged stimulation has a long history, but prior to the early nineteenth century it was confined principally to afterimages and color phenomena, and rarely included motion (see Wade, 1996). Indeed, it could be argued that the MAE was in the vanguard of modern research on visual motion. It has been variously called the aftereffect of seen movement, the movement aftereffect, successive motion contrast, and the waterfall illusion. Many of the major figures in visual science in the nineteenth century added to knowledge about the MAE, and it is now seen as a tool for linking the psychology of vision to its underlying physiology. A new type of dynamic stimulus, comprised of a matrix of computer-controlled moving dots, has directed attention to different cortical sites of motion processing, which are being investigated with modern imaging techniques. Despite the contemporary tone of such research, the MAE puzzled ancient as well as modern scholars.

Figure 1.1
Aristotle (ca 384–322 B.C.) after an illustration in Hekler (1912).

1.2 Ancient Reports

In the natural environment, objects, like the stones on the bank of a river, could appear stationary at one time and moving at another—following fixation on flowing water. In his book on dreams, Aristotle (ca 330 B.C., figure 1.1) described the MAE in just such circumstances: "when persons turn away from looking at objects in motion, e.g., rivers, and especially those which flow very rapidly, they find that the visual stimulations still present themselves, for the things really at rest are then seen moving" (Ross, 1931, p. 459b). There has been some debate about whether Aristotle either did not report on the direction of the MAE or reported its direction incorrectly. Verstraten (1996) compared a number of different translations from the Greek text and several interpretations of this section from Aristotle, and concluded that while the MAE itself was described, its direction was not adequately specified. The MAE is a successive phenomenon, whereas induced motion occurs simultaneously. Induced motion also displays a mismatch between the perception of the same objects under different conditions: a stationary object appears to move in the opposite direction to those moving around it, like the apparent motion of the moon when clouds pass by it. Almost three centuries after Aristotle, Lucretius (ca 56 B.C., figure 1.2) described both induced motion and the

Figure 1.2
Lucretius (ca 98–55 B.C.) after an illustration in Wood (1885).

MAE direction: "when our spirited horse has stuck fast in the middle of a river, and we have looked down upon the swift waters of the stream, while the horse stands there a force seems to carry his body sideways and pushing it violently against the stream, and, wherever we turn our eyes, all seems to be rushing and flowing in the same way as we are" (1975, p. 309). Verstraten (1996) compared different translations from the Latin and concluded that Lucretius was the first known writer to have specified the direction of the MAE. The reports of both Aristotle and Lucretius were in the context of water flowing in a river, and a critical nineteenth-century description of the phenomenon was following fixation on descending water in a waterfall.

Unlike most other visual phenomena described by Aristotle, the MAE did not become a staple entry in subsequent texts on optics. One possible reason for this could have been that it was not described by Ptolemy in his *Optics*, written in the second century. Ptolemy's *Optics* influenced those of Ibn al-Haytham (Sabra, 1989; Howard and Wade, 1996; A. M. Smith, 1996), who in turn influenced the medieval *Perspectiva*s of Bacon, Pecham, and Witelo, which provided the basis for Kepler's inquiries in the seventeenth century. By contrast, induced motion was described by Ptolemy and by Ibn al-Haytham, and it has a much more continuous history than the MAE (see Wade, 1998).

Figure 1.3
Jan Evangelista Purkinje (1787–1869) after a photogravure in Stirling (1902).

1.3 Rediscoveries in the Nineteenth Century

There do not seem to be any other descriptions of the MAE until early in
the nineteenth century when it was rediscovered frequently. The two
most notable accounts were by Purkinje (1820, 1825, figure 1.3) and by
Addams (1834). Purkinje first briefly described the MAE in an article concerned with vertigo: "Another form of eye dizziness can be demonstrated
if one observes a passing sequence of spatially distinct objects for a long
time, e.g., a long parade of cavalry, overlapping waves, the spokes of
a wheel that is not rotating too fast. When the actual movement of the
objects stops there is a similar apparent motion in the opposite direction"
(1820, pp. 96–97). He amplified one aspect of the MAE in a subsequent
book, and this is more frequently cited: "One time I observed a cavalry
parade for more than an hour, and then when the parade had passed, the
houses directly opposite appeared to me to move in the reversed direction to the parade" (1825, p. 60). Purkinje specified the direction of the
illusory motion, and he interpreted it in terms of involuntary eye movements over the houses. A few years later Robert Addams (about whom
very little is known; see Wade, 1994) observed at the *Falls of Foyers*
(see figure 1.4) in northern Scotland what later became called the waterfall
illusion. This was a noted, though remote, cascade visited in the eigh-
teenth century by Dr. Johnson on his Highlands tour and celebrated in

Figure 1.4
An engraving of the lower Fall of Foyers from Beattie (1838).

verse by both Robert Burns and William Topaz McGonigall. Addams (1834) described the waterfall illusion thus: "Having steadfastly looked for a few seconds at a particular part of the cascade, admiring the confluence and decussation of the currents forming the liquid drapery of waters, and then suddenly directed my eyes to the left, to observe the vertical face of the sombre age-worn rocks immediately contiguous to the water-fall, I saw the rocky face as if in motion upwards, and with an apparent velocity equal to that of the descending water" (p. 373). The full text of Addams's brief but insightful article can be found in Dember (1964) and in Swanston and Wade (1994).

Despite the fact that Purkinje's book was well known in Germany, and that Addams's article was translated into German (Addams, 1835), both were often overlooked by German sensory physiologists, and the MAE was rediscovered independently several more times (see Wade, 1994). Some of the rediscoveries were in the context of flowing water (Müller, 1838; Oppel, 1856; Aitken, 1878). Traveling on the railways also provided a platform for observing MAEs (Brewster, 1845; Helmholtz, 1867/ 1925; S. P. Thompson, 1877), and S. P. Thompson extended the MAE to depth as well as direction: "Thus, if from a rapid railway train objects from which the train is receding be watched, they seem to shrink as they are left behind, their images contracting and moving from the edges of the retina towards its centre. If after watching this motion for some time the gaze be transferred to an object at a constant distance from the eye, it seems to be actually expanding and approaching" (1877, p. 32). MAEs in the third dimension were examined more systematically by Exner (1888) and von Szily (1905). S. P. Thompson (1880) did make reference to Addams's report and was probably the first to refer to the phenomenon as the "waterfall illusion" (p. 294).

Addams (1834) appreciated that the waterfall illusion could be investigated experimentally, and he suggested that the motion of falling water could be simulated in the laboratory by moving stripes, but this was not put into practice until Oppel (1856) reached the same conclusion independently. Oppel had experienced the MAE initially at the dramatic *Rheinfall* at Schaffhausen, and this stimulated his interest in it. A few years earlier, Plateau (1849, 1850; figure 1.5) stumbled across the MAE in the course of conducting experiments using the phenakistoscope (or stroboscopic disk). He had been studying the effects of rotating patterns on perception and noticed the motion visible in stationary objects following prolonged exposure. He introduced the stimulus employed most widely throughout the second half of the nineteenth century—a black disk with a white Archimedes spiral on it—which became called the *Plateau spiral* (figure 1.5). Plateau described the MAE in the following way: "If the disc rotates in the direction indicated by the arrow, and one looks at it with

Figure 1.5
Plateau's spiral as illustrated in Plateau (1849), together with a portrait of Plateau after an engraving in the catalogue for the exhibition, Het wetenschappelijk en cultureel erfgoed van Joseph Plateau (1801–1883), held at the University of Ghent in 1996.

the eyes fixed on the centre for a time sufficiently long, but not long enough to tire the eyes, then one immediately directs the eyes to another object, such as the face of a person, for example, one experiences a singular effect: the head of the person appears to shrink for some time. If the disc is turned in the opposite direction, the resulting effect is opposite: it is as if the head of the person appears to expand" (1849, p. 257). The description is all the more remarkable because Plateau was blind at the time of writing it (see Verriest, 1990).

Many of the nineteenth-century studies of MAEs used the Plateau spiral, or some variant of it, like concentric counterrotating spirals (Dvorak, 1870). Other stimuli were introduced, however, some of which have a remarkably contemporary ring to them. Oppel (1856) constructed an instrument for producing continuous linear motion of parallel stripes. Bowditch and Hall (1881) added a further modification to the moving stripes, surrounding them with stationary ones (figure 1.6). It was with such a stimulus that Wohlgemuth (1911) carried out many of his experiments.

Linear motion in two directions simultaneously was examined by Exner (1887) and by Borschke and Hescheles (1902). Horizontal and vertical gratings were moved vertically and horizontally, respectively, behind a circular aperture. Exner (1887) reported that the motion seen during adaptation was in a diagonal direction, with an MAE in the opposite diagonal. Borschke and Hescheles (1902) developed the stimulus further with sets

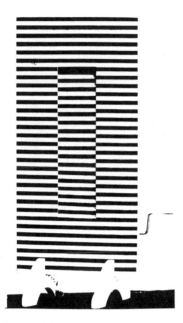

Figure 1.6
The apparatus employed by Bowditch and Hall (1881) for studying the MAE.

of vertical and horizontal rods: they systematically changed the relative velocity of the two components, thereby modifying the direction of the resultant vector and also of the MAE.

The sectored disk was described independently by Wundt (1874) and by Aitken (1878), although it was by no means as widely used as Plateau's spiral. Those employed by Aitken (1878) and by S. P. Thompson (1880) are shown in figure 1.7, together with Thompson's spiral. Rotating sectored disks continue to be used in experiments, and they are particularly good for demonstrating the paradoxical aspect of the MAE: following inspection the stationary sectors appear to rotate but not to change position.

1.4 Landmark: Wohlgemuth (1911)

Nineteenth-century studies of the MAE were reviewed by Wohlgemuth (1911) in what remains the most comprehensive single article on MAEs. The monograph was the first of those published by the British Psychological Society, and it composed his thesis for a doctor of science at the University of London. His mentor was William McDougall, who was also a subject in some of the experiments, as were Spearman, Read, Flügel, and

Figure 1.7
The sectored disks developed independently by Aitken (1878) and S.P. Thompson (1880),
together with S. P. Thompson's spiral.

Sully. Wohlgemuth's historical survey was chronological, and he repeated
many of the previous studies before reporting thirty-four experiments
of his own. However, there were some oversights in his survey. While
he mentioned Aristotle's account, he omitted reference to Lucretius;
Purkinje's 1825 description was given, but the earlier one of 1820 was
overlooked. Addams was mentioned at length, but his name was short-
ened to Adams! This error has resurfaced frequently in those reports
which have relied on Wohlgemuth rather than the original account.
Wohlgemuth confirmed many aspects of previous experiments showing
that: motion over the retina is necessary to generate an MAE; the
strength of the MAE is more marked with fixation; the MAE is restricted
to the retinal area stimulated by prior motion; it immediately follows

adapting motion and its visibility improves with practice; an MAE can be produced in each eye independently and what is seen with two eyes is a combination of the two monocular adaptations; adaptation of one eye transfers to the other; MAEs can be produced by a wide range of speeds, and by stroboscopic as well as real motion; following adaptation, motion can be seen with the eyes closed. This last distinction was referred to as the MAE in the subjective field (with the eyes closed or viewing a homogeneous surface) as opposed to the objective field (when viewing a stationary test pattern). The aftereffect in the subjective field was of shorter duration and it was phenomenally different from that in the objective field: "At no time does there appear to be such a rapid or tumultuous streaming in the objective field as in the subjective" (Wohlgemuth 1911, p. 31). As such, it is closely linked to the "streaming phenomenon" that can be seen during or after fixation on geometrically repetitive patterns (see Wade, 1977).

Wohlgemuth's first experiment demonstrated that the MAE is more readily visible in the objective than in the subjective field and, after its dissipation, it can be revived briefly by blinking. Moreover, if the eyes remained closed for a period longer than the MAE would normally last, then it was still seen on opening the eyes. This is now called *storage* of the MAE, and it is discussed more extensively in chapters 3 and 5. He also found that the MAE is more marked with a well-illuminated stimulus; it occurs with indistinct moving contours; its strength increases with spatiotemporal frequency, and is related to the velocity of the adapting motion; a stronger MAE is seen with square-wave than with rectangular-wave gratings; the MAE can be added to real motion; its initial velocity is comparable to that of the adapting motion; it occurs with both light- or dark-adapted eyes; it has different characteristics following adaptation of central and peripheral retina; an MAE is not seen if the adapting motion involves the whole visual field, but it does occur with motion over very small visual angles; following opposite simultaneous or successive motions over the same retinal area the motion observed is the resultant of the component MAEs; MAEs are restricted to the orientation of lateral motion; it does not require attention; and it does not occur for touch.

Wohlgemuth drew attention to the paradoxical feature of MAEs: "I hold that in an objective movement we have two factors, viz. (a) the experience of movement proper, similar to the after-effect, and (b) the change of position in space.... The after-effect is different from the experience of seeing an objective movement, in that the latter contains two components (a) and (b), as described above, whereas the after-effect contains (a) alone" (1911, pp. 108–109). This characteristic of MAEs has created problems with regard to its measurement, since it cannot be readily canceled by real motion. On the other hand, the possibility exists that it might provide a means of measuring a pure motion system in vision. Indeed, this was appreciated early by Bowditch and Hall (1881): "We cannot resist raising the question whether we may not be here very near the quale of real, pure sensation" (pp. 300–301).

Wohlgemuth classified the previous interpretations into physical, psychic, and physiologic. Eye movement explanations were considered to be physical; they had been proposed by both Purkinje and Addams, but they could not accommodate the occurrence of oppositely directed MAEs visible simultaneously. Wohlgemuth devoted most attention to the physiologic interpretations, particularly that advanced by Exner (1894), which is shown in figure 1.8. This model has been acclaimed as the first representation of a neural network (Dierig, 1994), although Alexander Bain had presented one some 20 years earlier (see Wilkes and Wade, 1997). Exner's model was expressed in terms of influences on eye muscles, but it could be interpreted more generally. The symbols a–f denote units receiving input from retinal receptors, which will be stimulated in succession, dependent on the direction of motion. Prolonged stimulation in a given direction (e.g., a–c) will lead to the fatigue of the summation cell E, but not of Jt; this imbalance will be displayed when a stationary stimulus is subsequently viewed. Wohlgemuth raised certain problems with Exner's model, and modified it slightly by incorporating inhibition as well as excitation (figure 1.9). Wohlgemuth's model was greatly influenced by McDougall, who was in turn in thrall to Sherrington's (1906) theory of integration within the nervous system. Exner was also the source of inspiration for a similar, but more generally stated, analysis of motion presented by Stumpf (1911; see Todorovic, 1996). Both Wohlgemuth and Stumpf presented precursors of Reichardt detectors (Reichardt, 1957), although Wohlgemuth formalized the model more fully.

1.5 Clinical Correlates and Observer Variables

Wohlgemuth did not pursue motion perception further but turned to emotion and clinical psychology; in 1923 he wrote a trenchant critique of psychoanalysis in which its scientific credentials were questioned. Research published at the time Wohlgemuth's article was in press has been neglected. This applies not only to Stumpf (1911) but more particularly to several studies by Basler (1909, 1910, 1911), who devised a novel way of measuring the phenomenon—by asking subjects to move a lever to represent the velocity of perceived motion. He also demonstrated that an MAE could be seen in a stationary pattern if motion had been induced in it by a moving surround. The next reviews of MAEs were in articles by Durup (1928) and Gates (1934), but a major survey was undertaken

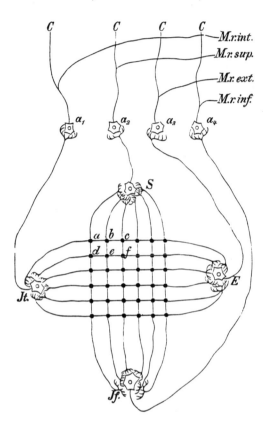

Figure 1.8
Exner's (1894) diagram and physiologic interpretation of the MAE: "Schema for a centre of optical motion detection. *a–f* and the analogous points are the locations at which the fibres from the retinal elements enter the centre. The cells *S, E, Jt* and *Jf* represent centres to which each and every point of excitation arrive and where they can be summated. The time required by the excitations to reach there from any one of these points would be approximately proportional to the distance given in the diagram. a_1–a_4 are centres which are closely related to, or perhaps identical with, the nuclei of the external eye muscles (only four are shown in the schema: M. rectus internus, superior, externus and inferior). *C* are fibres to the cortex, the organ of consciousness" (p. 193).

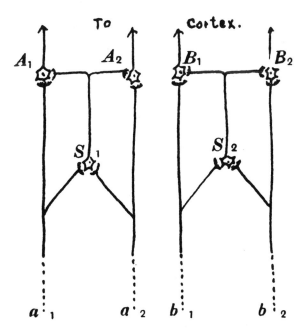

Figure 1.9
Wohlgemuth's (1911) model of motion detection: "Let a_1, a_2 and b_1, b_2 be connected retinal elements in a straight line and adjacent or nearly so. These elements are connected with series of neurones, as indicated by the dotted lines, giving off collaterals to the various centres of brightness, of colour, perhaps of 'local sign,' etc. Also a branch, as indicated by the drawn outline, towards a 'subcortical centre of movement,' consisting of summation-cells A_1, A_2, B_1 and B_2, etc., that pass their excitations on to the cortex, the organ of consciousness. Now, if a physical stimulus passes across the retina in such a direction that the stimulation takes place in the direction a_1, a_2 , etc., a_1 becomes first stimulated. The excitation passes on to A_1 and also to the 'Schaltzelle,' S_1. From S_1 two paths are open to the innervation, viz. towards A_1 and A_2. But the resistance at the synapse S_1–A_1 has been lowered owing to the direct excitation of A_1 from a_1, so by far the greater part of the excitation from S_1 will pass on to A_1 and comparatively little to A_2. Then a_2 is stimulated and the excitation passes on towards A_2 and S_1. Here, however, the resistance at the synapse S_1 is lower than at the synapse A_2, hence most of the excitation from a_1 passes on to S_1, and thence, for the same reason, to A_1. In other words, by the successive stimulation of a_1 and a_2, A_1 becomes more strongly excited than A_2.... If now the movement stops suddenly, then there is no difference in the excitations reaching A_1–A_2, B_1–B_2, but A_1 and B_1, being more fatigued than A_2 and B_2, owing to the previous excessive stimulation, send off less innervations to the cortex than these, and my theory is then that this fact of A_2 and B_2 having now more tonus than A_1 and B_1 constitutes the subcortical condition of an apparent movement in the opposite direction" (pp. 99–100).

by Holland in a book published in 1965, which was concerned principally with his experiments on the spiral MAE. Holland was influenced by Eysenck's theory of cortical inhibition, and so concentrated on the use of the spiral MAE as a tool for its measurement. His interests in applying the MAE to exploring the mysteries of vision seemed limited, since he stated that their "psychophysical aspects appear to be pretty straightforward" (1965, p. 94)! Only nine studies published between 1911 and 1950 were cited by Holland (although his survey was not exhaustive). The period between 1950 and 1965 saw a shift of emphasis from stimulus determinants of MAEs to its use as a tool for assessing personality differences and brain damage. Of the seventy-nine studies between 1950 and 1963 cited by Holland, well over 50 percent were concerned with the effects of brain damage, drugs, or personality on the MAE. Despite this resurgence of interest in spiral MAEs, Holland, in the preface to his book, expressed the dangers in expecting too much of it: "The mid-twentieth century emphasis on the use of the spiral after-effect in the diagnosis of brain pathology and the delineation of individual differences has been both a boon and a curse. On the one hand it has led to a large number of investigations and to the clarification of hitherto obscure sources of variance. On the other hand, however, it has been asked to do too much and risks the danger of becoming the deadest of all things—a psychological test which failed to live up to expectation" (1965, p. x). In general, it must be said that the other hand won! Subsequent research has focused on more specific correlates of brain activity, like dopamine levels and MAEs (see J. Harris, 1994).

In addition to the clinical application of spiral MAEs the phenomenon has been employed to assess characteristics of binocularity within observers. These inquiries started in the nineteenth century, and they continue to be used for this purpose. Dvorak (1870) reported that an MAE generated with only one eye open can be seen with the other eye; a translation of Dvorak's article may be found in Broerse, Dodwell, et al. (1994). Many early studies confirmed Dvorak's observation of interocular transfer: differences between monocular and interocular MAEs were remarked upon but not quantified until this century. Interocularly transferred MAEs are about 50 percent of monocular MAEs (Wade, Swanston, et al., 1993), although there are differences in the value according to the stimulus used (Heller and Ziefle, 1991; Steiner, Blake, et al., 1994; Symons, Pearson, et al., 1996). Interocular transfer of color-contingent MAEs can be difficult to measure (J. P. Harris and Potts, 1980). In common with other spatial aftereffects, little or no interocular transfer of MAE has been reported in stereoblind observers (Mitchell, Reardon, et al., 1975), although doubts have been cast on this relationship by Mohn and van Hof-van Duin (1983); the degree of interocular transfer has been used as an index of any residual binocularity (Moulden, 1980; Ziefle, 1992). Exner (1887, 1888) generated opposite MAEs in each eye (both with rotation and with linear motion); he found no MAE when viewing a stationary test pattern with two eyes, but opposite ones when viewing with each eye separately. This result has been confirmed several times, and theories of spatial aftereffects have become increasingly concerned with aspects of binocular combination (e.g., Moulden, 1980; van Kruysbergen and de Weert 1993, 1994). Contemporary approaches to issues of binocularity are elaborated on in chapter 4.

1.6 The Revolution in the Sixties

Use of the spiral aftereffect as an index of arousability or brain damage continued after Holland, but its pace abated. However, as Holland's book was being published the MAE received the impetus for its most intense phase. Barlow and Hill (1963) interpreted the waterfall illusion in terms of visual processing by single cortical cells, providing substance to support the earlier speculations by Sutherland (1961) as to its cause. Neurophysiologists had demonstrated that single cells in the visual cortex extracted features of stimuli, such as orientation, motion, and retinal disparity. The cortical neurons responded to edges moving orthogonally to their orientation; many responded more strongly to movement in one direction than to that in the opposite direction, and so have been called motion detectors. Consider what happens when an observer looks at the rocks by the side of a waterfall: the stationary rocks will have many contours which will stimulate motion detectors. For example, horizontal contours will excite different motion detectors for downward and upward movement, but the net effect of these would cancel. When the waterfall is observed, the downward motion detectors will be strongly stimulated, and if this stimulation is prolonged, the motion detectors will adapt or fatigue—that is, their rate of firing will decrease. Subsequent observation of the stationary rocks will produce a different net effect: the adapted downward-motion detectors will exert less influence than the unadapted upward-motion detectors. Therefore, the signal from the rocks would be similar to one produced by contours moving slowly upward, which corresponds to what is seen (figure 1.10).

The MAE, together with other spatial aftereffects, became designated the psychologists' microelectrode, because inferences regarding neural processes could be based on psychophysical experiments (see Frisby, 1979). This approach proved to be a tremendous stimulus for studies of MAEs: not only could the nature of motion detectors be inferred but speculations regarding their binocular combination could also be entertained (see Barlow, 1990). Between 1963 and 1993, almost 400 studies on

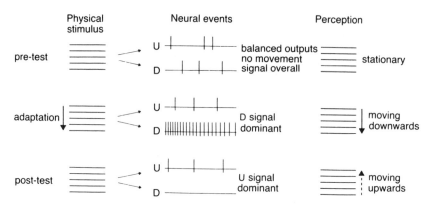

Figure 1.10
An interpretation of the motion aftereffect in terms of adaptation of cortical motion detectors (after the manner proposed by Barlow and Hill, 1963). In the pre-test a stationary grating will excite motion detectors for upward (U) and downward (D) directions equally; the net activity will favor neither, resulting in its stationary appearance. During adaptation the downward direction detectors are strongly excited resulting in a neural signal for that direction, which is reflected in perception. In the post-test a stationary grating is presented again, and the downward-direction detectors (having been adapted) are not responsive; the upward detectors signal as before, but since there is no equivalent output from the downward detectors the net activity signals upward motion, and the stationary grating is seen as ascending. (Adapted from Wade and Swanston, 1991).

MAEs were published (see Wade, 1994). Subsequent developments in both stimulus manipulation and in neural modeling find their parallels in experiments on MAEs (see chapter 6).

There are some similarities in Barlow and Hill's interpretation and earlier ones advanced by Exner (1894) and Wohlgemuth (1911). They speculated that eye movement centers that are sequentially stimulated can become fatigued, and provide the basis for MAEs. Exner's interpretation was extended by Wohlgemuth (1911), and it is taken as the precursor of modern motion detector interpretations (Frisby, 1979). Barlow and Hill (1963) suggested that MAEs "may result from the temporary imbalance of the maintained discharges of cells responsive to motion in opposite directions" (p. 1346). This ratio model has been modified into a distribution-shift model by Mather (1980) because adaptation to motions in orthogonal directions results in MAEs that are in the opposite direction to the resultant (see also Borschke and Herscheles, 1902; Exner, 1887, 1888; Riggs and Day, 1980). The site for such adaptation effects has been the subject of further inquiry using drifting plaids, and Wenderoth, Bray, et al. (1988) have argued that there are extrastriate contributions to the MAE. A similar conclusion follows from experiments on MAEs from second-order motion (Ledgeway and Smith, 1994a).

Since the mid-1960s MAE research has relied to a great extent on the classic ratio model, largely because of its simplicity and logical appeal (Mather, 1980). A strict ratio model (in terms of the relative activity of oppositely tuned detectors) now seems rather unlikely. Although Mather's distribution-shift model is not as well formalized, it accounts for many more aspects of the phenomenon. However, the biggest challenge to the classic ratio models—the MAE of transparent motion—does not necessarily rule out a ratio mechanism. There is ample evidence that there are different origins (gain controls) along the path of visual motion processing. It is not unlikely that the perceptual manifestation of motion adaptation (the illusory motion that is experienced) is an integration or a combined output of several gain controls which, at a local individual level, might act as predicted by the classic ratio model (see also chapter 7).

One feature of ratio models that has not received much attention is the fact that a ratio mechanism requires a reasonable baseline activity: neural activity cannot fall below baseline activity when there is none. Various alternative models have been proposed. For example, Cornsweet (1970) presented a recurrent inhibition model; this has the problem of assuming the equivalence between suppression of a motion detector's output and driving a motion detector tuned to the opposite direction. A functional magnetic resonance imaging (fMRI) study by Tootell, Reppas, et al. (1995) showed an interesting result that might shed some light on this problem. They found that after adaptation when the subject was presented with a stationary test pattern, the middle temporal area (MT/V5) remained active for a while, indicating that the MAE might be a result of "real" instead of "relative" activity (already reported in electrophysiologic studies by Petersen, Baker, et al., 1985). Although there are some ideas of how this could be implemented (e.g., Grunewald and Lankheet, 1996) the underlying mechanism is still subject to debate (see chapter 6).

1.7 Stimuli and Measurement

Rotating spirals have remained a popular stimulus for MAE studies during this century, but their complexities, both in terms of the perceptual effects elicited (Hunter, 1914) and of the motion vectors generated (Broerse, Dodwell, et al. 1992), have led to the more widespread use of simpler stimuli. Moreover, there is a marked asymmetry in the spiral MAE: following observation of an apparently contracting spiral the MAE seen in a stationary spiral is stronger than that following apparent expansion (Wohlgemuth, 1911; Scott, Lavender, et al. 1966).

The stimuli most favored for research on spatial vision since the mid-1960s, sine-wave gratings, have been widely adopted for experiments on MAEs (see chapter 2). Pantle (1974) produced an MAE with drifting sine-wave gratings, Keck, Palella, et al. (1976) demonstrated that MAE magnitude increased with contrast up to about 3 percent; its duration depended upon the contrast of the test grating (Keck and Pentz, 1977), and the MAE displayed spatial frequency specificity (Cameron, Baker, et al., 1992). Orthogonal drifting sine-wave gratings (plaids) yield MAEs in the direction of the resultant (Wenderoth et al., 1988). A further division of motion stimuli into first- and second-order stimuli has been proposed: first-order stimuli have spatiotemporal variations in luminance or color, or both, unlike second-order stimuli, which are defined by relative motion or contrast (see chapter 5). Mather (1991) reported that weaker MAEs are produced by second- than by first-order stimuli, but this would appear to depend on the test stimuli employed (McCarthy, 1993).

Random-dot stereosequences have been used to create cyclopean motion which yields an MAE after adaptation (Papert, 1964); the MAE requires relatively long periods of adaptation, can transfer to non-cyclopean stimuli, and is best elicited by dynamic test patterns (Patterson, Bowd, et al., 1994). Dynamic patterns, such as random-dot kinemato-grams, have been adapted for use in MAE studies (Hiris and Blake, 1992; Raymond, 1993a, b, 1994; Steiner et al., 1994; Wist, Gross, et al., 1994). These stimuli typically consist of an array of (say 100) dots each under computer control; the directions of motion can be random or biased so that a defined percentage move in a particular direction. Following adaptation to coherent motion (all dots moving in the same direction), a random-dot kinematogram appears to move in the opposite direction, and the proportion of dots moving in the adaptation direction required to make the test appear stationary can be determined. The MAE measured with dynamic test stimuli differs in a number of respects, like duration and interocular transfer, from that tested with stationary stimuli (see chapter 5).

It was mentioned in section 1.3 that Exner (1887) and Borschke and Hescheles (1902) used stimuli that could be described as constructed from two superimposed gratings. One grating moved vertically and the other horizontally behind a circular aperture. This would now be called a plaid (see Adelson and Movshon, 1982). The MAE following such stimulus motion is opposite to the perceived direction during the adaptation period, which is unidirectional. This aftereffect is readily explained by the classic ratio model. However, in the 1980s a variant of this kind of stimulus became popular; it is known as transparent motion or motion transparency. It refers to the visibility of two motion directions or speeds in the same part of the visual field. The surprising finding was that even if two motion directions were perceived during the adaptation phase, the MAE was unidirectional (Mather, 1980). For orthogonal motion directions the resulting MAE direction was the inverse of the vector sum of both inducing patterns (e.g., van Doorn, Koenderink, et al., 1985), a finding which challenges the classic ratio model. As a consequence, Mather introduced the distribution shift model: he proposed that not only is the activity of oppositely tuned motion sensors taken into account but also the activity of motion sensors tuned to all directions. Adaptation to orthogonal motion then results in a shift of the relative activity toward the non-adapted sensors, which is the perceived direction of the MAE of transparent motion.

Recently, more information has become available about the nature of this process. Verstraten, Fredericksen, et al. (1994a) showed that the MAE direction from transparent motion can be predicted from the motion sensitivity of the visual system to the individual speeds. Moreover, the MAE is not always an integrative phenomenon. For example, if depth from disparity is introduced between the two adapting patterns, it is possible to generate a transparent MAE: the patterns are segregated during adaptation as well as during testing (see Verstraten, Verlinde, et al., 1994d).

The influence of color on MAEs has emerged as a source of interest because of the suggestion that color and motion might be processed in different pathways (Ramachandran and Gregory, 1978). It has been examined in two ways: by making color and motion contingent upon one another and by the use of isoluminant stimuli. Following adaptation to motions in opposite directions, illuminated with different colors, Hepler (1968) found that a moving pattern in white light appeared in the color complementary to that presented during adaptation; and Favreau, Emerson, et al. (1972) found that the direction of motion changed with the color of the illuminant of the stationary test pattern. A variety of other contingent MAEs have been reported (Mayhew and Antis, 1972). Isoluminant borders are differentiated by color rather than brightness, and it has been suggested that motion perception is degraded under these conditions. However, both Mullen and Baker (1985) and Cavanagh and Favreau (1985) measured robust MAEs at isoluminance.

The measurement of MAEs has always proved problematic because of their paradoxical nature. The phenomenal characteristic of them that is so evident—how long they last—has been the most commonly employed measure of MAE strength. It was introduced by Oppel (1856), although he did not give any values; he did remark that the durations differ between individuals. Aubert (1886) reported MAEs lasting as long as 30 seconds following adaptation to linear motion, but he also found wide variations in the durations for the same observer. Despite the ready availability of a convenient measure, relatively few nineteenth-century studies made quantitative comparisons between MAEs observed under experimental conditions: most reported the presence or absence of the phenomenon and described its intensity verbally. While duration is the easiest aspect of

MAEs to report in the initial stages, it does introduce problems when the MAE has dissipated; determining when motion has ceased can be difficult. Nonetheless, MAE duration does correspond reasonably well with other measures (Basler, 1909; Keck et al., 1976; Heller and Ziefle, 1990). Duration was the principal measure used by Wohlgemuth, although he also derived ratings of vividness and speed. The duration of MAEs increases nonlinearly with adaptation times up to 15 minutes (Hershenson, 1989); apparent velocity declines exponentially (Taylor, 1963) and it can be very difficult to determine when motion in the test pattern ceases. The duration of MAEs can be described by the square root of adaptation time up to 90 s (Hershenson, 1993).

Cords and Brücke (1907) introduced a nulling method for measuring the velocity of MAEs following linear motion—low-contrast stripes could be moved in the same direction as previous motion until they appeared stationary. Basler (1909) measured the velocity of MAEs by manual tracking. The problem with nulling techniques is that they use real motion to cancel paradoxical motion: any nulling stimulus would involve displacement as well as motion, whereas the MAE appears to move without displacement. The nulling problem does seem tractable with random-dot kinematograms because the appearance of the region adapted to coherent motion can be matched with one adapted to random motion (Blake and Hiris, 1993). Kleiner (1878) reported that an MAE added to a real movement in a different direction, and such combinations were commented on anecdotally in several nineteenth-century studies. Peter Thompson (1981) confirmed this relationship with drifting sinusoidal gratings and proposed that MAEs are velocity-specific. A related approach to measurement derives from direction-specific threshold elevation: adaptation to a drifting grating raises the contrast threshold for a grating drifting in the same direction, but not for gratings moving in the opposite direction (Pantle and Sekuler, 1969; McCarthy, 1993); displacement thresholds are also elevated following adaptation (Stadler and Kano, 1970).

1.8 Interpretations

The earliest interpretations of the MAE were in terms of eye movements (Purkinje, 1820; Addams, 1834; Helmholtz, 1867/1925) despite the logical difficulty of accounting for the phenomenon in this way: any aftermovement of the eyes would affect all contours in the visual field, rather than being restricted to regions exposed to prior motion. Mach (1875) pointed to the problems associated with eye movement interpretations and the difficulty they would have in accounting for radial motion seen in the spiral MAE. Kleiner (1878) rotated a central sectored disk in the opposite direction to two adjacent ones, and reported oppositely directed MAEs that were visible simultaneously. Eye movements can be discounted experimentally because the MAE occurs with stabilized retinal images (Sekuler and Ganz, 1963; Drysdale, 1975) and eye rotations are not correlated with the rotary MAE (Seidman, Leigh, et al., 1992). It is clear that motion can be seen in an isolated stimulus following prolonged pursuit (Chaudhuri, 1991), and that this can be attributed to afternystagmus. However, this MAE does not exhibit a reduction in its duration under interocular transfer (Swanston and Wade, 1992).

An early interpretation in terms of tendencies to eye movements was proposed by Classen (1863, cited by Wohlgemuth, 1911), and this is related to the views of Mack, Goodwin et al. (1987) and Mack, Hill, et al. (1989) who suggested that the MAE is a consequence of adapting signals from a comparison of eye and image movement information. Evidence supporting this position was derived from differences between MAEs following object motion and eye movement, but this has been questioned by Swanston and Wade (1992).

The MAE was often compared to other contrast phenomena. For example, S. P. Thompson (1880) likened it to color contrast, and presented "an empirical law based on the physical fact of retinal fatigue, and on the psychological fact of association of contrasts. It is as follows:—*The retina ceases to perceive as a motion a steady succession of images that pass over a particular region for a sufficient time to induce fatigue; and on a portion of the retina so affected, the image of a body not in motion appears by contrast to be moving in a complementary direction*" (p. 296). Perhaps it was this relationship that led to Wohlgemuth's generalization that "the uniform passage of light-stimuli over the retina in any given direction for a certain time produces the after-effect of apparent motion in the opposite direction" (1911, p. 110), although this now requires some qualification. Aitken (1878) reported that stimulation of the whole retina with linear motion during adaptation did not produce an MAE, a result confirmed by Wohlgemuth (1911). However, this only applies to linear motion since Reinhardt-Rutland (1987b) did find MAEs following exposure to large spiral rotation. Day and Strelow (1971) directed attention to the importance of relative motion in the MAE by comparing equivalent adapting linear motions with and without a visible surround. Basler (1910) showed that an MAE can follow induced motion, and the interaction between these has been demonstrated by Anstis and Reinhardt-Rutland (1976) and Reinhardt-Rutland (1981, 1983a, b, 1984, 1987a). MAEs have been generated from the observation of stationary stimuli (Anstis, 1990) and with "phantom" gratings (Weisstein, Maguire, et al. 1977). The adequate stimulus for the MAE would appear to involve relative motion (Zöllner,

1860), even if this is restricted to some arbitrary boundary within which the motion is displayed (see Wade, Spillman, et al., 1996).

The MAE has become a tool for investigating the organization of functions within the visual system, such as the interaction of signals from the two eyes, or the sites at which increasingly complex adaptations occur. Few reports have dealt with another potentially interesting question, namely, whether the MAE reflects processes in addition to adaptation of neurons. For example, it is known that light and dark adaptation mechanisms enable an organism to operate under a wide range of illuminations. Does an analogous mechanism exists for motion processing? If so, is the MAE—as a sign of adaptation—related to that? It is not unreasonable to speculate that such a mechanism exists and that it might be related to the MAE, perhaps as a response to changes in environmental motions. An organism has to operate under a wide range of movement conditions and the MAE could reflect an adjustment or recalibration to the changed conditions (see chapter 7 for a more extensive discussion of this possibility).

A different type of recalibration process was suggested as the basis for the MAE by L. R. Harris, Morgan, et al. (1981). They proposed that the MAE arises as a result of a conflict between visual and vestibular information. Adaptation studies in laboratories typically involve a stationary observer looking at a moving pattern. According to L. R. Harris et al. this is not how the brain operates in more ecologically valid situations. A moving observer perceives motion for a prolonged time during which vestibular information is also available. L. R. Harris et al. found that if the conflict is removed by adapting observers to motion that is related to their movements (e.g., by placing both the display and the observer on a moving trolley), the magnitude of the MAE was significantly reduced. Also, Wiesenfelder and Blake (1992) speculated that the storage effect (Spigel, 1960) might reflect a delay in recalibration of motion mechanisms. The question whether adaptation aftereffects are outcomes of recalibration to new environmental conditions is still not answered (see also Pelah and Barlow, 1996, for a related phenomenon).

1.9 Conclusions

We have presented a history and overview of one of the most intensively studied phenomena in vision science—the motion aftereffect. This chapter is not intended to give a comprehensive account of the phenomenon, and several research results we have mentioned here have been successfully challenged. For example, Wohlgemuth's statement that the MAE does not require attention has recently been questioned (see Chaudhuri, 1990), as has the contention that motion over a particular part of the retina is a necessary precondition (see section 1.8). We have only touched on some of these recent developments, but they will be discussed in greater detail in the chapters that follow. However, one conclusion is justified here: although the MAE has been known since the time of Aristotle and much progress has been made since then, the MAE remains one of the mysteries of vision.

Chapter 2
How Do Measures of the Motion Aftereffect Measure Up?

Allan Pantle

Among the many effects of *adaptation to a moving stimulus* summarized by Sekuler (1975) are (1) the elevation of the threshold for detecting the moving stimulus, (2) the reduction of the apparent speed of the moving stimulus, (3) the distortion of the appearance of similar moving stimuli (e.g., their apparent contrast or motion direction), and (4) the apparent motion of a stationary pattern in a direction opposite to that of the moving adapting stimulus. The fourth effect is known as the motion after-effect (MAE) or waterfall illusion. These phenomena offer different measures of the visual system's altered state following prolonged exposure to a moving stimulus. Comparisons between them can certainly be valuable in understanding the ability of any one of them to reveal the nature of the processes underlying motion adaptation. But an in-depth analysis, from time to time, of the myriad studies falling in any one of the categories can also be enlightening. The goal of this chapter is to highlight some modern issues surrounding the measurement of the MAE. As more and more studies of motion adaptation are conducted, the distinctions among the MAE and the phenomena falling in the other categories become blurred. Studies which we will include in the MAE category are defined by (1) a prolonged period of adaptation to a moving stimulus, (2) a test stimulus whose visibility is clearly suprathreshold, and (3) a test stimulus which is stationary, or with a minimal directional bias (i.e., a test stimulus whose motion energy in different directions is the same, or nearly so).

2.1 The Variety of Measurement Procedures

As in any field of science, the body of knowledge about MAEs has developed as a result of the evolution of measurement procedures and theory. Measurement, the assignment of numeric values to observed entities or events according to some rule, can take place in the absence of theory, but the assigned numbers ultimately derive their meaning from a linkage with theoretical constructs. In the first half of the twentieth century, there were a number of measures of the MAE. In general, each measure was assumed

Table 2.1
Summary of the basic or most often used forms of motion aftereffect (MAE) measurement

Type of Test Stimulus	Dimension	Procedure
Neutral Test Method Stationary test or dynamic test with no direction bias	Presence/absence or probability	Verbal report
	Apparent speed	Matching with real visual motion or motor movement
		Direct scaling by magnitude estimation
	Duration	Timer
	Apparent direction	Setting an indicator
Null Test Method Dynamic test stimulus with a direction bias used to null MAE	Apparent strength or magnitude	Cancel MAE with real motion of variable speed
		Cancel MAE with moving random-dot pattern with constant speed, but variable percent coherence
		Cancel MAE with grating phase shift of variable magnitude
Transfer Method Test stimulus different from adapting stimulus	Any one of the above dimensions	Any one of the above procedures

to be little more than a reflection of some single underlying adaptation process which gave rise to illusory motion in a direction opposite to an adapting motion. As theory evolved, some of the measures were found wanting and others grew more sophisticated. The basic or most often used measures are summarized in table 2.1. The reader may wish to use the table as a hierarchical outline for the various MAE measures. In the remainder of this section, a general survey of the measures is provided first, and it is followed by a more detailed critical analysis.

Essentially, all procedures for measuring the MAE can be classified into one of three categories. *Neutral test methods* employ a test stimulus with no directional bias or energy, such as a stationary pattern, counterphase gratings, and incoherent random-element arrays. A counterphase grating is one whose dark and light stripes reverse periodically, typically about two times per second when used as an MAE test stimulus. An incoherent random-element pattern is a sequence of frames containing randomly positioned dots or checks, the positions of which are chosen anew for each frame. With any of these stimuli, an MAE manifests itself as motion in a direction opposite a previous adapting motion. The test stimulus appears to "float" in the opposite direction, quickly at first, then more slowly until it finally stalls. Attempts to measure the strength of to the MAE with the neutral test method take the form of estimates of the probability of seeing an MAE, subjective estimates of the speed or vividness of the MAE obtained by some form of matching or scaling procedure, or estimates of the duration of the MAE (see top of table 2.1).

Measurement procedures based on *null test methods* use a test stimulus with a directional bias or energy opposite to the MAE in an effort to balance, cancel, or null it (a variant of this class is the cancellation of one MAE by another). With the null test method, the strength of the MAE can be assessed by the properties of the test stimulus required to null the MAE. Those properties include the speed, percent coherence, or magnitude of the spatial shift of a test stimulus (see middle of table 2.1).

Finally, there is a class of studies which use the *transfer method*. In some sense, this method is nothing more than an adaptation of one of the other methods in which the relationship between the adapting and test stimulus is systematically varied. However, unlike the other measures, the transfer measure is a derived measure which compares, either implicitly or explicitly, the magnitude of an MAE obtained with different adapting and test stimuli to that obtained with the same adapting and test stimuli. Moreover, the transfer measure by its nature involves assumptions not required by the other measures. For these reasons, experiments using the transfer method have been placed in a separate category (see bottom of table 2.1). A more detailed description of the variety of MAE measurement procedures follows. Measures obtained with neutral test methods are discussed first.

The simplest measure of the MAE belongs to the neutral test class and is nothing more than a notation about its presence or absence under some adaptation condition. The difficulty with the measure is that it provides no information about the strength or magnitude of an MAE on a given trial. Without embellishment, this measure is not very useful in a modern context, except in cases when an MAE was present when none was expected (e.g., an aftereffect in an area where induced, but no real, adapting motion was present beforehand; Anstis and Reinhardt-Rutland, 1976) or when an MAE was absent when one was expected (e.g., no MAE after adaptation to a moving contrast-modulated pattern with a static test pattern; McCarthy, 1993). Early measures of MAE magnitude or strength took a number of forms. One procedure for measuring the strength or magnitude of an MAE which has never been widely adopted is a matching procedure used primarily to estimate the speed of an MAE. With this procedure an observer would adjust a real seen motion or make a motor movement of some type to match the speed of an MAE. The matching procedure is a difficult one to use because the speed of MAEs is slow and because the matching motion necessarily involves a change of position whereas the MAE does not. Moreover, as noted before, the speed of the MAE changes during the recovery period. Another procedure for quantifying the magnitude of an MAE dimension is the method of magnitude estimation. With this procedure an observer simply gives a direct subjective estimate of the dimension in question, usually with some anchor stimulus as a reference. With a few exceptions, this procedure too has not fared well in modern times. The lack of success of this measure probably owes to its classification as a type B experiment in Brindley's terminology (1970). Results of type B experiments are not as easily linked to underlying processes as are the results of simple detection or matching experiments (type A).

Other measures of MAE strength have fared better in modern times, owing as much as anything to controversies about their meaning in theoretical contexts. At least until modern times, and possibly even today, MAE duration has been the most popular choice of MAE magnitude. Given that an MAE is the result of some type of adaptation process, it seems logical that the greater the adaptation is, the longer the MAE will be if it is viewed as a manifestation of the recovery from adaptation. What complicates matters is the fact that the measurement of an MAE with a continuously present test stimulus may itself influence the measured process; that is, the measurement of MAE duration may be reactive or obtrusive. This is one of the major issues prevalent in today's literature and is the first major topic to which we devote extended attention in this chapter.

Let us now turn to the null test methods for measuring the MAE. In the simplest case the entire test stimulus is moved in a direction opposite to that of the MAE so that it appears stationary. In early research the null was achieved by an adjustment of the speed of the test stimulus. In some sense this was problematic and remains so because there is no a priori reason why a stronger aftereffect (resulting from a greater degree of adaptation) must necessarily be a faster aftereffect. The relationship between direction and velocity coding is still unresolved. Newly developed measures of "energy" nulling circumvent this problem. The percentage of dots which move coherently in one direction in a test pattern of otherwise randomly moving dots can be varied so as to offset any motion of the dots due to an MAE. The higher the percentage required to offset the MAE, the greater the presumed magnitude of the MAE (Blake and Hiris, 1993). All the dots always move at the same speed. Just the coherence of their motion is varied. Another measure of "energy" nulling can be used with periodic test patterns like sine-wave gratings. The contrast of the grating can be made to reverse over time; or alternatively, its phase can be shifted by 180 degrees in discrete time steps. In either case, the dynamic grating has equal motion energy in directions perpendicular to stripes, and the grating will appear to flicker while remaining stationary in space, or else appear to move randomly back and forth. An MAE will cause the dynamic test pattern to appear to move in one direction. In the case of the stepped grating, the phase shift can be made slightly greater or less than 180 degrees to favor one direction of motion over the other (phase test). Then the amount by which the phase has to be increased or decreased from 180 degrees in order to make the test stimulus appear stationary (or to move as much in one direction as the other) constitutes a measure of MAE strength (McCarthy, 1993). The problem with the use of dynamic test stimuli is that they can lead to results apparently at odds with those obtained using static test stimuli (e.g., McCarthy, 1993; Nishida and Sato, 1995; Ashida and Osaka, 1995b). Theoretically, one solution has been to suggest that the different test stimuli tap different adaptation processes. The role of multiple sites and pathways in the generation of MAEs and the manner in which the new nulling measures bear on this problem is the second major topic discussed in this chapter.

Early anecdotal descriptions of the MAE gave the impression that the similarity of adapting and test stimuli was unimportant. One could watch a continuously moving waterfall or river and turn one's gaze to the surrounding scenery and see an MAE. While there were some early laboratory reports of MAEs observed with different adapting and test stimuli (e.g., the report of moving images with the eyes closed after motion adaptation), early scientific studies of the MAE were typically conducted with test stimuli that were stationary versions of adapting stimuli. Thus, it was not known to what extent MAE measurements depended upon the similarity of adapting and test stimuli. With the advent of computer displays which made it easier to generate different kinds of visual stimuli, more and more different kinds of adapting and test patterns have been used to generate MAEs (e.g., first- and second-order stimuli, Cavanagh and Mather, 1989; or three-dimensional stimuli, e.g., Petersik, 1984). Bolstered by neurophysiologic findings of multiple sites and pathways for signaling motion, researchers became increasingly interested in knowing whether, and to what extent, an MAE would be manifest when adapting and test stimuli were different; that is, in measuring the degree to which an MAE would transfer from adaptation with a stimulus of one class to a test stimulus of a different class. On the one hand, the transfer measurement is nothing more than an extension or elaboration of experiments on the degree of interocular transfer of the MAE; that is, the degree to which an MAE could be observed in one eye after an adapting stimulus had been presented to the other eye. On the other hand, the sheer number of ways in which the transfer measurement has been employed makes it seem like an entirely new type of measurement. The use of transfer measurement to infer the properties of visual motion mechanisms is discussed later in this chapter.

The direction of an MAE did not receive serious attention as a dependent measure until recent years. Adapting motion in the early years of study of the MAE was unidirectional, and the MAE observed was opposite to the one adapting direction. Adapting patterns with more than one moving component overlaid in the same area of the visual field made it meaningful to ask how the adapting directions would combine to determine MAE direction, if indeed they did combine. Studies on MAE direction are the third major topic receiving special attention in this chapter.

As will become clear, the new or evolved measures are a requirement for studying MAEs in the context of theories which describe the experience of motion as a consequence of processing at multiple sites (stages and pathways) in the visual system.

2.2 Measurement Reactivity or Obtrusiveness

The very act of measuring an MAE may itself influence the processes of adaptation and recovery, as mentioned earlier. A study by Spigel (1965) can be taken as evidence that the MAE is reactive or obtrusive in this way, though Spigel did not necessarily see his work in this way. Spigel recorded durations of aftereffects in the usual way by presenting a test stimulus immediately after exposure to an adapting stimulus. He also recorded durations for aftereffects whose measurement was delayed by the insertion of a dark or contourless field between the inspection of the adapting and test stimuli. MAEs with the delayed test were almost as long as MAEs with the immediate test, even when the delay was as long as the duration of the MAEs tested immediately. Spigel concluded that the "normal rate of decay of a movement aftereffect may be inhibited by the interpolation of conditions which markedly reduce or eliminate contour ..." (p. 221).

There are two potential, and perhaps related, problems with this interpretation. The first problem is an implicit assumption that the state of the visual motion system after the cessation of the MAE (S-AC) is the same as its state before adaptation (S-BA). If one accepts this assumption, then the only way an interspersed contourless field in the delayed test condition can extend the MAE is by inhibiting (prolonging) the system's return to the S-BA. The *inhibition* of the decay is in turn a corollary of choosing to view the MAE duration with an immediate test as the reference or baseline duration.

Subsequent research by Keck et al. (1976) and by Keck and Pentz (1977) cast doubt on Spigel's interpretation. Keck et al. (1976) generated MAEs with sine-wave adapting gratings moving in a uniform direction. Both the duration and initial speed of MAEs measured with stationary test gratings were a function of their contrast. The duration and initial speed of MAEs decreased as test grating contrast rose in the range of 0.9 to 10.5 percent. Following Spigel, one might attempt to argue that lower test contrasts merely inhibit the decay of MAEs and result in longer durations. However, the fact that the MAEs are faster at onset (initial speed), as well as have different offset times, militates against a simple interpretation in terms of a differential decay to a common preadaptation state. Rather, MAEs with different test contrasts are different from the beginning, and this leaves open the possibility that the S-ACs with stimuli of different test contrasts are not the same, nor the same as the S-BA. That different equilibriums or balanced states underlie the cessation of the MAE with different test stimuli was corroborated by the work of Keck and Pentz (1977).

The novel feature of the first experiment of Keck and Pentz (1977) was a switch from one level of test contrast to another during an MAE. In one condition observers adapted to a moving sine-wave grating, and subsequently an MAE was measured with a stationary grating whose contrast was switched from 10.5 to 1.7 percent 8 seconds into a test period. When the test contrast switched, the apparent speed of the MAE increased abruptly, and it took a longer time to dissipate than an MAE for a condition in which the contrast remained at 10.5 percent. Keck and Pentz concluded that the MAE is as much influenced by the effect of the test stimulus on the visual motion system as it is by a change of its state due to adaptation. Just as important, the contrast-switch effect suggests that the visual motion system might arrive at different balanced states when the MAE ceases in the switch and no-switch conditions because the test stimuli affected the visual motion system differently.

In the second experiment of Keck and Pentz (1977), a delay interval filled with a spatially uniform field was inserted between the adapting period with a moving grating and a test period with a stationary grating. They estimated the speed of an MAE at the very beginning of the test period for a number of different delay conditions. Interestingly, there were MAEs with measurable initial speeds for delays which were longer than MAEs would have lasted had they been measured immediately. This must mean that the S-AC of a typical (immediately measured) MAE cannot logically be the same as the S-BA. Otherwise, there would be no residual changed state which could serve as the substrate for an MAE remaining after the intervening blank interval. Furthermore, Keck and Pentz found that the initial speed of residual MAEs decreased exponentially with the duration of the delay interval between adapting and test periods. The initial speed reached zero for delays which were three to four times the duration of an immediately measured MAE. These results suggest a different perspective on Spigel's original findings. Rather than characterizing the immediately measured MAE as a baseline or reference for the "normal" decay of the MAE and the delayed MAE as representing some type of inhibition of the normal decay, it may make more sense to view (1) the decay of the initial speed of residual MAEs for longer and longer delay intervals as the baseline decay of adaptation (recovery) back to the S-BA (a decay only minimally influenced by a test stimulus), and (2) the more rapid decay of any other more immediate measurement of the MAE in the continued presence of a test stimulus as a result of some further adapting effect of the test stimulus itself. The combined effect of adaptation to the original adapting stimulus and to the test stimulus probably would not return the system to the S-BA, but to some other balanced directional state. If this analysis is correct, then the prescription for watching the system return to the S-BA would be to use short (nonadapting), intermittent test stimuli interspersed between blank periods until an MAE is no longer present.

While no one has yet attempted to construct a dynamic model of the MAE in the presence of a prolonged test stimulus, Sachtler and Zaidi (1993) successfully modeled a steady or equilibrium state of the MAE. After an initially long (10 minutes) period of motion adaptation, attempts were made to maintain a steady state of motion adaptation by readapting the system to motion for 5 seconds after each 1/2-second test period. A test grating was present for only 75 ms during each test period, so it was not likely that the test stimulus added much adaptation of its own. Motions of the test stimulus required to cancel any MAE could be explained by a change of gain in motion units sensitive to the adapting direction. In order to fit the data, motion units sensitive to two different speeds in each direction were required, and each motion unit had to have a tuning curve which included a significant response to a *stationary* stimulus.

The analysis of the decay of the MAE and the Sachtler and Zaidi model both implicitly assume that an MAE is the result of adaptation at one site in the visual system, or that, at the very least, a test stimulus must be capable of activating those motion units (area of the brain) whose state was altered by an adapting stimulus. It is this assumption to which we now turn our attention, and we will return later to the issue of the obtrusive nature of an MAE test stimulus.

2.3 Multidimensional Aspects of Motion Aftereffect Encoding and Measurement

There are a number of recent studies which demonstrate that the type of test stimulus itself, or the relationship between test and adapting stimuli, affects the measurement of the MAE. The general thrust of all these experiments is to suggest that MAEs arise from adaptation or state changes at more than one site (stage or pathway) in the visual system. Among other things, the assumption of multiple sites can have implications for the generalization or transfer of MAEs from one type of stimulus to another. The interocular transfer of the MAE provides a prototypal example which can be used to investigate the assumptions about multiple sites underlying the MAE.

In studies of the interocular transfer of an MAE, the MAE is measured with a test stimulus presented to one eye after the other eye has been exposed to a moving adapting stimulus. The implicit assumptions underlying the interocular transfer experiment are made clear by an examination of the possible results of the experiment. Suppose that no MAE is observed in the interocular transfer experiment. Indeed, this is what often happens in an interocular transfer experiment with stereoblind strabismic observers (e.g., Mitchell, Reardon, et al., 1975; Wade, 1976; Keck and Price, 1982). One interpretation of the absence of an MAE is that the adapting stimulus is ineffectual in bringing about any significant state changes in the system. In the case of the lack of interocular transfer in stereoblind strabismic observers, this possibility is easily rejected because one can readily measure an MAE with a test stimulus presented to the adapted eye even though none is present in the opposite eye. A second interpretation is that activity (response) underlying the perception of the test stimulus is not anatomically, or functionally, linked to any state changes produced by the adapting stimulus. The different nuances of the second interpretation are highlighted in a study of interocular transfer of the MAE by Barlow and Brindley (1963).

As in most studies of the interocular transfer of the MAE, Barlow and Brindley found that an aftereffect was present interocularly. Unlike others, however, they did not accept the usual conclusion that the interocular transfer necessarily implied that the state change underlying the MAE was central; that is, that the test stimulus in one eye acted directly on some binocular mechanism(s) (central site) whose state had been altered by the adapting stimulus in the opposite eye (common-site hypothesis). Instead, Barlow and Brindley entertained an alternative hypothesis, that some form of motion imbalance signal from one retina was combined with the test stimulus signal from the other retina at some central site (separate-site hypothesis). The common-site hypothesis places the state change at a central site, whereas the separate-site hypothesis places the state change at a peripheral site and does not assume that the test stimulus signal ever impinges upon the site where the state change occurred. In order to decide between the alternatives, Barlow and Brindley pressure-blinded the adapted eye during the inspection of the test stimulus so as to suppress any retinal motion imbalance signal. The MAE was unaffected, suggesting that the state change responsible for the MAE was located at a central site.

The above analysis of the interocular transfer of the MAE applies at least in principle to all MAE experiments whose adapting and test stimuli differ and in which transfer is measured. At first glance, the separate-site hypothesis seems plausible given evidence that stimulus motion is encoded in an area of the brain which is separate from areas encoding other stimulus characteristics (e.g., Zeki, 1993). State changes in a motion area responsible for MAE signals would simply be linked to other characteristics of the test stimulus encoded in other areas of the brain by whatever means is used to solve the binding problem (e.g., Treisman, 1986; von der Malsburg and Schneider, 1986). Viewed in this way, a test stimulus that is different from an adapting stimulus could give rise to an MAE even though it never impinged on the motion site altered by the adapting stimulus. The difficulty with the separate-sites interpretation is that, under it, there is no a priori reason to expect (1) that some test stimuli would give rise to MAEs, while others would not (e.g., McCarthy, 1993; Nishida and Sato, 1995), (2) that MAE magnitude would vary in a systematic way with the relationship between adapting and test stimuli (e.g., spatial frequency selectivity; Cameron et al., 1992), or (3) that adapting stimulus characteristics which lead to measured MAE invariance would be dependent upon the test stimulus (e.g., Pantle, 1974; Ashida and Osaka, 1995b).

The common-site hypothesis fares better when applied to the results of MAE experiments with different adapting and test stimuli. A few examples should suffice to demonstrate this point.

1. A number of researchers have found that contrast-modulated stimuli do not produce MAEs with a stationary test stimulus, but do produce MAEs with a dynamic test stimulus (e.g., McCarthy, 1993; Nishida and Sato, 1995). Under the common-site hypothesis, this result can be explained if it is assumed that the adapting stimulus produces a change of state in a motion area which, because of its temporal response characteristics, cannot be stimulated with a stationary stimulus, but can be stimulated with a dynamic stimulus. This is not an unreasonable assumption for an extrastriate motion area.

2. There is human psychophysical evidence that directionally selective motion cells are spatial frequency–tuned (Pantle, Lehmkuhle, et al., 1978). For this reason, the expected overlap of the set of cells whose state is changed by an adapting stimulus and the set of cells stimulated by a test stimulus would be greater, the more similar the spatial frequency of the adapting and test stimuli. If the magnitude of an MAE is positively related to the overlap, then MAE magnitude ought to be positively related to the similarity of adapting and test spatial frequencies, as has been demonstrated by Cameron et al. (1992). Still other procedures for measuring MAE transfer across stimulus domains such as first- (Fourier) and second-order (non-Fourier) stimuli can be explored to determine whether the different classes of stimuli are processed by overlapping mechanisms or not. Again, the underlying assumption is that the degree of the transfer of the MAE from an adapting stimulus chosen from one stimulus domain to a test stimulus chosen from a different stimulus domain will be positively related to the extent to which the test stimulus taps a state change in mechanisms responsive to the adapting stimulus.

3. Pantle (1974) measured MAEs as a function of the speed of sine-wave gratings at different spatial frequencies. With a stationary test stimulus (hereinafter, static MAE), MAE magnitude was invariant with spatial frequency provided that the speed of the adapting stimulus was expressed as temporal frequency. Nishida and Sato (1995) replicated Pantle's static MAE findings, but in addition they found that MAE magnitude was invariant with speed expressed in degrees per second when the test stimulus underwent counterphase flicker (hereinafter, dynamic MAE). Nishida and Sato explained their results by assuming that the adapting gratings produced state changes in at least two sites, that the cells at the different sites had different functional properties, and that each of the test stimuli (stationary or counterphase) primarily stimulated a different site leading to different static and dynamic MAEs.

More puzzling aspects of MAE behavior seem difficult to accommodate theoretically even if one combines the concept of multiple adaptation sites and the concept of the reactivity of MAE measurements. Consider the major results of a study by Verstraten, Fredericksen, et al. (1996) using random pixel arrays. In one condition the duration of a static MAE (static test pixels) was measured after a dynamic MAE (test pixels refreshed at random) had run its course. In a second condition, measurement of the dynamic MAE followed the measurement of the static MAE. In the first condition, the interposition of the dynamic MAE between the adaptation period and the static MAE hardly affected the duration of the static MAE. If one assumes that both MAEs depend upon a state change at a single site and that the cessation of the dynamic MAE represents a return to the

S-BA, then any residual static MAE in the first condition is paradoxical. However, if one assumes that the static and dynamic MAEs constitute probes of state changes at different adaptation sites, then the duration of the static MAE might very well be independent of the achievement of an equilibrium state at the site tapped by the dynamic test stimulus, that is, any effect of measuring the duration of the dynamic MAE during an intervening period. Thus, the results of the first condition are in qualitative agreement with the assumptions of multiple adaptation sites and measurement reactivity. However, in the second condition, the duration of the dynamic MAE was affected by the intervening measurement of the static MAE. The asymmetrical effect of static and dynamic MAEs on each other when their order of measurement is switched is difficult to explain even with the more complex assumptions about multiple adaptation sites and measurement reactivity.

2.4 Can Motion Aftereffect Measurements be Linearly Combined?

The original purpose of a study by Pantle (1978) was to compare data on detection, motion adaptation, and speed discrimination over a range of temporal frequencies using sine-wave stimuli. In the present context the results are important for a couple of reasons which were not stressed at the time of the study.

First, the motion adaptation experiment employed a new titration measure of the MAE. It was a type of aftereffect nulling. Instead of canceling an MAE with real motion in a direction opposite to the aftereffect, as had been done in many past studies, a standard MAE in one direction was balanced by a second MAE in the opposite direction. In order to accomplish this, Pantle had observers adapt to a complex stimulus containing two superimposed sine-wave grating components moving in opposite directions. One component, the standard, always had the same characteristics. The second component, the variable one, moved at different temporal frequencies. At each temporal frequency the contrast of the variable component was adjusted until the MAE it produced just canceled the MAE produced by the standard component. At the balance point, the test stimulus appeared stationary. Implicit in this procedure was the assumption that the MAEs would add, even when the adapting stimulus contained components which moved transparently through one another. The manner in which the individual MAEs produced by the multiple components of an adapting stimulus combine to determine perceived MAE direction has since been studied extensively.

Second, in Pantle's study, MAEs in opposite directions could not only be balanced but the contrasts of the variable component which produced a null (no MAE) at different temporal frequencies were a constant multiple of the contrasts required to detect the variable component on its own. With a simple adjustment of contrast scale the null contrast and detection contrasts could be brought into register, and no complex interaction between the motion of the standard and variable components of the adapting stimulus need be proposed. In this respect, the system behaved linearly. Other researchers have since attempted to determine whether MAEs generated by more than one adapting component sum linearly, that is, obey the principle of superposition.

Mather (1980) had observers adapt to two motions simultaneously, but unlike Pantle (1978), the two motions were not limited to opposite directions. Mather used isotropic random-dot patterns, so as not to confound orientation of the patterns with their direction of motion, and he combined adapting motions whose directions were between zero and 180 degrees apart. Importantly, for all combinations of adapting motions, the MAE was unidirectional. It was not made up of two simultaneous MAEs, nor of an MAE whose direction alternated over time between the directions opposite the adapting motions. Some underlying integrative process is implied by the results, and the nature of the integrative process could be studied by an examination of the manner in which the two components of the adapting motion combined to determine MAE direction.

In one experiment, Mather (1980) measured the perceived direction of MAEs generated with random-dot adapting patterns containing two components of equal contrasts and equal speeds. The MAE direction was predicted by the vector sum of the adapting components. In taking the vector sum, the vectors representing the adapting components had directions equivalent to their physical directions, and magnitudes corresponding to the durations of their individual MAEs. In another experiment, Mather found that the empirically measured durations of two individual MAEs could be used to predict, to a first approximation, the durations of the combined MAE arising from the two individual MAEs.

Verstraten et al. (1994a) confirmed and extended the findings of Mather (1980). They used random pixel arrays as adapting and test stimuli. The adapting stimulus contained two superimposed components. One component had a fixed direction and speed in all experimental conditions. The direction of the second component was 90 degrees away from that of the first component, and its speed was varied across experimental conditions. Verstraten et al. found (1) that MAE direction varied as a function of the speed of the second component of the adapting stimulus, and (2) that, for *different* as well as equal speeds of the adapting components, the direction of the combined MAE could be predicted from the vector sum of the adapting components provided that their magnitudes were made proportional to the MAEs they produced individually.

In view of the conventional assumption that the adaptation produced by a stimulus is positively related to one's sensitivity to it, it was natural for Verstraten et al. (1994a) to ask whether sensitivity to the variable speed component of their adapting stimulus could also be used to compute its contribution to the combined MAE. Recall that Pantle (1978) had found that sensitivity to one component (moving at different speeds) of an adapting stimulus predicted its ability to null the MAE of a second adapting component moving in the opposite direction. In the paper of Verstraten et al. (1994a), the direction of a combined MAE generated by an adapting stimulus with transparent components 90 degrees apart was reported to be less well fit by a vector sum when the components were normalized by their individually measured luminance signal-to-noise ratio sensitivities (van Doorn and Koenderink, 1982) than when they were scaled by the MAE durations they produced individually. However, some of the sensitivity data used in this report were obtained on a different day than the MAE data. When Verstraten (1994) revisited the problem later, new sensitivity data collected on the same day as the duration data showed that the "conclusion [in Verstraten et al., 1994a] that MAE duration is a better predictor of the MAE of transparent motion than directional sensitivity does not hold...." (p. 80).

To a first approximation the vector addition model, with components normalized by threshold sensitivity or by duration of MAE induction, provides a reasonable fit to data in the first few studies of MAEs generated by adapting stimuli with more than one direction or speed component. It is somewhat surprising that the process of integration seems relatively simple, because MAE magnitude is a highly nonlinear function of stimulus contrast (Keck et al., 1976). Undoubtedly, measures of integration will remain an important tool for the discovery of mechanisms underlying MAEs. For example, what rules of integration would describe the MAEs generated by a complex adapting stimulus made up of first- and second-order components with a dynamic test stimulus?

2.5 Summary and Conclusions

For the resulting numbers to be useful or meaningful, psychophysical measurement procedures must reflect current knowledge and theory about the behavioral phenomenon in question. Thus measurement procedures for the MAE have evolved to keep pace with the changing theoretical climate. Early on, the MAE was largely viewed as the consequence of a single adaptation process with a simple passive recovery back to an initial unadapted state. In the 1960s this view took the form of an imbalance in the responsiveness of directionally selective neurons brought about by the inspection of what was conceived as a single-component adapting stimulus moving in a uniform direction. The degree of adaptation depended upon the characteristics of the adapting stimulus. It was assumed that one could measure the adaptation by simply presenting a stimulus (usually the same as the adapting stimulus, but stationary) and making some unidimensional measurement of its motion, or by canceling its apparent motion with some real motion varying along some single dimension. With time the responsiveness of the putative neurons recovered, and when the system had returned to its state before adaptation, the MAE ceased (e.g., Sekuler and Pantle, 1967).

Much has changed in recent years in the way in which researchers think about the encoding of motion, so procedures for measuring MAE characteristics have necessarily changed as well. In general, attempts intended to probe the motion system with a suprathreshold stimulus to determine its state after adaptation to a moving stimulus must necessarily recognize the possibility that the act of measurement itself produces changes (adaptation, gain control, etc.) in the state of the system being measured. One consequence of this is that the system after the cessation of an MAE is probably not returned to the state in which it was before adaptation, if the measurement is anything but almost instantaneous. Evidence from diverse areas of motion research indicates that visual motion is multiply encoded at more than one site by mechanisms with different response characteristics. As a consequence the specific form in which an MAE manifests itself will in large part be determined as much by the test stimulus and the site it activates as it is by the adapting stimulus. Finally, with the increased sophistication with which mathematical methods have been applied to the description of visual stimuli, it has become possible to ask whether the individually measured MAEs from the components of a complex stimulus can be linearly combined to explain the unidirectional MAE it generates. If the linear methods fail, more complex measurement techniques derived from nonlinear systems analysis will have to be adopted.

Chapter 3
Tuning of the Motion Aftereffect

Peter Thompson

Visual aftereffects generally show some tuning. That is, some adaptation configuration induces the greatest effect and some test pattern elicits the greatest effect. Generally speaking, the greatest effects are seen when the test stimulus most closely resembles the adaptation stimulus.

To understand what "tuning" of the motion aftereffect (MAE) might tell us about mechanisms underlying motion perception, it is necessary to consider some very general underlying assumptions.

1. When we "adapt" to a pattern we assume that some mechanisms, neurons, or synapses in the visual pathways are excited, stimulated, or activated.
2. The greater the excitation, stimulation, or activation during adaptation, the greater the mechanisms, neurons, or synapses are adapted, fatigued, or habituated.

It follows from these assumptions that one would expect the greatest effects of adaptation to be manifest upon test patterns that involve the same mechanisms as those fatigued during adaptation. If we consider the example of adaptation to stationary spatial stimuli, we can see the extent to which this is true. In 1969 Blakemore and Campbell reported that adapting to a sine-wave grating elevates contrast thresholds. They found that the greatest elevation was found on test gratings that shared their spatial frequency and orientation with the adaptation pattern. Figure 3.1A–C illustrates this. However, if one examines the perceived shift in spatial frequency following adaptation (Blakemore and Sutton, 1969; Blakemore, Nachmias, et al., 1970) or the shift in orientation following adaptation (the tilt aftereffect; Gibson and Radner, 1937), then the picture is different (figure 3.1D). The reasons are straightforward: a shift in (say) the perceived spatial frequency arises from an imbalance in the relative contributions of channels above and below the adaptation spatial frequency, whereas around the adaptation spatial frequency itself, the relative contributions are balanced.

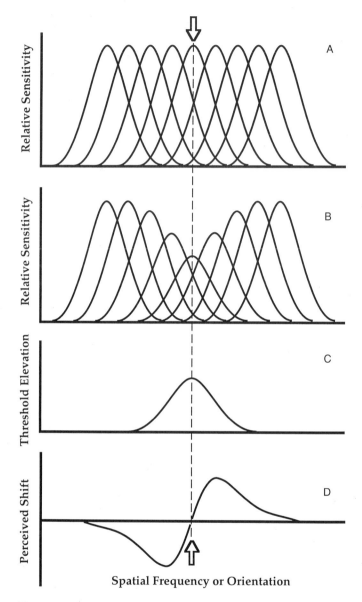

Spatial Frequency or Orientation

Figure 3.1
A shows a collection of bandpass spatial channels before adaptation. Relative sensitivity is plotted on the ordinate, spatial frequency (or orientation) along the abscissa. B, Following adaptation at the spatial frequency (or orientation) indicated by the arrows and vertical dashed line, the relative sensitivity is altered. C, The subsequent contrast threshold elevation reflects the reduction of sensitivity of the channels. D, The perceived shift in spatial frequency (or orientation) reflects the change in relative contributions from the various channels following adaptation.

Before moving on from this example two points should be noted. First, the tuning of the aftereffect provides us with an indication of the bandwidth of the underlying channels. Second, the typical example we have illustrated assumes that there are channels both above and below the range we are investigating. What will happen then when we start to run out of channels? Blakemore and Campbell (1969) clearly felt they *had* run out of channels when they reported that adapting to a spatial frequency of less than 1.5 cycles/degree led to the peak threshold elevation remaining at 1.5 cycles/degree and not at the adaptation spatial frequency. Although the authors did not make the point clear, the expression "lowest adaptable channel" does not mean "lowest channel" but the "lowest channel that can be adapted." This point has been made succinctly by Stromeyer, Klein, et al. (1982):

> The displacement of the peak observed with stationary test patterns does not imply that there are no shape analyzing mechanisms optimally sensitive to low spatial frequencies, but rather that these mechanisms may *not be readily adapted*. If there were *no* such mechanisms, then the threshold elevation at the adapting frequency should remain high, for adapted mechanisms tuned to a higher spatial frequency would be used to detect the low spatial frequency patterns. And, thus the adaptation function would have a low-pass spatial frequency. Only if there were low spatial frequency mechanisms that do not adapt would there be little threshold elevation at the adapting frequency. (p. 225)

Evidence from adaptation experiments investigating the spatial tuning of mechanisms in human vision is consistent with what we know of single-cell tuning functions in visual cortex, namely, that there exists a number of fairly narrowly tuned mechanisms in both the orientation and spatial frequency domains (see Hubel and Wiesel 1962, 1968; Campbell, Cooper, et al., 1969). This consistency and clarity has made spatial adaptation experiments among the most influential in visual psychophysics. Given such success it is no surprise that flicker adaptation experiments were carried out to establish the temporal tuning of mechanisms in human vision as well. However, the same level of success was not forthcoming. R. A. Smith (1970, 1971), Pantle (1971), and Nilsson, Richmond, et al. (1975) all looked at the effects of flicker adaptation, but little consensus about temporal tuning emerged, save that any flicker tuning must be extremely broad. Once temporally modulated stimuli other than uniform flicker were investigated, things improved; we now have some idea about the spatial frequency tuning of motion mechanisms from aftereffect studies and we have gone a little way toward unraveling the temporal tuning characteristics as well.

3.1 Spatial Tuning of the Motion Aftereffect

From the earliest reports of the MAE it became clear that spatial tuning of the effect could not be very narrow. Both Purkinje (1825), adapting to a cavalry parade and testing the effect on stationary houses, and Addams (1834), adapting to the waterfall at Foyers and testing on the "sombre age-worn rocks immediately contiguous to the waterfall," demonstrated that the spatial frequency content of the test pattern did not have to match that of the adapting pattern. Later reports suggest there need not be any test pattern at all—David Brewster (1845) showed that the MAE can be observed with one's eyes closed during the test phase and Grindley and Wilkinson (1953) reported on the MAE on a uniform bright test field; following adaptation they likened the aftereffect to "a rice pudding getting nearer to you in a fog." (This is a useful analogy as previously I had no idea what a rice pudding approaching me in a fog would look like.)

Unfortunately, Spitz (1958) found no effect when a clear blue sky was used as a test field and Cameron et al. (1992), while reporting spatial frequency tuning of the MAE, found no measurable effect on test spatial frequencies below 0.25 cycle/degree. My own prejudice is that an MAE can be seen against uniform unpatterned light and dark backgrounds, especially if the adaptation pattern is revolving or, if in a linear drift, has a stationary surround.

If MAEs can be observed with a blank test field it might seem odd that Over, Broerse, et al. (1973) found some evidence for spatial frequency tuning of the effect in a series of experiments that varied the spatial frequency of both adaptation and test stimuli. Unfortunately, their experiment was constrained by a restricted range of stimuli, their use of square-wave gratings, and poor control of the drift rate of the adaptation stimuli. A more comprehensive range of experiments employing a wide range of spatial frequencies by P. Thompson (1976) confirmed the spatial frequency tuning of the MAE (figure 3.2). Foolishly, he never published his results, though they are to be found in the depths of his Ph.D. thesis and were generously acknowledged by Cameron et al. (1992) who also report spatial frequency selectivity of the MAE. Cameron et al. did find one set of circumstances under which spatial frequency tuning to the MAE appears to break down: at all adaptation spatial frequencies below about 0.5 cycle/degree, the optimal test spatial frequency remains at 0.5 cycle/degree. The authors point to the apparent similarity between this effect and the "lowest adaptable channel" phenomenon reported by Blakemore and Campbell (1969). More recently, Bex, Verstraten, et al. (1996) have also examined the spatial frequency tuning of the MAE, particularly at low spatial frequency. They found, in agreement with other studies, that

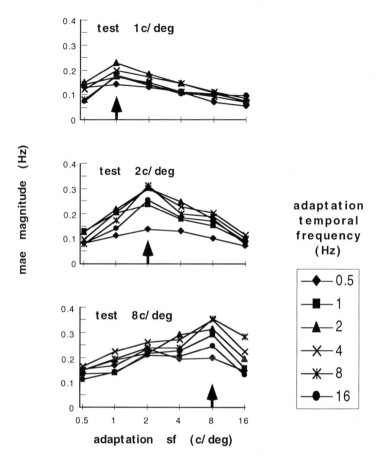

Figure 3.2
Experiments by P. Thompson (1976) showing the spatial frequency tuning of the motion aftereffect (MAE). The aftereffect was measured by a matching procedure following adaptation conditions in which adaptation gratings of a range of temporal frequencies (0.5 to 16 Hz) and spatial frequencies (0.5 to 16 cycles/degree) produced MAEs on stationary test gratings of spatial frequencies 1, 2, and 8 cycles/degree. Each point represents the mean of eight readings. Subject: PT.

there is spatial frequency tuning, but they also found no evidence for a "lowest adaptable channel" phenomenon. Even investigation of spatial frequencies as low as 0.125 cycle/degree produced no evidence that the best spatial frequency of the test pattern was anything other than the spatial frequency of the adaptation pattern. This seeming contradiction with the work of Cameron et al. may be explained by the different test stimuli used in the two experiments: Cameron et al. employed a stationary test field while Bex et al. used a counterphase flickering grating. There is good reason to suppose that the MAE measured with flickering test patterns is different from that seen with stationary test patterns (see below and chapter 5).

The consensus of these studies is that the greatest MAE is found when the spatial frequency of the test pattern is the same as that of the adapting stimulus. The tuning of the effect appears to be such that moving one octave from the adaptation spatial frequency reduces the MAE by approximately half. This is not qualitatively different from the contrast threshold elevation tuning reported by Blakemore and Campbell (1969, figure 8). Intriguingly, the narrowest spatial frequency tuning of the MAE to have been reported is probably that of Brigner (1982). A 2.5-turn arithmetic spiral was used as the adaptation and the various test patterns. Brigner claims that the test patterns had "spatial frequencies, in cycles/degree of visual angle, .32, .43, .53, .64, .85, 1.07, 1.29, 1.72, 2.15, 2.58, 3.44, 4.3, and 5.16." The author does not make it clear what he means by "spatial frequency" here. Following adaptation to a rotating spiral of "1.29 cycles/degree," Brigner's three subjects on average saw an aftereffect when the spatial frequency of the test spiral was less than one octave different from the adaptation pattern. This narrow tuning is odd when we consider that the spiral patterns used by Brigner must have had a wide spatial frequency content.

This review of spatial tuning seems to conclude that although one does not require any spatial structure in the test pattern to see the MAE, it is nonetheless quite narrowly tuned with respect to spatial frequency. Clearly we have a problem here. I regret that the most likely resolution to this seeming paradox is that we are dealing not with one MAE but with (at least) two. This is an idea with a long history, but it was stated most clearly by Favreau (1976). Essentially, one component of the MAE is shortlived and very broadly tuned for spatial parameters. This component shows interocular transfer and thus must involve binocularly driven cells. It probably is not color-selective. The second component is long-lived and shows spatial frequency specificity. This component can be induced in opposite directions in the two eyes simultaneously (a "dichoptic" MAE in Favreau's terminology) and thus probably involves monocularly driven cells. It probably is color-selective.

Thus the paradox of the spatial frequency specificity is solved at a stroke! As has been noted by Masland (1969), immediately after adaptation the MAE can be observed on a wide variety of test patterns, while later the effect is specific to the adapting stimulus. Inevitably a similar observation had been made by Wohlgemuth (1911).

3.2 Temporal Tuning of the Motion Aftereffect

When it comes to temporal tuning, the very nature of the MAE—adaptation to a moving adaptation pattern producing perceived motion on a stationary test pattern—seems to deny the possibility of narrow tuning. However, we can determine whether some adaptation rates of motion produce greater MAEs than others. If we might extend our definition of the MAE to include the effects of motion adaptation on moving and flickering as well as stationary patterns, then considerations of temporal tuning become more meaningful.

As might be expected, just about every possible pattern of relationship between adaptation velocity and subsequent MAE magnitude has been found. The most popular result is that the MAE magnitude shows an inverted U-shaped function plotted against adaptation velocity. In the limit, this may seem trivial—a stationary adaptation pattern will produce no MAE, nor will adaptation at speeds beyond the resolution of the visual system; the optimal adaptation velocity must lie somewhere in between. Such a conclusion was reached by Wohlgemuth (1911) in his incomparable monograph, with the optimal adaptation velocity around 7 to 10 cm/second, but Wohlgemuth was not the first to arrive at this conclusion, an honor that may belong to Kinoshita (1909). Granit (1928) supported this view, claiming a maximum MAE following an adaptation velocity of 1.5 degrees/second, and by the time Scott and Noland (1965) collated data from several studies, the optimal adaptation velocity for the MAE seemed to lie in the region of 2 to 3 degrees/second. Moulden (1974) investigated the magnitude of the MAE on a noise field and found that the magnitude of the effect was a function of adaptation velocity, but only for adapting temporal frequencies greater than about 4 to 5 cycles/second.

Support for the idea that the MAE *increases* in magnitude with increasing adaptation velocity is somewhat thin, but interestingly this was one of the earliest proposals, emerging in a paper by Budde (1884), cited by Wohlgemuth (1911). Budde believed that MAE magnitude increased with adaptation velocity until flicker fusion was reached. Dureman (1962) also found that increasing adaptation velocity increased MAE, but as the adaptation stimulus was a rotating disk it is unclear what the adaptation velocity was in any condition. Sekuler and Pantle (1967) found that increasing adaptation velocity *reduced* the MAE, but as their slowest adaptation velocity was over 2 degrees/second, their finding is perfectly consistent with the idea that there is a peak velocity at approximately 2 degrees/second, as Scott and Noland (1965) suggested.

Another school of thought suggests that the MAE is independent of adaptation velocity. This was reported by Johansson (1956), but as Johansson reports that his apparatus "is described in an unpublished paper" but not the published one, it is hard to evaluate his findings.

The studies described above might be regarded in the main as "early findings." Where the stimuli are described in detail it is clear that results from one study cannot be compared with those in another study. All too often there is too little detail to determine what was done at all. Only when the scourge of the sine-wave grating swept psychophysics did a stimulus emerge that was reasonably consistent across studies and one that was appropriate for answering questions about the importance of velocity, spatial frequency, and temporal frequency tuning. An early paper to examine the magnitude of the MAE as a function of adaptation temporal frequency and velocity was by Pantle (1974). This highly cited paper concludes that adaptation temporal frequency, not velocity, determines MAE magnitude. Pantle adapted subjects to a sine-wave grating of 3 cycles/degree drifting at a range of rates between 0.3 and 40 Hz. The peak aftereffect was found with an adaptation temporal frequency of 5 Hz (or 1.6 degrees/second). Repeating the experiment with grating of a spatial frequency of 6 cycles/degree, Pantle found that the peak MAE was still found at 5 Hz and not at 10 Hz, the latter rate being the same velocity as the optimal in the 3 cycle/degree condition.

Thus the spatiotemporal tuning of the MAE can be summarized as follows: the greatest MAE is found with an adaptation temporal frequency of about 5 Hz (Pantle, 1974), with the adaptation spatial frequency matching the test spatial frequency (Cameron et al., 1992; Bex et al., 1996). P. Thompson's data (1976) referred to in the previous section, manipulated both spatial and temporal frequencies. His results are completely in accord with the spatial tuning reported by Cameron et al. (1989), but while they do confirm that the MAE is greatest with an adaptation temporal frequency around 5 Hz, they do not appear to show the dramatic temporal tuning reported by Pantle. One reason may be that Pantle examined a wider range of adaptation temporal frequencies (seven octaves) than did Thompson (five octaves).

3.3 Dynamic Aftereffects

In recent years the suggestion has been made that the nature of the MAE depends upon the type of test pattern employed. Specifically, Hiris and Blake (1992) have suggested that when dynamic visual noise is used as a test pattern for the MAE, it ensures that the neural mechanisms affected during adaptation are implicated in the aftereffect, in contrast to the traditional stationary test display; thus, they claim, the MAEs elicited by each sort of test pattern are distinctly different. A number of other differences have now emerged that seem to depend on the static vs. flicker test display. First, adaptation to second-order motion does not produce an MAE on a static display, but does on a flickering display; see, for example, Nishida, Ashida, et al. (1994). Second, the spatial frequency tuning described above is only found on static test patterns; no such specificity is found with flickering test patterns (see Ashida and Osaka, 1994). Third, it seems likely that the MAEs with flicker tests show complete interocular transfer, whereas with stationary tests the interocular transfer is a more traditional 70 percent (see Raymond, 1993a). Finally, using flicker test patterns it appears that the MAE is partially velocit-tuned (Ashida and Osaka 1995b), rather than showing a maximum at some adaptation temporal frequency (see section 3.2). Intriguingly, this finding marries very neatly with findings on velocity aftereffects that are looked at in the next section.

3.4 Velocity Aftereffects

If we extend the definition of the MAE to include the effects of motion adaptation on subsequently presented moving patterns, as well as on stationary patterns, then we can examine velocity tuning of the test pattern as well as of the adaptation pattern. These effects have a long and distinguished history and have been called "velocity aftereffects" by P. Thompson (1976,1981) because the magnitude of the aftereffect seems to be determined by the adaptation velocity rather than by its temporal frequency, spatial frequency, or speed.

The first report of such effects comes (almost inevitably) from Wohlgemuth's monograph; in his experiment fifteen subjects fixated between two vertical belts of horizontal black-and-white stripes. The left-hand belt was stationary while the right-hand belt was set in motion at a constant velocity. After about 30 seconds of adaptation the left-hand belt was set in motion at the same speed as the right-hand belt. Wohlgemuth noted that the perceived speed of the two belts was not equal, the previous adaptation reducing the perceived velocity of the right-hand belt. This effect was "rediscovered" by Gibson (1937) who reported:

> Two contiguous openings with shutters are cut in a screen and a moving surface is set up behind them. The observer, who should fixate a point on the screen, will find the two fields will appear to move at the same speed when both shutters are opened at the same

time. But if one field is exposed first for a short time and then the other window is opened, the first field will look slower that the second, and the two areas of movement may not coincide in apparent speed for some seconds. (p. 325)

These two studies, and a third by Goldstein (1959), only examined the effects of movement adaptation upon a stimulus moving at the adaptation velocity. The consistent finding of a reduced perceived velocity in the test stimulus fitted well with Gibson's view that the motion dimension was shifted by adaptation so that the "null point" of the dimension (a stationary pattern in the case of motion) was shifted toward the adaptation condition (figure 3.3). A clear prediction of this general model is that after adaptation all stimuli moving in the adaptation direction will be reduced in perceived speed and all stimuli moving in the opposite direction will be increased in perceived speed.

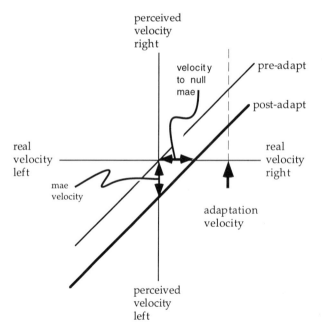

Figure 3.3
A possible model of the effects of adaptation to motion on the perceived speed of subsequently presented motion. The whole velocity dimension is shifted to bring the null point (a stationary pattern) toward the adaptation velocity. This will perceptually slow all speeds in the adaptation direction and increase the perceived speed of patterns in the opposite direction.

It was not until 1962 that Carlson tested this type of model further by investigating the effects of adapting to one rate of motion upon a range of test velocities, both in the same and in the opposite direction as the adaptation motion. Carlson's subjects estimated the time it would take for a line to travel from its point of disappearance after crossing a window to reach a point beyond the window. Three adaptation and test velocities were used—30, 40, and 53 degrees/second; test stimuli were investigated both in the same and in the opposite direction as the adaptation motion. Two significant results emerged. First, when the adaptation velocity matched the test velocity the perceived velocity was reduced by adaptation, confirming the previous results of Wohlgemuth (1911), Gibson (1937), and Goldstein (1959). Second, when adaptation velocity was greater than the test velocity (in the same direction), the perceived test velocity was also reduced, again in accord with the model shown in figure 3.3. Although the other conditions did not produce significant results, there were interesting trends in the data. Following adaptation in motion in one direction there was a trend for test stimuli in the opposite direction to be perceived as slower, a result that clearly is in conflict with the model, and test stimuli that are in the same direction but faster than the adaptation motion tended to be overestimated, again an unexpected result. Rapoport (1964) carried out an experiment that was similar to Carlson's except that rotary movement was used and a magnitude estimation technique was employed to quantify the effect. The results in which adaptation and test directions were the same supported Carlson: tests equal to or slower than the adaptation were perceptually slowed and faster tests were now significantly faster. When adaptation and test stimuli moved in opposite directions, the results were inconclusive, but the speeding up of test stimuli predicted by the model was not found. These findings were supported by Clymer (1973) who, further, found a significant slowing of test stimuli after adaptation in the opposite direction. Thus, the accumulated results of these early studies suggest the pattern of results shown in figure 3.4.

These findings suggest some tuning of the aftereffect in that when the test pattern is similar to the adaptation pattern, there is usually a perceived reduction in speed, whereas test stimuli moving at very different speeds are either unaffected or actually look faster. This pattern of results was confirmed in an extensive series of experiments by P. Thompson (1976, 1981), with further elaboration coming from A. T. Smith (1985). When Thompson measured the perceived velocity of moving patterns following adaptation to patterns moving in the same direction, he found that (1) the magnitude of the aftereffect is determined by the velocity of the adaptation stimulus regardless of the spatial and temporal frequencies of the stimulus, and (2) for a given adaptation velocity the aftereffect

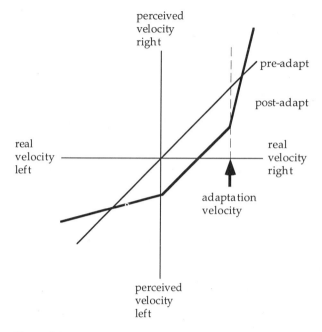

Figure 3.4
A summary of the findings of velocity aftereffect studies. The effects of adaptation upon patterns moving at the same velocity or slower than the adaptation velocity conform with the predictions of figure 3.3. However, faster movement and movement in the opposite direction do not.

magnitude remains constant for test patterns moving at equal velocities. This velocity tuning is unlike the tuning found when stationary test patterns are employed, though it shares similarities with the results of Ashida and Osaka (1995b) who employed flickering test patterns (see section 3.2).

3.5   Contrast

It is well established that several aftereffects are greatest in magnitude when the adaptation pattern has a high contrast and the test pattern has a low contrast, for example, in the case of the tilt aftereffect (see Parker, 1972; Tolhurst and Thompson, 1975), and in the spatial frequency aftereffect (see Blakemore et al., 1970). The same dependence in the MAE has a long history going back at least to von Szily (1905, 1907) who reported that the greatest MAEs are seen with weak contours, though in his experiments adaptation and test contours always had the same contrast. More recently, Keck et al. (1976) have shown that, as a rule of thumb, increasing adaptation contrast increases the aftereffect and reducing the test contrast does the same. P. Thompson (1976) found the same relationship in the velocity aftereffect. Recently there has been considerable interest in the effect of contrast on the MAE. Physiologic recordings of cells in the primate magnocellular pathway reveal cells whose response saturates at low contrasts, around an average of 9 percent according to Sclar, Maunsell, et al. (1990). Some of the Keck et al. (1976) results have been taken to be a psychophysical manifestation of this saturation, specifically one finding that MAE duration increases rapidly as adaptation contrast rises to 3 percent, but thereafter contrast has little effect on MAE duration. Unfortunately, this evidence may not support the notion that the motion system is contrast independent quite as strongly as some hope when it is taken into consideration that in the same paper Keck et al. find that initial MAE speed continues to increase with adaptation contrast beyond 3 percent. Later work by Keck, Montague, et al. (1980) found that at low spatial frequencies MAE speed increased linearly with log adaptation contrast up to 80 percent. Only when much higher spatial frequencies were used did signs of saturation occur—hard to reconcile with the predilection for lower spatial frequencies of the magnocellular pathway.

The most thorough investigation of the dependence of the MAE upon contrast, a study by Nishida, Ashida, et al. (1997a), effectively demolishes the notion that some rapidly saturating motion system is revealed by the interaction of adaptation and test contrasts in the MAE. They examined the effects of adaptation and test contrast on both static and flicker MAEs, finding that although the MAE magnitude saturates at low adaptation contrast when the test pattern is of low contrast, no such saturation is found when the test contrast is high. The authors see this interaction as being consistent with the hypothesis that adaptation is a gain control process rather than a fatigue process. Furthermore, they report that the seemingly complex dependency of the MAE on adaptation and test contrasts is well described by a single dependency "of adaptation contrast normalised by test contrast on a logarithmic axis". This general conclusion is supported by a number of other experiments (e.g., see Raymond and Darcangelo's, 1990, study of the effects of contrast on induced movement) that have been reviewed by P. Thompson (1993).

3.6 Storage of the Motion Aftereffect

Wohlgemuth (1911), having measured the duration of the MAE, instructed subjects to close their eyes immediately after adaptation for a period of time longer than the expected aftereffect. Upon opening their eyes the subjects reported a residual effect, albeit one somewhat shorter than the original MAE. Thus the decay of the MAE appeared to have been retarded by the period of darkness. This effect is known as "storage" and has been examined in some detail by Spigel (1960, 1962a,b, 1964) and more recently by Verstraten and colleagues (1994b) and Thompson and Wright (1994b) who have suggested that storage can occur not only if the time period between adaptation and test is spent in darkness but also if a wide range of patterns other than the stationary adaptation pattern are present.

There are several other studies that suggest that recovery from the MAE can be extremely slow. Masland (1969) reported the MAE to be visible some 26 hours after a 15-minute adaptation period. Effects of this length are reminiscent of the McCollough effect (McCollough, 1965) which has been demonstrated to persist over several months (Jones and Holding, 1976). Further support for this view comes from the fact that the decay of contingent aftereffects, investigated by Skowbo, Gentry, et al. (1974), exhibits many of the properties of MAE storage.

3.7 Retinal Specificity

Most aftereffects show retinal specificity. That is, the aftereffect is only manifest when the area of the retina that was adapted also receives the test pattern. Wohlgemuth (among others) showed that MAEs in opposite directions could be produced from adjacent parts of the retina, demonstrating the importance of retinal specificity; those wanting a more recent quantification of this should look at Masland (1969). However, any statement that the MAE is only manifest when the area of the retina exposed to adaptation motion is tested needs to be qualified. There are at least four caveats. First, as has been mentioned already, the MAE shows interocular transfer. Thus an area of the retina that has not been exposed to motion can give rise to the MAE. Second, it appears that real object movement need not occur during adaptation in order for an MAE to be observed during the test. That is, there is evidence that moving the eyes over a stationary pattern will elicit an MAE. Addams (1834) concludes his paper by reporting that the MAE can be generated "by moving the head up and down or laterally; but to particularize all the circumstances would make this communication inconveniently long." A model of brevity to us all as the paper can be scarcely 500 words long! Third, tracking real movement may not give rise to an MAE according to Anstis and Gregory (1965) who claimed that although moving the eyes over a stationary pattern does produce an MAE, tracking a moving grating does not. This last result was challenged by Morgan, Ward, et al. (1976) who found an aftereffect following the tracking of a moving pattern. They reconciled these differences by proposing that while tracking the moving stripes the stationary periphery moved across the retina and the subsequent MAE in the periphery induced an MAE in the central retina.

This leads us to the fourth caveat, the role of surrounds in generating the MAE. Aitken (1878) first demonstrated that adapting to whole-field motion produces no MAE—a result confirmed by Wohlgemuth but challenged by Thalman (1921). Later work by Day and Strelow (1971) stressed the importance of a surround in producing the MAE, and recent work by Swanston and Wade (1992) and Wade et al. (1996) has demonstrated that the MAE is only manifest when nonadapted as well as adapted regions of space are tested. Fifthly, L. R. Harris et al. (1981) report that adaptation to an expanding pattern of dots when yoked with forward motion of the subject produces almost no aftereffect; this, the authors suggest, is because "the correct metrical arrangement is maintained ... between the expanding visual field and other cues to forward motion." This perhaps explains why the MAE is rarely reported by motorists. Five caveats are enough for anyone, though we could point to more; we might even refer to the MAE as an example of a retinally contingent MAE, but that way madness lies.

3.8 Conclusions

The MAE in its various guises does depend upon the spatiotemporal parameters of adaptation and test patterns. However, although there is generally a good degree of agreement between the various studies that have investigated such aspects of the MAE, the results have shed little light on the nature of the underlying motion mechanisms in the visual pathway compared with the insights gained from studies investigating spatial aftereffects. Why should this be? The answer may be that motion tuning is broad and we have little idea of how different aspects of motion speed and velocity are coded in the visual cortex. It may be that different aspects of motion are encoded at different sites which have different properties and different adaptation characteristics It may be that when we talk of adaptation we are talking of a range of phenomena, from the fatigue of single units to the adjustments of sophisticated gain control mechanisms. These issues are taken up in chapter 7. Of course it may be that the certainty of the results derived from spatial aftereffects is itself an illusion.

Chapter 4

The Retinal Image, Ocularity, and Cyclopean Vision

Bernard Moulden, Robert Patterson, and Michael Swanston

One measure of progress in a field is the degree to which research questions that once seemed fundamental and crucial now seem naive and simplistic. Sometimes this may only reflect differences in the available technology, or—worse—the assumption that scientific progress is necessarily entailed by the passage of time (see Wade, 1996). However, it is also possible that such a change in view is an indication of real progress in understanding. In the case of visual movement perception, the questions we now ask do seem, on the whole, to demonstrate the richness of the knowledge gained over the last two or three decades. In parallel with the advance in our understanding have come technological developments that have permitted us on the one hand to generate and to exploit very sophisticated stimuli, and on the other hand to make subtle explorations of the electrophysiologic response properties of neurons in visual systems of animals.

One question that does still seem fundamental is the following: To what extent is the extraction of visual information about motion in the environment carried out by mechanisms that are "tuned," or specialized, to respond to motion, and to what extent are processes involved which have less rigidly defined operating characteristics, and whose properties cannot be predicted from relatively simple transforms of the retinal image?

The basic philosophy, usually implicit, underlying much research on the motion (and other) aftereffects was encapsulated crudely but effectively by Mollon (1974) with the aphorism, "If it adapts, it's there."

The broad notion is that any low-level filtering mechanism is likely to lose sensitivity with prolonged firing (e.g., by a gain reduction; see, e.g., Greenlee, Georgeson, et al., 1991; Wilson and Humanski, 1993; reviewed in chapter 7). As a result of this adaptation the pattern of firing in an array of filters in response to any stimulus will be distorted compared with its unadapted response. The distortion in the response pattern will be reflected by a change in the appearance, including the detectability, of a subsequently viewed stimulus. This change in appearance is the aftereffect. The existence of an aftereffect is taken as evidence for the existence of an adaptable filter specifically tuned to the stimulus property in question, and by manipulating the degree of similarity between the adapting stimulus and the test stimulus the degree of stimulus specificity of the adaptation, and therefore the filter's response selectivity, may be inferred.

One logical weakness of this approach, rarely made explicit, is of course that any mechanism that did not exhibit adaptation could never be revealed in this way. It is worth bearing in mind that even if the existence of an aftereffect can be taken to indicate the existence of special-purpose low-level mechanisms (and some would debate even this; see below), the absence of an aftereffect may not be taken necessarily to demonstrate the absence of such mechanisms. All of the conclusions described in this chapter are subject to this caveat.

As hinted above, the logical position has been further blurred by two intriguing recent studies (Culham and Cavanagh, 1994; Lankheet and Verstraten, 1995) which challenge even the notion that only low-level mechanisms adapt. For example, Lankheet and Verstraten (1995) required observers to adapt to a bidirectional motion display composed of superimposed leftward and rightward moving dot arrays. The observers were required to "attentively track" one or the other direction of movement—that is, to pay exclusive attention to one of the directions, but without moving their eyes as they would in normal tracking. Upon viewing a dynamic test pattern, Lankheet and Verstraten found a shift of the baseline psychometric function for direction sensitivity but little or no phenomenal aftereffect as in the classic case. Because the adapting motion was bidirectional, and therefore should have produced no net adaptation effect in the preattentive motion system, the argument is that it must have been the attentive tracking that induced the aftereffect.

Until the nature of the mechanisms underlying this phenomenon is firmly established, its precise implications are going to remain unclear. There are just too many possible explanations. For example, perhaps "attention" is a mechanism for suppressing unwanted neural activity. If this mechanism were to operate so as to suppress the response of low-level filters signaling, say, rightward movement, then only the leftward-signaling filters would be active, become adapted, and mediate an aftereffect. It would then still be possible to argue that the motion aftereffect (MAE) reflects the operation of low-level mechanisms even in an "attentive tracking" paradigm. The jury is out, but in the meantime we need to be circumspect in drawing inferences in this respect.[1] A detailed discussion of research on attentional effects in motion adaptation may be found in chapter 5.

Nevertheless, we can still glean important insights from such studies if these caveats are kept in mind. Accordingly, what follows is a review of studies investigating different stages of processing as reflected in the MAE, such as the importance of retinal image motion for inducing the MAE, whether motion is encoded before or after (or before *and* after) the point of binocular fusion, and whether the answers depend on the precise nature of the movement in question. All of these issues arise in the context of a review of studies of ocularity and cyclopean vision as they relate to the MAE.

4.1 The Importance of Retinal Image Motion

One venerable question to which the rationale described earlier has been applied is the following. Imagine a grating moving from left to right. Whether an observer visually tracks one bar of the grating so that the retinal image is effectively immobile on the retina, or whether he or she fixates some stationary point so that the image of the grating flows across the retina, the subjective impression of motion is to all intents and purposes the same. Are the two identical impressions of motion, then, mediated by identical visual mechanisms?

One way of approaching the question is to ask whether retinal image motion is or is not essential for the generation of an MAE. If it is, one might infer that the adaptable mechanism responds only to retinal image motion. As will be seen below, however, the question as posed above is deceptively simple. Even though the issue is central to an understanding of how evolution has shaped the solution to this basic visual problem, the situation is considerably more complex than might have been suspected, and the review below will indicate that the last word on this topic has yet to be written.

Although a venerable phenomenon in its own right, the most important role of the MAE has been to inform us about the mechanisms used by the human visual system to extract information either about the motion of the observer with respect to the environment, or about the motion of objects with respect to the observer and the environment. This is the broader philosophical context for the specific questions that have been posed in the laboratory. The following provides an outline of one instantiation of this broader theoretical context, as a background to some research findings. It also illustrates the latent complexities that may be hidden even in what are apparently the most simple questions and observations.

Further, the characteristics of the visual field against which the MAE is observed can be manipulated, and have been shown to produce independent influences on the measured aftereffect (see, e.g., Wade et al., 1996). Many of the effects of these variables can be understood in terms of processes leading to the recovery of object motion with respect to the environment, which we call geocentric motion. Swanston, Wade, et al. (1987,

1990) and Wade and Swanston (1987) have identified stages in the transformation of retinal motion information from a retinocentric to a geocentric coordinate system, and have also identified the extraretinal information needed for this transformation.

Essentially, the model describes the successive frames of reference with respect to which motion information may be represented, and predicts the perceptual consequences of error at the various stages. According to this approach, motion aftereffects can be attributed to the functioning of mechanisms at one or more of these stages (Swanston, 1994).

Consider the situation in which retinal stimulation is uniform, that is, all points in the retinal image move with the same velocity and in the same direction. Under this condition the "uniform process" is the component of the motion processing system that is responsible for the recovery of object motion with respect to the environment, irrespective of movements of the eyes in the head, the head with respect to the trunk, or of the observer with respect to the environment. Uniform stimulation is not normally encountered except under laboratory conditions, since there will typically be relative motion between visual objects, as, for example, when a bird flies through a scene. It is true that if smooth pursuit eye movements are made across a stable scene, then there will be uniform retinal stimulation from enviromental features. However, such eye movements are normally generated voluntarily in the presence of a smoothly moving target (Carpenter, 1988) and this will result in relative motion between the target and the environment.

The model of the uniform process has been extended to include the motion of one visual object relative to another, which has been termed "patterncentric" motion (Swanston, 1994; Wade and Swanston, 1987; Wade et al., 1993). This term retains the sense of a frame of reference, in this case a purely visual one. Extraction of patterncentric motion implies that one set of visual objects acts as a frame of reference for another. Thus the motion is represented entirely in terms of the relative motion of one set of visual objects. Since a frame of reference is necessarily assigned a velocity of zero, motion of both sets of visual objects can only be represented in terms of a further superordinate frame of reference.

The extended model is illustrated diagrammatically in figure 4.1. All boxes except those labeled as, or falling between, "patterncentric" boxes form part of the uniform process. The model proposes that patterncentric information is merged with retinocentric information after the latter has been adjusted to take into account movements of the eyes with respect to the head. These signals are equivalent in that they are both in principle independent of such eye movements if the small effect of ocular parallax on image motion during eye movements with objects at different distances is ignored.

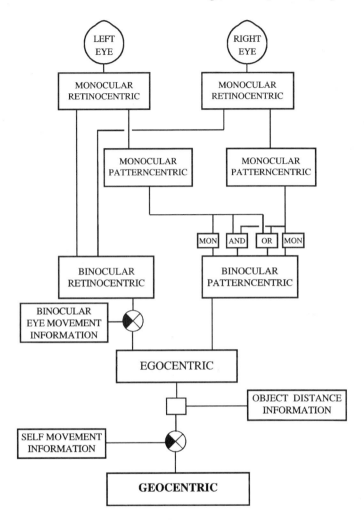

Figure 4.1
Representational framework for motion perception. Retinal motion information is transformed from a retinocentric to a geocentric coordinate system by means of a series of intermediate stages that take into account extraretinal information. See text for details.

The resulting egocentric representation expresses motion with respect to the head, independently of eye movements in the head, but in terms of an effectively angular displacement, because at this stage no information is available to determine the spatial extent of object motion. This can be achieved by scaling egocentric motion for the perceived egocentric distance of the moving object. There is considerable evidence that the human visual system does indeed carry out such a process (e.g., Gogel, 1990). This spatial motion can then be compensated for the spatial extent of head motion. The resulting motion information is specified with respect to the environment and is therefore geocentric, as required. Observers' reports are always geocentric, but may correspond to representations at other levels if the necessary controls are present.

The functional, experimental, and theoretical significance of this is made clear by a consideration of typical displays used to examine the MAE. If the adapting motion is linear, it is almost invariably viewed within a visible stationary surround. Consequently, there will be information both about the motion of the adapting stimulus with respect to the retina and about its motion with respect to other visual features. The relative contributions of uniform and patterncentric motion cannot in these circumstances be logically separated.

Moreover, if the observer's eyes are in motion, then retinocentric effects cannot be differentiated from egocentric or geocentric ones. If the velocity of the adapting motion is nonuniform (e.g., rotary or spiral), then the gradient of relative motion with respect to a stationary center of rotation will ensure that there is always patterncentric information available.

The difficulties of interpreting results from experiments without strict control over these factors is illustrated by the long-running controversy over whether retinal motion per se is sufficient to produce an MAE.

Motion of the image of an object over the retina is neither a necessary nor a sufficient condition for the perception of motion (Gogel, 1990). However, it is possible that such image motion could still give rise to an MAE, even if it had not been perceived as motion during the inspection phase. Such a condition arises when, for example, an observer's eyes move over a stationary surface.

Anstis and Gregory (1965) and Tolhurst and Hart (1972) reported that motion of contours over the retina could produce an MAE, even when the contours themselves were stationary and the image motion was solely the result of eye movements. Observers tracked a moving point across a stationary field of stripes, and subsequently reported a normal MAE in a stationary test field. However, this seemingly straightforward finding is not what has been reported in circumstances that in all functional characteristics might appear at first sight to be identical.

Morgan et al. (1976) and Mack et al. (1987, 1989) did not obtain the expected MAE after eye movements in pursuit of a grating moving across another stationary grating. If the tracked grating had been functionally interchangeable with the tracked spot in the studies described above, an MAE would have been generated that was in the same direction as the movement of the eyes in the inspection phase—that is, of course, in the opposite direction to the relative motion of the physically stationary grating.

What observers actually reported was an MAE associated with the pursued grating, the contours of which were (approximately) stationary on the retina throughout the inspection phase. This MAE was in the opposite direction to that of the movement of the eyes during the inspection phase. Mack et al. (1989) suggested that this MAE was, in part, a consequence of adaptation to a motion signal derived not from any single source such as the retinal image motion, but from a comparison of the eye motion and the retinal image motion. Swanston and Wade (1992) reported an experiment (their experiment 1) which confirmed the results of Mack et al. (1987), using a similar display.

However, with the acuity of hindsight it is clear that neither of these studies was without blemish. In both cases the static fixation condition and the tracking conditions did not produce equivalent stimulation of all retinal regions, as they were notionally designed to do. In the static fixation condition, the moving and stationary fields covered equal areas on either side of the fixation point throughout adaptation, but this was not the case when observers pursued a fixation point moving from one side of the display to the other. Since there were visible features other than the adaptation field, it was also not possible to differentiate uniform from patterncentric effects; even if a display is observed in an otherwise dark laboratory, motion of contours within a fixed screen window creates boundaries by dynamic occlusion and disclosure.

Swanston and Wade (1992) developed an experimental procedure which addresses these issues. All visible features were eliminated other than rectangular fields consisting of vertical gray bars. These fields moved bodily so that there was no boundary at which bars appeared and disappeared. In one experiment there were three grating fields consisting of a central field, with one above it, and one below. In one condition the upper and lower gratings moved from the right to the left while the central field remained stationary. When the upper and lower fields reached the limit of their motion, the screen was briefly blanked and the cycle repeated. In the other condition, the upper and lower gratings were stationary and the central grating moved from the left to the right in a similar cyclic manner. In both conditions fixation was maintained on a small cross located within the middle bar of the central grating; the retinal stimulation was therefore identical in the two conditions.

MAE duration was measured for the central and the surround fields on separate trials, with a test field consisting of all three fields in alignment. Despite the fact that only the images of the surround fields moved on the retina, the MAE was confined to the retinally stationary central field. This distribution of the MAE was the same whether the central field was physically moving or stationary, or whether the eyes moved or were stationary.

These results, together with those of other studies reviewed by Reinhardt-Rutland (1987a) and Swanston (1994), demonstrate the importance of patterncentric, rather than just local retinal, information for the MAE. Anstis and Reinhardt-Rutland (1976) showed that adaptation to an induced movement can result in an MAE. A large field of random dots rotated alternately clockwise and counterclockwise around a stationary target, which consisted of two concentric annuluses. The inner annulus was filled with texture when the field rotated clockwise, and the outer one was blanked. When the field direction was reversed, the inner annulus was blanked and the outer one was filled with texture. There was a strong induced movement within the annuluses, and corresponding oppositely directed MAEs. The authors concluded that the relative motion between the surround and the annulus, which was perceptually attributed almost entirely to the stationary texture, was sufficient to produce an MAE. This study addressed the issue of whether misattributed patterncentric information can produce an MAE, and there was extensive relative motion in all conditions, during both adaptation and testing. Wade et al. (1996) used the procedure described earlier to eliminate patterncentric information in adaptation or test. The center and surround gratings could each be either present or absent in the adaptation or test phase. Thus, in one experiment, adaptation was only to the movement of the upper and lower gratings (the surround), and the central field was black with a small faintly luminous fixation cross. In the test phase all three fields were present, and observers were asked to report on the MAE, if any, in the central field.

In this and other experiments, it was found that no MAEs could be measured in either the center or the surround gratings when the test stimulus was the center grating alone or the surround gratings alone, but that an MAE was reported in the surround gratings when they were themselves surrounded by stationary gratings during testing.

It seemed that the picture, though more complex than had been suspected, was nevertheless becoming clear—the aftereffect depended on adaptation of a retinal region to motion, but the MAE would only be expressed when the test field consisted of a stimulus that had contours covering previously unadapted parts of the retina, as well as previously adapted parts. However, as it turns out, the picture is even more complex yet.

The results described above were obtained with linear motion. A different conclusion was reached by Symons et al. (1996), who presented observers with a random-dot pattern moving horizontally within a circular field. This field, which was presented monocularly, either was or was not surrounded by a stationary annulus containing random dots, presented either to the same or to the opposite eye, during either the adaptation or the test phase or both. They reported that the stationary surround only increased the duration of the MAE in the central field if it had also been present, in the same eye, during adaptation.

This finding implies that at least some aspects of adaptation can occur as the result of monocular relative motion and be specific to the eye of adaptation. The display contained patterncentric information even when the annulus was not present, due to the boundary of the central field at which dots appeared and disappeared, and the experimental comparisons were between conditions with varying strengths of information for relative motion between visual elements. Support for this account is given by the findings of Ashida, Susami, et al. (1996) and Ashida and Susami (1997). They used a display which permitted the analysis of the contribution from relative motion to the MAE, and which was derived from that used by Swanston and Wade (1992). In both studies, it was found that adaptation occurred to both local and relative motion, and that for a MAE to be present in testing, previously adapted areas needed to receive patterned stimulation. Ashida and Susami (1997) concluded that the MAE should be regarded as "a composite phenomenon reflecting multiple sites of adaptation." Swanston (1994) reached a similar conclusion.

In the light of the foregoing discussion, it appears that two distinct kinds of MAE may exist: (1) an MAE based upon pursuit eye movements whose characteristics may not directly reflect the operation of direction-selective cells; and (2) an MAE based upon patterncentric information whose characteristics do directly reflect the operation of direction-selective cells. Although it is not known to what degree the pursuit-derived MAE entails a binocular substrate, it is likely that the patterncentric MAE does entail a binocular substrate because many pattern-related attributes (e.g., texture, binocular disparity) are probably coded by extrastriate binocular mechanisms. In the following sections we examine a number of topics related to binocular MAEs.

4.2 Preattentive Motion Processing and Binocularity

The seemingly simple question of whether and how motion processing is binocular is difficult to answer, perhaps impossible, because it is likely that the perception of motion is mediated by multiple processes—in other words, that there is more than one kind of motion processing. These processes include lower-order (i.e., passive) operations involving arrays of localized motion detectors that act preattentively and mechanistically (see, e.g., Adelson and Bergen, 1985), as well as higher-order (i.e., active) attentional processes that select stimulus features for motion processing (Lu and Sperling, 1995a,b; Shulman, 1993) or whose operation itself generates motion signals when moving objects are tracked (Anstis, 1978, 1980; Braddick, 1980; Cavanagh, 1992, 1995). A more rewarding question may be whether binocular motion-detecting mechanisms are different from monocular ones.

A pervasive assumption underlying all of these studies has been that preattentive, low-level processes are monocular, while postattentive processes are binocular. A number of techniques other than adaptation and aftereffect have been used to address the question. One piece of evidence suggesting a monocular substrate for preattentive motion processing is the following. When successive frames of a motion sequence are presented to different eyes (i.e., dichoptically) motion perception is specifically degraded for visual displays which are thought to reveal early motion processing, such as random-dot kinematograms (Braddick, 1974) or pedestal displays (Lu and Sperling, 1995b).

However, the failure of interocular integration of motion frames with random-dot kinematograms or pedestal displays could be due to factors other than the lack of a binocular substrate. Such factors include the difficulty of establishing perceptual correspondence across eyes as well as frames of a motion sequence involving many elements (Cavanagh and Mather, 1989) or the use of a task involving the identification of motion-defined boundaries, as in the original kinematogram study by Braddick (1974; see Carney and Shadlen, 1993).

One approach thought likely to help resolve this issue was to employ an MAE paradigm which involved information that is intrinsically binocular. Until recent years it has been assumed that only the preattentive, low-level process displays adaptation effects. On this basis, it would be reasonable to infer that MAEs possessing binocular characteristics would reflect the binocularity of the preattentive system. The work of Culham and Cavanagh (1994) and Lankheet and Verstraten (1995), which showed the existence of attentive-tracking MAEs and which is discussed above, now suggests at least that such an interpretation needs to be treated with caution.

The purpose of this section is to review the psychophysical literature on certain aspects of the MAE which speak to the question of whether motion processing in general is mediated by a binocular substrate, and in particular whether the preattentive process, the postattentive process, or both, are mediated by such a substrate. Note that there are reasons to suspect that both levels of processing are to be found at neural levels beyond the point of binocular convergence. As pointed out by Carney and Shadlen (1993), neurophysiologic studies of cats and monkeys show that directionally selective responses first arise in cortical cells that are binocular (e.g., Hammond and Pomfrett, 1989; Hubel and Wiesel, 1962; Maunsell and Van Essen, 1983a,b; Schiller et al., 1976). Direction selectivity and binocularity are properties that coexist at higher cortical stages as well (Roy, and Wurtz, 1990; Roy, Komatsu, et al., 1992; Zeki, 1978).

Like most mammals, humans have two spatially distinct primary visual detectors. Each eye separately projects to some neurons that are purely monocular; and both eyes together project to some common binocular neurons. This provides a unique opportunity for some functional neuroanatomical analysis, via two logical routes.

First, the existence of two independent input channels offers the opportunity to examine the qualitative and quantitative differences between visual effects generated by stimuli presented to either eye alone or to both eyes together. This in turn permits us to draw inferences about any quantitative or qualitative commonalities or differences between the mechanisms that are assumed to mediate those effects. This in itself has proved a very fruitful line of inquiry, but the paradigm is even richer than it might have seemed at first sight.

The second opportunity arises from the fact that it is possible to generate percepts that are *only* available to mechanisms that are at or beyond the point of binocular fusion: they simply do not exist for either of the monocular channels alone. Such stimuli are known, since Julesz (1971), as "cyclopean" stimuli. The best-known such stimulus is the random-dot stereogram pair. A percept of depth emerges only because of the structured *differences* between the two monocular images; by definition, this difference information cannot be available to either monocular channel alone. Such stimuli provide a powerful tool for the exploration of binocular channels. The paradigm related to these stimuli is called the cyclopean MAE paradigm.

We turn now to a consideration of the kinds of questions that have been asked by these two paradigms, some of the answers that have been obtained, and a few of the many remaining mysteries.

4.3 Ocularity

In 1691 Isaac Newton wrote a letter to John Locke in which he described at some length his observations of a persistent afterimage (almost certainly a scotoma) engendered by observing the sun through his spyglass. He commented:

... though I looked upon ye sun with my right eye and not with my left, yet my phansy began to make ye impression upon my left eye as well as upon my right. For if I shut my right eye and looked upon a book or the clouds with my left eye I could see ye spectrum of the sun almost as plain as with my right eye.... (Newton, 1691/1961, p. 153)

This may be the first recorded observation of the interocular transfer (IOT) of an aftereffect, though the first unequivocal description of the IOT of an MAE was by Dvorak in 1870 (see Broerse et al., 1994). The mechanism of transfer has only recently been understood; even as recently as 1953 the possibility of signals being literally transferred from one eye to the other was taken sufficiently seriously to be judged worthy of refutation on the grounds that "There is no known anatomical opportunity for a retina-to-retina transfer...." (Walls, 1953, p. 59).

The core of the current view, that IOT is mediated by the adaptation of binocular neurons, was published by three different research groups virtually simultaneously, in the early 1970s (Coltheart, 1971; Movshon, Chambers, et al., 1972; Mitchell and Ware, 1974).

In 1980 Moulden proposed the first well-elaborated model designed to account for what was then known about the existence and relative magnitude of the aftereffects generated under various combinations of using one or the other or both eyes during inspection or test phases (figure 4.2). This model may be conveniently referred to as the "intersection of sets model" since it is based upon which sets of (monocular and binocular) neurons are involved in both adaptation and test phases: it proposes that the magnitude of an aftereffect is determined by the proportion of the units stimulated in the testing phase that have previously been adapted during the inspection phase. For example, the BIN-MON condition should generate just as large an aftereffect as the MON-MON or BIN-BIN conditions because all of the tested neurons have been previously adapted. The TRANSFER condition should generate the smallest aftereffect of all because (according to this, a logical OR model; see below) it has the smallest proportion of tested units that have previously been adapted.

Wade et al. (1993) reviewed a very large number of studies that had involved IOT of an aftereffect. Consistent with the prediction above, and despite wide variation in stimulus conditions, the aftereffect measured when the test stimulus is viewed through the eye that was not exposed to the adapting stimulus (the transferred effect) is almost invariably smaller than the same-eye effect: a median value of around 60 percent IOT emerges from studies reported over more than 100 years. (There are three

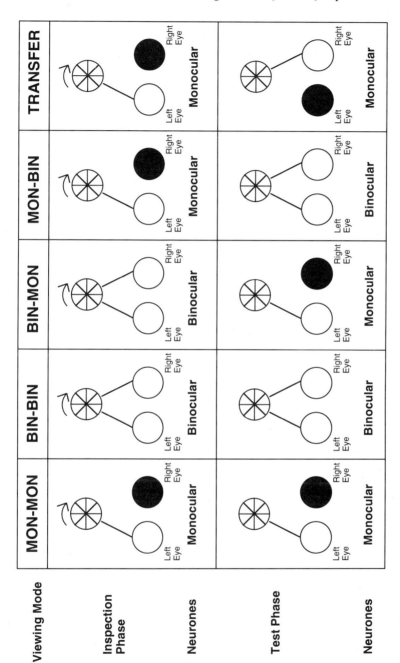

Figure 4.2
Five possible viewing modes in MAE experiments, with populations of monocular and binocular neurons involved in each. (Adapted from Moulden, 1980).

main exceptions; they are all informative, and are described later.) The explanation for partial IOT is the following.

It has been suggested that binocular interaction, as expressed through spatial aftereffects, may involve two types of binocular combination (Moulden, 1980; Wilcox, Timney, et al. 1990, Wolfe and Held, 1981). One type [Bin (OR)] involves the stimulation of either monocular channel or both channels, and is the equivalent of a logical inclusive OR operation. The other binocular channel [Bin (AND)] behaves like a logical AND operation in that it is activated by simultaneous stimulation with similar contours in each eye but not by stimulation of either eye alone.

It is possible to test for the existence of a binocular AND pathway that would be activated only by stimulation of both eyes together. This may be done in the following way. It is assumed that different viewing conditions activate different sets of neural units. Left- and right-eye monocular units are activated by stimulation of the left and right eyes, respectively. Binocular (inclusive) OR cells are activated by stimulation of either the left eye or the right eye or both eyes together. It is also assumed that an adaptation aftereffect is mediated by the pooling of activity from adapted and nonadapted pathways during the test phase (Moulden, 1980). An attempt is then made to dilute the strength of various aftereffects by activating the putative binocular AND pathway during the test phase via binocular viewing. Since this pathway would not have been adapted during the inspection phase the response of the additional unadapted units during the test phase should reduce the aftereffect.

For example, an observer may adapt to monocular stimulation in one eye and test for the aftereffect with the same eye (direct testing), the opposite eye (IOT or indirect testing), or both eyes together (binocular testing). As discussed by Timney, Wilcox, et al. (1989), if a binocular AND pathway exists, following monocular adaptation the strength of the aftereffect should be greatest with direct testing (because all pathways engaged with direct testing would have been adapted) and less with binocular and indirect testing (because not all pathways engaged with binocular and indirect testing would have been adapted), with the latter two conditions yielding equal aftereffects. However, as discussed by Moulden (1980), if there is no binocular AND pathway, following monocular adaptation the aftereffect should be greatest with direct testing, intermediate with binocular testing, and least with indirect testing (because the proportion of the pathways engaged with these testing conditions that would have been adapted would respectively decrease).

The empirical evidence is contradictory: Wolfe and Held (1981, 1983) found that the strength of the tilt aftereffect across conditions was consistent with the existence of a binocular AND pathway, but as Moulden (1980) had found, and as Wade et al. (1993) subsequently confirmed, the strength of the motion MAE (as well as the tilt aftereffect in the Moulden study) across conditions was not consistent with the existence of a binocular AND pathway. One reason for these differing results may be that the monocular-adaptation paradigm yields unreliable results (see Wilcox et al., 1990).

An observer may also adapt to alternating monocular stimulation in the two eyes and test for the aftereffect with one eye (monocular testing) or both eyes (binocular testing). If a binocular AND pathway exists, following alternating monocular adaptation the strength of the aftereffect should be greater with monocular testing than with binocular testing (because in the former case all of the pathways engaged with monocular testing would have been adapted, whereas in the latter case not all of the pathways engaged with binocular testing would have been adapted). However, if there is no binocular AND pathway, the aftereffect should be equal with monocular and binocular testing (because all of the pathways engaged with either monocular or binocular testing would have been adapted; see Timney et al., 1989).

Again, the empirical evidence is contradictory: Wolfe and Held (1981, 1983) and Wilcox et al. (1990) studied the tilt aftereffect and obtained results consistent with the existence of a binocular AND pathway. However Blake, Overton, et al. (1981a) investigated the contrast threshold elevation aftereffect and obtained evidence that was not consistent with the existence of a binocular AND pathway. Possible reasons for this discrepancy include the speculation that the binocular AND pathway, if it exists, is not activated at threshold (Wolfe and Held, 1981, 1983; Timney et al., 1989).

That the strength of an aftereffect may be diluted with binocular testing relative to monocular testing has been assumed to be due to the inclusion of a nonadapted binocular AND pathway during binocular testing. However, the strength of an aftereffect may be diluted under binocular testing for an entirely different reason, namely, binocular synergism of the OR pathway (Blake and O'Shea, 1987; Burke and Wenderoth, 1989; Timney et al., 1989). According to this idea, during binocular testing the binocular OR pathway might exhibit binocular facilitation and respond vigorously, thereby diluting the signals from the adapted monocular pathway. (During monocular adaptation the binocular OR pathway would be only slightly activated and therefore only slightly adapted.)

Thus, a given aftereffect could in principle be diluted by synergistic or facilitative activation of a binocular OR pathway during binocular testing, and it might be unnecessary to postulate the existence of a separate binocular AND pathway to account for such effects.

There is other evidence relevant to the question of a binocular AND pathway. Anstis and Duncan (1983) adapted each of their observers' eyes separately to motion in one direction and both eyes together to motion in the opposite direction; they were subsequently able to elicit separate aftereffects according to whether they tested with either eye alone or with both eyes together. These results may be explained by postulating the existence of either a binocular AND pathway or a binocular OR pathway with the latter exhibiting binocular facilitation (Anstis and Duncan, 1983).

Wolfe and Held (1982) studied the tilt aftereffect induced with a cyclopean (i.e., random-dot stereogram) adapting pattern and obtained an aftereffect with binocular testing but not with monocular testing. These results suggested the existence of a binocular AND pathway that was engaged by cyclopean stimuli but not by monocular stimuli. However, Burke and Wenderoth (1989) obtained the tilt aftereffect with a monocular adapting pattern and a cyclopean test pattern. These results suggested that a binocular OR pathway was engaged with the cyclopean stimuli.

Finally van Kruysbergen and de Weert (1994) adapted observers to a consistent motion signal presented synchronously to the two eyes (but no consistent motion presented to either eye alone nor to the two eyes asynchronously) and obtained an MAE. Although the authors assumed that the synchronous binocular information would stimulate only the binocular AND pathway, such information would likely stimulate a binocular OR pathway as well, and thus the MAE may have been mediated by a binocular OR pathway.

To summarize, the current psychophysical evidence that is taken to support the existence of a binocular AND pathway can also be explained by postulating the operation of a binocular OR pathway that displays strong binocular facilitation or binocular synergism (Blake and O'Shea, 1987; Burke and Wenderoth, 1989; Timney et al., 1989). More generally, certain stimuli that may be defined by information requiring a binocular ANDing operation could still be processed by a binocular OR pathway: it is important not to confuse stimulus with process. Results from neurophysiologic studies show that the vast majority of binocular cells in cat and monkey cortex display OR properties; very few (typically less than 10 percent) binocular cells display true AND properties (Timney et al., 1989). Taking the evidence by and large, it would probably be premature at this stage to declare the existence of a separate binocular AND pathway that serves a functional role in vision.

In an earlier section on IOT we reported that a typical figure for the magnitude of the IOT aftereffect was about 60 percent of the nontransferred aftereffect, but that there were some important exceptions.

The first exception is a case that produces IOT which is below that typically reported. Wade et al. (1993) used the three-grating display de-

scribed earlier, and varied the eye or eyes to which the central or surround gratings were presented. In one experiment, adaptation was
monocular (left eye), and testing was with the same stimulus configuration
either to the left or the right eye alone. The MAE with testing of the
unadapted eye was about 30 percent of that found with the adapted eye, a
value which recurred in the other reported experiments based on the same
methodology. As it happens, the authors' prediction was that IOT under
these conditions would actually be zero, but the fact that it is so small is
still a puzzle; this latter result could be due to the lack of common binocular features in their stimuli.

The second exception is an aftereffect described by Chaudhuri (1991).
After repeated tracking of a vertically moving luminous point, a stationary, isolated point then appears to move in the opposite direction to the
previous pursuit eye movements. Swanston and Wade (1992) found that
this aftereffect was of relatively long duration (about 30 seconds), and
that it showed 100 percent IOT. Swanston (1994) has suggested that
the aftereffect is due to continuing activity in the pursuit eye movement
system, rather than to adaptation of motion detectors. This is of considerable interest in its own right, but may not pose a challenge to theoretical orthodoxy.

The third exception certainly does raise such a challenge, and for that
reason is perhaps the most fascinating of all. The observation, reported by
two independent groups (Raymond, 1993a; Nishida et al., 1994) is this:
with dynamic (flickering) test stimuli the IOT of the MAE is 100 percent.

According to the intersection of sets model (Moulden, 1980) this
would imply that of the neurons stimulated during the testing phase, all
had previously been adapted during the inspection phase. For this to be
so, some rather interesting assumptions would have to be met. For example, the model would hold if all neurons became functionally binocular
when stimulated by dynamic stimuli; or if only binocular neurons, and
not monocular ones, were to be driven by dynamic stimuli. This is pure
speculation suggested by the apparent inconsistency between the intersection of sets model and the data described above, but the speculation
may not be entirely wild.

It is indeed possible that it is primarily binocular cells that are engaged
by dynamic stimuli. This would explain why Raymond reported 100 percent IOT with dynamic test stimuli. Raymond's suggestion was that
dynamic test patterns activate extrastriate cells (all of which are binocular), whereas static test patterns engage V1 cells (which are monocular
and binocular). Moreover, Hiris and Blake (1992) have made the stronger
claim that only a dynamic test pattern appropriately engages the motion
system (arguing that a static test pattern activates the sustained "form"

system to which the sense of motion is somehow appended). If most or all motion cells are binocular, then by extension, dynamic test patterns should engage the binocular system. It is a possibility worth pursuing.

As the above survey shows, we have a much clearer understanding today than we had just a few decades ago about the nature of mechanisms involved in coding visual movement, and about how neural signals may be integrated, but it will be clear that there are many details as yet unsettled. It may be that one key to further understanding will be the use of the complex and sophisticated stimuli employed in some of the experiments we describe next.

4.4 Cyclopean Vision

Motion can be perceived from displacement of boundaries defined by differences in other attributes besides luminance or texture (e.g., Cavanagh and Mather, 1989; Chubb and Sperling, 1989a,b; McCarthy, 1993; Turano and Pantle, 1989). A difference in disparity (a depth cue whose processing necessarily requires binocular integration) is one kind of boundary whose displacement in space and time provides information for motion processing (Cavanagh and Mather, 1989; Patterson, Ricker, et al., 1992). Motion from disparity information supports a number of motion phenomena well known in the luminance domain: bistable apparent motion in a Ternus display (Patterson, Hart, et al., 1991; Petersik, 1995); repulsive MAEs that transfer between the cyclopean and luminance domains (Patterson and Becker, 1996); direction-specific threshold elevation from adaptation (Phinney, Bowd, et al., 1997); coherent plaid motion (Bowd, Donnelly, et al., 1996a); the barber pole illusion (Bowd et al., 1996a); and classic MAEs that are retinotopic and that transfer between the cyclopean and luminance domains (Bowd et al. 1996a; Fox, Patterson, et al., 1982; Lehmkuhle and Fox, 1977; Patterson et al., 1994; Patterson, Bowd, et al., 1996; Stork, Crowell, et al., 1985)

Motion derived from stereoscopic disparity information is called "cyclopean" motion. The term "cyclopean" was coined by Julesz (1960, 1971) to refer to a mechanism which represents information existing only at binocular-integration levels of vision. He identified two kinds of cyclopean vision, strong and weak. Strongly cyclopean phenomena require input from both eyes; weakly cyclopean phenomena require input from one or the other or both eyes but are nevertheless centrally mediated, such as orientation discrimination; orientation tuning is found only at cortical levels of processing. The bulk of Julesz's work was concerned with phenomena of the strongly cyclopean kind. Note that, as discussed earlier, cyclopean information may be processed by a binocular OR pathway or by a binocular AND pathway.

An early study of what we now know as cyclopean perception can be found in the work of Sherrington (1906), who investigated the integrative action of the central nervous system within the context of spinal reflexes. As an extension of his work on reflex arcs, Sherrington examined binocular summation of flicker by presenting flickering lights alternately to the two eyes of observers while manipulating interocular phase to examine binocular summation of flicker.[2]

Since by definition cyclopean information exists only centrally at binocular-integration levels of vision (Sherrington, 1906; Julesz, 1960, 1971) the paradigm permits us functionally to partition the operation of the visual system into cyclopean vs. monocular processing, or into central vs. peripheral processing, by employing cyclopean stimuli which restrict the information to binocular-integration levels (Anstis and Moulden, 1970; Julesz, 1960, 1971; Papert, 1964).

In the following sections the emphasis is on the use of the MAE as a tool for investigating the properties of cyclopean motion detectors. Two complementary phenomena are discussed which address the issue of the binocularity of motion processing. The first phenomenon is the *cyclopean motion aftereffect*, which refers to the MAE induced by adaptation to cyclopean motion. The existence of a cyclopean MAE is proof that the visual system contains cells which code for direction of motion subsequent to binocular integration.

The second phenomenon is the *stereoscopic disparity-contingent motion aftereffect*, which refers to the induction of an MAE which is contingent upon binocular disparity. The very existence of a disparity-contingent aftereffect strongly suggests that the visual system contains cells which code for both direction of motion and binocular disparity. The specificity of the contingency can give information about whether there are different groups of cells tuned to differing values, rather than just different signs, of disparity that can be selectively adapted.

4.4.1 *The Cyclopean Motion Aftereffect*
The cyclopean MAE refers to the MAE induced by adapting to cyclopean motion, whose existence by definition depends upon binocular integration. As discussed below, there are several ways in which cyclopean motion can be created.

In the original study on the cyclopean MAE, Papert (1964) investigated whether adapting to moving cyclopean bars defined by differences in binocular disparity would induce an MAE when viewing a stationary test pattern. The cyclopean stimuli were created from a dynamic random-dot stereogram (Julesz, 1960). Using an adaptation period of 30 seconds Papert found that a cyclopean aftereffect of only a few seconds' duration was induced: "The AE [aftereffect] time with centrally produced inducing motion is very much shorter. Times of more than a second are rare with induction times (e.g., 30 seconds) that regularly give rise to long AE's with real movement . . . ."

Anstis and Moulden (1970) developed an apparent motion display in which lights making up frames of a motion sequence stimulated the two eyes in combinations that produced monocular or interocular (cyclopean) apparent motion. Adaptation to monocular apparent motion induced a monocular MAE, while adaptation to interocular apparent motion induced a "brief but definite" cyclopean aftereffect. Similar results were reported by Steinbach and Anstis (1976, cited in Anstis, 1980). Cavanagh (1995) reported no cyclopean aftereffect with stereoscopic stimuli.

Much the same finding was reported by Zeevi and Geri (1985), who generated cyclopean motion by viewing dynamic visual noise with a neutral-density filter placed over one eye. This is a variant of the Pulfrich effect, generally attributed to the fact that the dimmer image suffers a transduction delay (Δt) so that the binocular signal results from the integration of stimulus frames (t) and (t $-\Delta t$) received via the separate monocular channels. The perceptual consequence is that the dynamic noise appears to segregate into two sets of oppositely moving depth planes, one set of planes appearing behind the display monitor and the other set of planes appearing in front of the display monitor. The duration of adaptation was 20 seconds, and Zeevi and Geri reported that a cyclopean MAE of only a few seconds' duration was induced. (It is worth remarking upon the fact that the motions of the two sets of planes moving in opposite directions apparently do not cancel each other's adaptive effect as they would if they were in the same plane. This fact alone suggests the possibility that there exist mechanisms that are simultaneously specific both to a particular direction of motion and to a particular depth; this possibility is discussed in more detail below.)

All of the above studies have in common the fact that the reported cyclopean MAEs were very brief. Could it be that the nature of the adaptation, perhaps the nature of the underlying mechanism, involved in cyclopean motion is different in kind from that involved in noncyclopean motion? The answer is, probably not. A number of investigators have reported strong and long-lasting cyclopean MAEs.

Lehmkuhle and Fox (1977) and Fox et al. (1982) used dynamic random-dot stereograms, as Papert had done, to generate cyclopean grating patterns defined by binocular disparity differences. They wanted to discover whether motion of these disparity-defined bars would induce an aftereffect in a stationary cyclopean test pattern. Adaptation duration was 45 seconds in the former study and 90 seconds in the latter study. Both groups found that a strong cyclopean aftereffect lasting many seconds was induced. Similar results were reported by Stork et al. (1985).

Carney and Shadlen (1993) investigated whether adapting to cyclopean motion, created from dichoptically viewed flickering gratings presented in spatiotemporal quadrature, induced an MAE when viewing a noncyclopean test pattern. Their motion stimuli were based upon the principle of decomposing traveling sine-wave gratings into the sum of two standing waves in spatial and temporal quadrature. The interocular quadrature phase relationship engages motion sensors at binocular-integration levels of vision without the presence of binocular disparity. An aftereffect-nulling procedure was used to measure aftereffect strength. Adaptation duration was an initial 5 minutes followed by top-up periods of 4 seconds following each subsequent trial. The authors reported strong cyclopean aftereffects.

Clearly, cyclopean MAEs are not necessarily brief and weak. Apparent contradictions in the results of different studies may be largely attributable to differences in the duration of adaptation. Of the studies reporting weak or nonexistent cyclopean aftereffects, the two studies which reported the duration of adaptation employed durations of 30 seconds or less (Papert: 30 seconds; Zeevi and Geri: 20 seconds). Of the four studies reporting strong aftereffects, the three studies which reported the duration of adaptation used durations longer than 30 seconds (Lehmkuhle and Fox: 45 seconds; Fox et al: 90 seconds; Carney and Shadlen: 5 minutes). It appeared that adaptation durations greater than 30 seconds might be needed to generate marked cyclopean MAEs, and that the difference in the mechanisms underlying cyclopean and noncyclopean motion might simply be a difference in adaptation rate.

This duration hypothesis was tested directly by Patterson et al. (1994), who varied the duration of adaptation within the range 15 to 120 seconds. The aftereffect was induced by moving cyclopean grating patterns defined by binocular disparity differences (created from a dynamic random-dot stereogram), and a similar but stationary cyclopean pattern was used as the test stimulus. Only adaptation durations longer than 30 seconds produced significant aftereffects. The fact that long, strong cyclopean aftereffects can be generated provided the inspection period is long enough suggests that the underlying mechanisms are not different in kind from those that underlie luminance aftereffects. This conclusion is strengthened by a subsequent finding in a slightly different experiment by Bowd, Rose, et al. (1996b). They discovered that the duration of a cyclopean aftereffect was proportional to the square root of the adaptation duration, as was the aftereffect induced by adaptation to luminance-defined motion.

The effects of inspection are intriguing, and a moment's reflection reveals how little we know about some of the fundamentals of neural coding as reflected in aftereffects. What properties of a system might make it slow to generate a large (marked, long-lasting) aftereffect? One possibility might be a low density of filters. If cyclopean disparity-specific motion detectors were just a subset of the set of all motion detectors, or if the more highly specific filters were simply less common than those with less specific tuning, then they would be relatively sparse and their neural chorus might be relatively feeble. But there is no current model of adaptation and aftereffect that explicitly addresses this issue; the ratio model (Sutherland, 1961) and all of its variants, and the "intersection of sets" model (Moulden, 1980) are silent on this point.

However, it is interesting to note that a recent study by Donnelly, Bowd, et al. (1997) showed that, in a random-walk cinematogram display involving coherently moving signal dots embedded in incoherent noise dots , five times more signal dots were required to detect the presence of cyclopean global motion than to detect luminance-defined global motion. This suggests that cyclopean motion detectors, for whatever reason (sparsity is just one possibility), send a weaker signal to higher motion-processing centers than luminance motion detectors.

It seems likely, too, that factors other than duration may be significant. The use of a dynamic test display may be one of these. In the Patterson et al. (1994) study, as well as other studies showing a significant cyclopean MAE (e.g., Lehmkuhle and Fox, 1977; Fox et al., 1982), the test displays were not static. Even though the cyclopean test pattern was stationary, the luminance dots composing the structure of the random-dot stereogram display were dynamic. In some studies reporting little or no cyclopean aftereffect (e.g., Cavanagh, 1995), the test displays were static. However, though clearly important, this may not be a necessary factor because the study by Zeevi and Geri (1985) reported a weak cyclopean aftereffect despite having employed a dynamic test display.

Nishida and Sato (1995) investigated this question directly. Subjects adapted to a moving cyclopean grating pattern defined by binocular disparity differences and then inspected either a flickering or a static non-cyclopean test pattern. Although adaptation duration was relatively brief (30 seconds), Nishida and Sato found that strong cyclopean aftereffects of many seconds were elicited by the flickering, but not by the static, test pattern.

The authors suggested that flickering and static test stimuli both elicit reliable MAEs induced by first-order (e.g., luminance-defined) motion that reflects adaptation of a low-level motion-processing mechanism, while only flickering test stimuli elicit reliable MAEs induced by higher-order motion (such as cyclopean motion) that reflects adaptation of a higher-level motion-processing mechanism. A similar result and conclusion was reached by Nishida, Edwards, et al. (1997b) for the phenomenon of simultaneous motion contrast. The issue of first-order and second-order contributions to MAEs is discussed at length in chapter 5.

This speculation by Nishida and Sato is at least consistent with the available evidence, but prompts the obvious question: Why? Why might higher-order motion detectors be accessed by flickering but not by static stimuli? The answer might provide important clues about the characteristics of these mechanisms. The findings certainly suggest that while the mechanisms encoding cyclopean and luminance motion stimuli may have elements in common, they also possess some elements that are not common because they respond differentially to static and flickering stimuli.

Three recent studies by Patterson and co-workers offer support for the idea that some common elements are involved in the processing of cyclopean and luminance motion. First, Patterson et al. (1994) found that motion adaptation transferred between the cyclopean and luminance domains: MAEs were reported when cyclopean and luminance patterns were employed as adapting and test stimuli respectively, and vice versa. Second, Patterson and Becker (1996) investigated "direction-repulsion effects" (Levinson and Sekuler, 1976; Mather and Moulden, 1980), in which inspection of motion in a particular direction can cause the apparent direction of test motion to be shifted away from the axis of the adapting motion. They obtained repulsion effects not only when the two directional components were cyclopean but also when one component was cyclopean and the other was luminance-defined. The purely cyclopean effect was much larger than the luminance-mediated effect (20 to 30 degree angular shifts, as opposed to 10-degree shifts). Third, Donnelly, Bowd, et al. (1996) investigated cross-domain adaptation using random-walk cinematograms that contained cyclopean or luminance-defined elements. The effective strengths of the two kinds of cinematogram were equated by presenting each of them at equal multiples above global motion-detection threshold (signal-to-noise ratio). An MAE nulling paradigm was used to measure aftereffect strength (i.e., cyclopean motion nulling a luminance aftereffect and vice versa). Results showed that the luminance adapt–stereoscopic test combination induced a weaker aftereffect than the stereoscopic adapt–stereoscopic test, luminance adapt–luminance test, and stereoscopic adapt–luminance test combinations. Donnelly et al. proposed that only part of the substrate engaged by stereoscopic test motion was adapted by luminance adapting motion and that there exists a purely cyclopean global motion mechanism that is activated exclusively by moving disparity-defined boundaries.

These results further strengthen the belief that cyclopean and luminance motion perception are mediated at least in part by a common neural substrate. In particular, it is likely that such cross-domain adaptation effects are expressed at multiple sites along the visual pathway, especially at the site involving global integration of signals from multiple motion cues. For further discussion, see chapters 5 and 7.

As mentioned earlier, it has been suggested (see Cavanagh, 1992) that attentive tracking might form the basis of an explanation for cyclopean motion adaptation as opposed to the existence of low-level mechanisms. According to this idea, the process of tracking objects by moving a window of attention itself generates motion signals but little or no phenomenal aftereffect (see Lankheet and Verstraten, 1995). Bowd et al. (1996b) set out to examine this possibility. They investigated whether prolonged simultaneous adaptation to two oppositely moving cyclopean grating patterns (a rightward-moving grating pattern above the fixation point with a leftward-moving grating pattern below it) would lead to two correspondingly opposite MAEs when subsequently viewing stationary cyclopean test patterns. The cyclopean grating patterns were defined by binocular disparity differences created from a dynamic random-dot stereogram. Adaptation duration ranged from 30 seconds to 64 minutes per trial. Bowd et al. found that two opposite phenomenally strong cyclopean aftereffects of many seconds' duration were induced—the aftereffects were retinotopic. Given the assumption that an attentional tracking mechanism would not generate phenomenally strong retinotopic aftereffects, these results are entirely consistent with the notion that cyclopean motion is encoded by binocular mechanisms at a preattentive level of motion processing.

4.4.2 Stereoscopic Disparity-Contingent Motion Aftereffects

The disparity-contingent MAE is a special case of the classic MAE. It is an MAE, generated via adaptation to cyclopean or noncyclopean motion that is contingent upon the binocular disparity of the adapting and test stimuli. As stated earlier, the existence of a disparity-contingent aftereffect in itself suggests that the visual system contains cells which respond selectively to a particular direction of motion at a given binocular disparity. The precise specificity of the contingency can give information about whether there are different groups of cells tuned to different values, rather than just different signs, of disparity that can be selectively adapted.

It is important to distinguish between a contingency based upon binocular disparity and a contingency based upon perceived depth. *Disparity* is defined as an interocular difference in the position of corresponding monocular images. *Depth* is defined as the perceived z-axis interval between a given stimulus and fixation (horopter). To derive a metric of perceived depth, disparity must be scaled or calibrated by viewing distance information. Disparity scaling is necessary because disparity is an inherently ambiguous depth cue: the same value of disparity will yield different magnitudes of perceived depth, depending on viewing distance. Thus, disparity must be scaled for different distances for veridical depth to be perceived (Ono and Comerford, 1977; Patterson and Martin, 1992; Wallach and Zuckerman, 1963).

The distinction between disparity and depth is important in the present context because it has implications for the level of processing at which the motion system becomes binocular. If the MAE is contingent upon disparity, then this would suggest that its substrate is located prior to the locus of disparity scaling. However, if the MAE is contingent not upon disparity but upon perceived depth, then its substrate would have to be located subsequent to the locus of disparity scaling. It has been suggested that cells in cortical area V1 of monkey provide the substrate for disparity scaling (see Trotter, Celebrini, et al., 1992). Psychophysicists cannot yet attain this level of precision in their predictions—it is still unclear whether the MAE is contingent upon disparity or depth. In what follows, we simply use the term "disparity contingency" for convenience, without intending to imply any presumptions about precise locus.

In an early investigation of disparity contingency, Anstis and Harris (1974) had observers adapt alternately to clockwise rotary motion which appeared in crossed depth with respect to the fixation point, and to counterclockwise motion which appeared in uncrossed depth (the exact magnitude of the disparity or the depth involved was unspecified). They found that the direction of the aftereffect depended upon the disparity of the stationary test stimulus. When the test stimulus appeared in crossed depth, the MAE appeared counterclockwise, and when the test appeared in uncrossed depth, the MAE appeared clockwise.

R. A. Smith (1976) set out to discover whether adapting to dynamic stimuli (moving Lissajous figures or dynamic visual noise) with a 1.5 neutral-density filter placed over one eye induced a disparity-contingent aftereffect when the neutral-density filter was removed. The duration of adaptation was 8 or 30 seconds. Smith reported that a brief cyclopean aftereffect was induced (i.e., illusory reversal of motion in depth) which was contingent upon the disparity produced by the neutral-density filter.

Lehmkuhle and Fox (1977) and Fox et al. (1982) required observers to adapt to moving grating patterns lying in one depth plane and then to view stationary test patterns lying in the same or in a different depth plane. The grating patterns were defined by binocular-disparity differences created from a dynamic random-dot stereogram. The difference in disparity of the bars of the grating between adapting and test stimuli was either 0 or 30 arc minutes in the 1977 investigation or from 0 to 18 arc minutes in the 1982 study. Adaptation duration was 45 or 90 seconds, respectively. In both studies, differences in disparity between adapt and test stimuli lessened the aftereffect duration by about one-half.

In an investigation of the transparent MAE (the MAE induced by adaptation to two overlapping transparent dot arrays moving in different directions and in different depth planes), Verstraten, Verlinde, et al. (1994d) examined the effect of manipulating the disparity of the adapting and test stimuli on the duration and frequency of occurrence of the MAE. The difference in disparity between adapting and test stimuli was 14.1 arc minutes and the adaptation duration was 30 seconds. The difference in disparity between adapting and test stimuli lessened the duration of the aftereffect by about one-half and reduced the percentage of trials on which it was reported by about one-third.

The most straightforward interpretation of disparity contingency is that common mechanisms are engaged when the adapting and test stimuli possess the same or similar disparity, whereas at least some separate mechanisms are engaged when adapt and test stimuli possess very differing disparities. Such a model can provide a good qualitative account for the fact that the aftereffect typically declines with differences in disparity between adapt and test stimuli, in terms of the proportion of the number of units stimulated by the test stimulus that have previously been adapted by the inspection stimulus: if the proportion is large the aftereffect magnitude should be large. Such a "union of sets" model of aftereffect magnitude was proposed by Moulden (1980), where the sets were classes of monocular neurons and binocular neurons of various degrees of dominance. The model is immediately applicable to the case where the sets are classes of neurons with particular preferred disparities.

A recent study by Patterson et al. (1996) reported results that support the general thrust of this model but suggest the need for certain refinements. Patterson et al. (1996) employed cyclopean grating patterns, created from dynamic random-dot stereograms, to discover whether it is indeed just the *difference* in disparity between adapt and test stimuli that is the single relevant variable, or whether the *absolute* disparity values of the stimuli are a significant factor. The disparity relationships between the adapting, test, and fixation stimuli were manipulated, with disparity differences ranging from 0 to 11.4 arc minutes. The adaptation duration was 2.0 minutes. Results showed that aftereffect duration was greatest when adapting and test stimuli were presented with zero relative disparity *and* in the plane of fixation (i.e., is with zero disparity with respect to the fixation point). The most important and surprising feature was that the duration of the aftereffect declined by about one-half as soon as the absolute disparity of the adapting stimulus or the test stimulus became non-zero—that is, moved out of the plane of the fixation point—even when adapt and test stimuli had the same value of disparity. (Similar findings had been reported incidentally from other investigations: Fox et al., 1982; Lehmkuhle and Fox, 1977; Verstraten et al., 1994d).

In other words a strong cyclopean MAE only occurs when both the adapting and test stimuli are presented at or very close to the plane of fixation (i.e., is close to the horopter). Outside this plane, it seems, only relatively weak MAEs can be generated or elicited.

Why should this be? It recalls the question (see above) of why cyclopean stimuli in general appear to generate weak MAEs, requiring much longer inspection durations to produce clear aftereffects. The point was made then that current models are silent on such matters. The speculation was mooted that detectors for cyclopean motion are sparse, and that the resultant neural chorus might be sotto voce. In the present case, the detectors signaling non-zero disparity values may be relatively sparse compared to the number of detectors signalling zero disparity. The speculation is perhaps worth repeating here, despite the fact that there is no obvious way of reconciling it with the ratio principle and its variants, including the intersection of sets model, which depend upon the relative magnitudes of two or more sets of signals; according to such models the absolute signal magnitudes are irrelevant.

4.5 Conclusions and Suggestions for Further Research

The following specific conclusions can be drawn from the preceding sections : (1) two kinds of MAE can be distinguished, one based on pursuit eye movements and the other based on responses in direction-selective cells; (2) current evidence is consistent with the existence of a binocular AND pathway in the visual system, or at least an OR pathway exhibiting strong binocular facilitation; (3) cyclopean MAEs are likely to be mediated by direction-selective mechanisms that partially overlap with mechanisms that mediate luminance-defined aftereffects; and (4) disparity-contingent MAEs only occur near the plane of fixation.

More generally, both the cyclopean MAE and the disparity-contingent MAE clearly show that some specifically binocular mechanisms also carry out motion processing. Results from studies on the cyclopean MAE suggest that binocularity is a feature of motion processing at the preattentive level of processing and possibly at the postattentive level. This suggests that motion processing involves an even greater degree of complexity than had been thought and that an understanding of the nature of binocular vision will be necessary for a full understanding of the nature of motion processing in all its ramifications. Characteristics of both preattentive and postattentive motion processing may be demonstrated by binocular mechanisms, and this is consistent with neurophysiologic studies of cats and monkeys which show that direction selectivity and binocularity are properties that coexist at both early and late cortical stages of vision (Hammond and Pomfrett, 1989; Hubel and Wiesel, 1962;

Maunsell and Van Essen, 1983a,b; Roy and Wurtz, 1990; Roy et al., 1992; Schiller et al., 1976; Zeki, 1978).

Finally, the discussion has also unearthed a number of outstanding issues for future research to lay to rest:

1. Does motion adaptation transfer between cyclopean stimuli and other kinds of second-order stimuli such as texture patterns? We expect that motion adaptation would transfer between cyclopean and texture stimuli because motion adaptation transfers between cyclopean and luminance stimuli (Patterson and Becker, 1996; Patterson et al., 1994) as well as between texture and luminance stimuli (McCarthy, 1993; Nishida and Sato, 1995; Turano, 1991), but the expectation has yet to be confirmed.

2. Is the postattentive motion process indeed binocular, as some have suggested? This could be addressed by repeating the Lankheet and Verstraten (1995) attentive-tracking adaptation study, this time using cyclopean stimuli. If this motion process is binocular, we expect that the Lankheet and Verstraten study would be replicated with cyclopean stimui.

3. Are there individuals who possess otherwise normal binocular function but who are selectively blind to cyclopean motion? If so, does this deficiency make their motion detection different in any other ways from that of normal observers?

4. Are other kinds of motion adaptation phenomena, such as direction repulsion or threshold elevation, disparity-contingent, and do their absolute magnitudes vary in the same way as a function of distance from the horopter?

5. There still remains the broad general question (see above) of whether such motion-adaptation phenomena are disparity- or depth-contingent; as has been mentioned, this has important implications about the site of the coding involved.

Notes

1. The speculation that in this type of attentional manipulation experiment the output of low-level filters is being suppressed (rather than, say, merely being ignored in some sense) is open to experimental test: following attentional tracking of rightward motion in a bidirectional composite, the threshold for leftward motion should not be elevated as much as it would be if the stimulus were viewed with no attentional bias.

2. Sherrington found no evidence of binocular summation, and however prescient his use of the paradigm might have been, his findings are nevertheless puzzling in the light of recent studies that have reported evidence for binocular summation in a variety of contexts. For reviews, see Blake and Fox, 1973; Blake et al., 1981b.

Chapter 5
Higher-Order Effects

Jody Culham, Shin'ya Nishida, Timothy Ledgeway,
Patrick Cavanagh, Michael von Grünau, Michelle
Kwas, David Alais, and Jane Raymond

In this chapter we consider some potential high-level influences on the strength and direction of the motion aftereffect (MAE), and their implications for psychophysical and neural theories of motion perception. We focus on a wide range of stimuli and paradigms, including dynamic tests, higher-order stimuli, multivectorial motion, and brief adaptation periods. We also consider the effects of the observer's state of attention and the demands of the task, showing that both can influence the direction and size of the effect. These issues suggest that the MAE is not necessarily a unified phenomenon resulting only from low-level, preattentive processing of unidirectional motion from luminance cues. Rather, the MAE may have a wide range of influences and consequences, some of which are dependent on the particular stimuli and the observer's state of mind.

5.1 Static vs. Dynamic Motion Aftereffect Tests

Prolonged exposure to moving stimuli generates illusory backward motion in test stimuli presented subsequently at the same location. This MAE conventionally has been studied using static test patterns, although recent studies have also employed dynamic test patterns such as counterphasing gratings and random dots which are directionally ambiguous (figure 5.1). Dynamic test stimuli were originally used for a number of technical reasons. For instance, directional components within the stimuli are easy to manipulate, a useful property when MAE magnitude is evaluated in terms of the motion signals required to cancel the aftereffect (von Grünau, 1986; Blake and Hiris, 1993; Ledgeway, 1994). The illusory opposite motion seen in dynamic tests is perceptually indistinguishable from real motion (Levinson and Sekuler, 1975; Hiris and Blake, 1992), so it is easier for subjects to judge than that seen in static tests. In addition, it was suggested that perceptually unstable test stimuli might provide a more sensitive technique for revealing weak adaptation effects (von Grünau and Dubé, 1992).

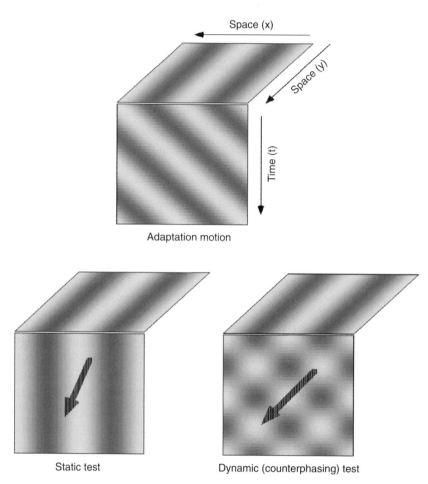

Figure 5.1
Motion aftereffects measured using static and dynamic (counterphase) gratings. Top: Adaptation stimulus. A rightward drifting sinusoidal grating is shown by a space (x)–space (y) and space (x)–time (t) plot. Bottom left: Static test grating. Arrow indicates the direction of the aftereffect. Bottom right: Counterphase test grating.

It has been suggested that the MAE is a result of selective adaptation of directionally selective mechanisms that respond continuously to the adaptation motion. A parsimonious explanation of the induction of MAEs either in static or dynamic test stimuli is that they both result from adaptation at the same site of visual motion processing. There appears to be no a priori reason to doubt this assumption, and it is implicit in several studies that have used dynamic test stimuli mainly for technical reasons. It has recently been found, however, that the MAE measured using dynamic test stimuli (dynamic MAE) demonstrates a number of differences from the MAE measured using static test patterns (static MAE). This is hard to reconcile with the proposition that a single mechanism is responsible for both types of MAE. A marked difference concerns the effects of second-order stimuli and higher-order motion, which are discussed later in this chapter. In this section, we first compare the properties of static and dynamic MAEs revealed by studies that have mainly employed first-order (luminance-defined) motion stimuli.

5.1.1 Contrast Dependency
Luminance contrast is one of the stimulus parameters that strongly control the magnitude of the classic static MAE (Keck et al., 1976). The effects of contrast on the duration of the dynamic MAE (seen in a 2.0-Hz counterphasing grating presented in the central visual field) were found to be quite similar to those known for the static MAE (Nishida et al., 1997a). In each case, as the adaptation contrast is increased, MAE duration steadily increases, leveling off when adaptation contrast approaches test contrast. As test contrast is increased, the MAE duration decreases, with a slightly steeper slope in the case of the dynamic MAE. These results appear to favor the suggestion that a common process is responsible for both static and dynamic MAEs, although the similarity could, in principle, arise from analogous adaptation processes occurring at different sites of visual motion processing. Another notable point with regard to the effects of contrast is that adaptation contrasts as low as two times the detection threshold can induce reliable MAEs in either type of test stimulus (Nishida et al., 1997a). This suggests that such differences that are present in sensitivity to the two types of test stimulus are moderate, at least in the case of simple luminance gratings.

5.1.2 Spatial Frequency
Static MAE magnitude measured with luminance gratings is typically strongest when the adaptation and test stimuli are matched for spatial frequency (Over, Broerse, et al., 1973; Cameron et al., 1992). This implies that the static MAE is spatial frequency–selective, and therefore that the underlying mechanisms responsible for this MAE are each narrowly tuned

to a limited range of spatial frequencies. Ashida and Osaka (1994) and Bex et al. (1996) investigated whether such selectivity is also obtained with dynamic MAEs. Ashida and Osaka found that the duration of MAE measured with sinusoidal counterphasing gratings was affected by the spatial frequencies of the adaptation and test stimuli. Nevertheless, when their data are plotted as functions of the adaptation spatial frequency, the maximum MAE generally occurs at a frequency lower than the test frequency. On the other hand, Bex et al. found clear spatial frequency selectivity of the MAE even though they also used counterphasing tests. One important procedural difference between these two studies was the test temporal frequency: Ashida and Osaka used 5.0 Hz while Bex et al. used 0.25 Hz. A follow-up study (Mareschal, Ashida, et al. 1997) found that the spatial frequency selectivity of the MAE broadened as the test temporal frequency increased, and almost disappeared at temporal frequencies equal to 2 Hz. These results indicate broad spatial-frequency tuning of the underlying mechanisms that give rise to MAEs with counterphasing gratings equal to 2 Hz. Von Grünau and Dubé (1992), however, using a nulling method and plaid adaptation stimuli, reported results that appear to indicate spatial-frequency selectivity of MAE seen in a 2-Hz counterphasing test.

5.1.3 Location Specificity
The static MAE is typically observed only in the region directly stimulated during adaptation (Anstis and Gregory, 1965). However, the dynamic MAE does not show such retinotopic specificity. Von Grünau and Dubé (1992) measured the magnitude of the dynamic MAE for tests presented at the adapted location and at another location equidistant from fixation. They reported dynamic MAEs at both locations, though the remote MAE was weaker and showed larger intersubject variability. Furthermore, MAEs at the test location were tuned for the direction and spatial-frequency of the adapting grating or plaid; however, remote MAEs showed no such direction tuning (responding with approximately the same magnitude even to gratings differing in orientation and direction by up to 60 degrees) nor spatial-frequency tuning.

5.1.4 Temporal Frequency
As the speed or the temporal frequency of the adaptation stimulus increases, the magnitude of the MAE first increases and then decreases. When this inverse-U function is measured for various spatial frequencies, it is possible to tell whether the speed or the temporal frequency characterizes this effect. Previous studies using static test stimuli (Pantle, 1974; Wright and Johnston, 1985) showed that MAE magnitude depends on adaptation temporal frequency. That is, MAE magnitude generally peaks

at adaptation temporal frequencies of 5 to 10 Hz regardless of the adaptation spatial frequency. On the other hand, Ashida and Osaka (1995b) reported that the duration of the dynamic MAE (measured using 2.5- and 5.0-Hz counterphasing gratings) depends on the adaptation speed, rather than temporal frequency, and peaks at adaptation speeds of 5 to 10 degrees/second irrespective of the adaptation spatial frequency. These results suggest that the mechanism underlying the static MAE codes temporal changes in luminance in terms of temporal frequency, while that underlying the dynamic MAE codes speed.

In the case of the dynamic MAE, the effects of test temporal frequency have also been examined. Bex et al. (1996) found a decrease in MAE duration with increasing test temporal frequency (except when the test was nearly static; i.e., at very low temporal frequencies). The shape of this function was not affected by the spatiotemporal frequency of the adaptation stimulus and thus the effect was selective neither for speed nor for temporal frequency. On the other hand, Verstraten, van Wezel, et al. (1994c) reported results that suggest an interaction between the temporal frequencies of the adaptation and test stimuli. They measured the direction of the MAE using dynamic random-dot tests after adaptation to a transparent motion stimulus in which two random-dot patterns drifted in orthogonal directions at different speeds. Their results suggest that the influence of the slower components in the adaptation stimulus is reduced as the test temporal frequency is increased.

5.1.5 Interocular Transfer

The magnitude of interocular transfer (the extent to which adaptation presented to one eye produces aftereffects measured with the other eye; see chapter 4) has been used as a tool to investigate the binocularity of the mechanisms responsible for aftereffects. It is known that the static MAE transfers interocularly, although the magnitudes of the MAE measured with the nonadapted eye are about half those measured with the adapted eye (Wohlgemuth, 1911; Moulden, 1980; see chapter 4). This result, called partial transfer, indicates that the mechanism subserving the static MAE is neither totally monocular nor binocular. In comparison, Nishida et al. (1994) found that transfer of the dynamic MAE, measured with a 2-Hz counterphasing grating presented in the central visual field, is nearly perfect regardless of the type of adaptation stimuli. This result led them to conclude that the dynamic MAE reflects adaptation at a site where binocular signals are completely integrated and eye-of-origin information is lost.

However, interocular transfer is not perfect for all MAEs measured using dynamic tests. Green, Chilcoat, et al. (1983) found no interocular transfer for the MAE that is seen in a homogeneous rapidly flickering test field after adaptation to a drifting grating of low spatial frequency. On the other hand, Steiner et al. (1994) found interocular transfer using a different type of dynamic test stimulus composed of random dots moving incoherently in all directions, but the magnitude of transfer was significantly less than perfect (76 percent on average) after adaptation to translational motion. The lack of interocular transfer reported by Green et al. (1983) is incompatible with the results of all other studies. It appears that the MAE seen in patterned dynamic stimuli and that seen in patternless flicker are different phenomena. This idea is strengthened by the finding that second-order motion is differentially effective in producing these two MAEs (Nishida and Sato, 1995). As for the discrepancy between Nishida et al. (1994) and Steiner et al. (1994), a notable difference is the method used to evaluate the magnitude of MAEs: Nishida et al. measured the MAE duration, while Steiner et al. measured the amount of motion signal required to null the adaptation effects.

To test whether different methods could give rise to different magnitudes of interocular transfer, Ashida and Nishida (unpublished) compared the MAE duration and the nulling motion strength obtained under the same stimulus conditions (adapting with a drifting grating, and testing with a counterphase grating). Their preliminary results suggest that interocular transfer is nearly perfect when measured by MAE duration, but less than perfect when measured by nulling motion strength. Another factor that may be relevant to the discrepancy between studies is the temporal structure of the test stimulus. While the temporal frequency of a counterphasing grating is localized at the modulation frequency, incoherently moving dots contain a broad range of temporal frequencies, including static and very slowly drifting components. Transfer (based on MAE duration measured with counterphasing gratings) is perfect only when the modulation rate is higher than 1 Hz (Ashida, Verstraten, et al., 1997); thus slow components in the test stimulus of Steiner et al. (1994) might allow the mechanism generating the static MAE to play a significant role. This possibility is in line with the nearly perfect transfer found by Raymond (1993a), who examined the effect of adaptation on motion coherence thresholds using dynamic random-dot patterns that had less slowly drifting components than those used by Steiner et al. (As discussed later, however, the phenomenon investigated by Raymond and her colleagues appears to have a number of properties distinct from those found in traditional MAE paradigms.)

In addition to the spatiotemporal properties of test stimuli and the methods used to measure MAEs, retinal eccentricity exerts a significant influence on the interocular transfer of the dynamic MAE. Ashida et al. (1997) found that transfer of the MAE (based on duration measured using counterphasing gratings) was nearly perfect in the central visual field, but was drastically reduced in the peripheral visual field. They suggested that this reduction might partially reflect difficulties in feature tracking or the loss of involuntary attention to the adaptation motion presented in the periphery. This hypothesis is in line with their preliminary results demonstrating that, even in the central visual field, interocular transfer of the dynamic MAE is significantly reduced when subjects cannot attend to the adaptation motion. The role of attention in the dynamic MAE is further addressed in later sections.

5.1.6 Storage

Verstraten et al. (1996) reported almost complete storage of the static MAE when the static test was preceded by a dynamic test. In their experiment, a dynamic random-dot test stimulus was presented immediately after adaptation, for as long as the MAE was perceived, and then the test was replaced by a static pattern. Although the dynamic MAE had disappeared by the time the static pattern was presented, subjects perceived an MAE in the static test which had nearly the same duration as when the static pattern was presented immediately after adaptation. On the other hand, the dynamic MAE was not stored when the dynamic test was preceded by a static test. This is a good demonstration of a dissociation in the time course of recovery from adaptation between static and dynamic MAEs. It has since been replicated using narrow-band stimuli (static and counterphasing gratings; Culham, unpublished observations).

5.1.7 Surround Motion

It is known that the magnitude of the static MAE depends upon the background stimulus presented during adaptation. For instance, the static MAE is enhanced when the moving adaptation stimulus is surrounded by a static pattern (Day and Strelow, 1971), and the static MAE is far stronger when the adaptation stimulus is surrounded by oppositely moving stimuli than when it is surrounded by stimuli moving in the same direction (Murakami and Shimojo, 1995). It has been suggested that relative movement is an important requirement for generating static MAEs (Anstis and Reinhardt-Rutland, 1976; Swanston and Wade, 1992). Nishida and Ashida (1997) recently found that the surround modulation of the dynamic MAE duration was as strong as that of the static MAE duration when measured in the peripheral visual field, but the modulation was reduced (and nearly disappeared for some observers) in the central visual field. This suggests that the role of relative motion is smaller in the generation of dynamic MAEs.

5.1.8 Separate Mechanisms?

The discrepancies between the properties of the static MAE and the dynamic MAE are summarized in table 5.1 (along with a number of other factors to be discussed later). These differences are difficult to reconcile with the notion that a single common mechanism is responsible for both types of MAE. Although the only physical difference is the temporal structure of the test stimulus, these discrepancies support the idea that the two types of MAE reveal adaptation at separate sites of visual motion processing. The properties of the static MAE indicate that it reflects adaptation of a mechanism that is spatial frequency–selective, temporal frequency–tuned, and partially monocular. On the other hand, the dynamic MAE appears to reflect adaptation of a mechanism that is non-spatial frequency-selective, velocity-tuned, and completely binocular.

It should be noted, however, that the distinction between the static MAE and the dynamic MAE may not be strict. As mentioned above, even when the test stimulus is a counterphasing grating, the properties of the MAE are similar to those obtained with a static test when the temporal frequency of the dynamic test is lower than 1 Hz (Bex et al., 1996; Ashida et al., 1997). This change in properties with test temporal frequency seems to be accompanied by a change in the appearance of the MAE. When the test stimulus is static or has a low temporal frequency, the MAE is manifest as an apparent gradual shift in the spatial positions of the bright and dark bars. On the other hand, the MAE elicited in a rapidly counterphasing grating appears to have a drift speed almost comparable to that of the individual drifting components composing the test stimulus.

Another notable issue with respect to the multiplicity of MAE mechanisms concerns the effects of retinal eccentricity on the dynamic MAE. The dynamic MAE measured in the periphery is different from that measured in the central visual field, at least in terms of the degree of interocular transfer and the modulatory effect of motion in the surround (Ashida et al., 1997; Nishida and Ashida, 1997). This raises the possibility that two mechanisms are responsible for the generation of the dynamic MAE: one predominates in the central visual field, and the other predominates in the periphery. That the dynamic MAE in the periphery is similar to the static MAE with regard to interocular transfer and the effect of surround motion may imply that the static MAE and dynamic MAE are both mediated by a common mechanism in the peripheral visual field, but by separate mechanisms in the central visual field. The low-level mechanism may generate dynamic MAEs also in the central visual field, but it presumably decays more rapidly than that generated by the high-level mechanism. This could be a reason why the interocular transfer is not perfect when the MAE magnitude is measured in terms of the nulling motion strength.

Table 5.1
Comparison of four types of motion aftereffect (MAE)

	Static MAE	Dynamic MAE[a]	DS threshold elevation	Speed aftereffect
Test contrast	Supra-threshold	Suprathreshold	Threshold	Supra-threshold
Test temporal structure	Static	Dynamic (ambiguous)	Dynamic (drifting)	Dynamic (drifting)
SF selectivity	Yes[1]	No[2]	Yes[3]	No[4]
TF/speed	TF[5]	Speed[6]	TF and speed[7]	Speed[8]
Spatial specificity	Yes[9]	No[10]		
IOT	Partial[11]	Complete[12] [partial][13]	Partial[14]	Partial[15]
Storage effect	Yes[16]	No[17]		
Relative motion	Effective[18]	Ineffective [effective][19]		
SO motion	Ineffective[20]	Effective[21]	Effective[22]	Effective[23]
FO-SO cross-adaptation	No[24]	Yes[25]	No[26]	Yes[27]
Long-range motion	No[28]	Yes[29]		
Modulation by attention	No[30] Yes[31]	Yes[32]		
Generated by attentive tracking	No[33]	Yes[33]		

[a] DS, direction-selective; SF, spatial frequency; TF, temporal frequency; IOT, interocular transfer; FO, first-order; SO, second-order; Properties of dynamic MAE in brackets are those obtained mainly in the peripheral visual field.
[1] Over et al. (1973), Cameron et al. (1992a); [2] Ashida and Osaka (1994), Mareschal et al. (1997); [3] Pantle et al. (1978), Nishida et al. (1997a); [4] Thompson (1981); [5] Pantle (1974), Wright and Johnston (1985); [6] Ashida and Osaka (1995b); [7] Sekuler (1975); [8] Thompson (1981); [9] Anstis and Gregory (1965); [10] von Grünau & Dubé (1992); [11] Moulden (1980); [12] Nishida et al. (1994); [13] Ashida et al. (1997); [14] A. T. Smith (1983); [15] A. T. Smith and Hammond (1985); [16] P. Thompson and Wright (1994); [17] Verstraten et al. (1996); [18] Anstis and Reinhardt-Rutland (1976), Swanston and Wade (1992); [19] Nishida & Ashida (1997); [20] Anstis (1980), Derrington and Badcock (1985); [21] McCarthy (1993), Ledgeway and Smith (1994a); [22] Turano (1991), Nishida et al. (1997a); [23] Ledgeway and Smith (1997); [24] Nishida and Sato (1995); [25] Ledgeway (1994), Ledgeway and Smith (1994a), Nishida and Sato (1995); [26] Nishida et al. (1997a); [27] Ledgeway and Smith (1997); [28] Anstis (1980); [29] von Grünau (1986); [30] Wohlgemuth (1911); [31] Chaudhuri (1990); [32] Shulman (1993), Lankheet and Verstraten (1995); [33] Culham and Cavanagh (1994).

5.1.9 Relation to Other Motion Aftereffects

A promising explanation of dynamic MAEs, especially those observed with a counterphasing grating, is that adaptation causes a direction-selective reduction in contrast sensitivity. Since a counterphasing sinusoidal grating can be decomposed into two oppositely drifting components of half-amplitude, a decrease in contrast sensitivity to one component would enhance the relative salience of the other component, possibly resulting in a percept akin to the dynamic MAE. Another phenomenon that indicates a direction-selective sensitivity reduction is the direction-selective elevation of contrast threshold after adaptation to moving stimuli (Sekuler and Ganz, 1963; Pantle and Sekuler, 1969). Levinson and Sekuler (1975) suggest that this threshold elevation and the dynamic MAE, one prominent near-threshold and the other prominent at suprathreshold contrast levels, result from adaptation at the same site. However, unlike the dynamic MAE, threshold elevation is spatial frequency–selective (Pantle et al., 1978; Nishida, Ledgeway, et al., 1997c). Threshold elevation clearly occurs only when the adaptation and test stimuli are both first-order or second-order motion patterns (Nishida et al., 1997c), while the dynamic MAE occurs for all combinations of stimulus type (Ledgeway, 1994). These discrepancies suggest that these two phenomena have separate origins. In addition, the differential efficacy with which second-order motion stimuli give rise to direction-selective threshold elevation and the static MAE suggests that these two phenomena are distinct. It appears that the three types of MAE, the static MAE, the dynamic MAE, and direction-selective threshold elevation, reflect processes occurring at different sites of adaptation.

Another effect of motion adaptation is a change in the perceived speed of moving suprathreshold stimuli (Carlson, 1962). The magnitude of the speed aftereffect depends on the speed of the adaptation stimulus regardless of its spatial frequency (P. Thompson, 1981). In addition, it occurs with second-order patterns even when first-order patterns are used for adaptation or test stimuli (Ledgeway and Smith, 1997). These properties are similar to those obtained with the dynamic MAE (see table 5.1).

The existence and characteristic properties of these different types of MAE could, in principle, be used to elucidate the underlying functional architecture of motion processing in human vision. In the next section, we focus on one area where this approach has recently been widely adopted, namely, the study of second-order motion.

5.2 Motion Aftereffects from Second-Order Motion

Moving objects in the visual world may give rise to drifting contours in the retinal image that are defined in terms of local variations in intensity or wavelength (first-order motion) or by variations in more complex derived characteristics (second-order or "non-Fourier" motion) such as local contrast, orientation, and binocular disparity (Chubb and Sperling, 1988; Cavanagh and Mather, 1989). The study of second-order motion is important theoretically because intensity-based motion analyzers, which have been modeled as quasi-linear filters that are oriented in space-time or spatiotemporal frequency (e.g., Adelson and Bergen, 1985), should be incapable of detecting second-order motion. Yet stimuli that give rise to second-order motion (figure 5.2), such as a drifting modulation of the contrast of a stationary luminance grating (carrier), typically produce vivid percepts of movement, and this poses a problem for conventional motion-detecting schemes.

5.2.1 Theories and Models of Second-Order Motion Perception

Since second-order motion stimuli undoubtedly contain "features" (e.g., texture edges and boundaries), motion perception could, in principle, be mediated primarily by a high-level, cognitive strategy involving the explicit tracking or matching of image features over space and time (Anstis, 1980; Braddick, 1980; Cavanagh, 1992). However, several computational models have been proposed which detect second-order motion on the basis of low-level, preattentive mechanisms without the need to track, or calculate correspondences between, features in the image. For instance, it has been suggested that first-order and second-order motion are detected by a single (common) low-level mechanism, an approach which is exemplified by the spatiotemporal gradient model of Johnston, McOwan, et al. (1992). An alternative class of model suggests that first-order and second-order motion are detected by independent (distinct) low-level mechanisms in the visual system (e.g., Derrington and Badcock, 1985, 1986; Chubb and Sperling, 1988, 1989a,b; Badcock and Derrington, 1989; Wilson, Ferrera, et al., 1992; Werkhoven, Sperling, et al., 1993; Zanker, 1993; Fleet and Langley, 1994; Nishida et al., 1994; Nishida and Sato, 1995). These models typically exploit the principle that a nonlinear transformation (e.g., rectification) applied to the luminance profile of many second-order motion stimuli is sufficient to expose their motion to analysis by sensors which utilize the same principles as those used for detecting first-order motion. Adaptation techniques have proved to be useful tools for discriminating between these different classes of model.

5.2.2 Motion Aftereffects Measured with Static, Second-Order Test Patterns

It is well established that following adaptation to stimuli that give rise to second-order motion, the presentation of a stationary test pattern typically fails to elicit a compelling MAE. Indeed, adaptation to several

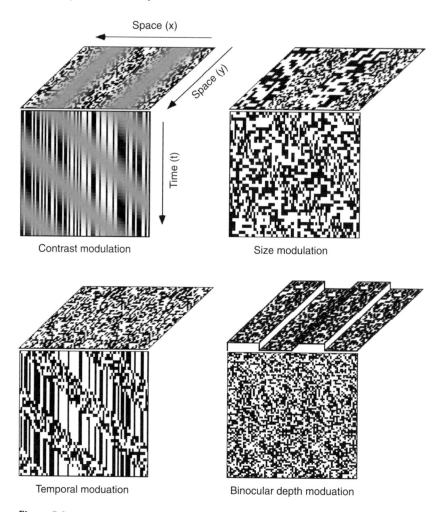

Figure 5.2
Space (x)–space (y) and space (x)–time (t) plots of typical second-order motion stimuli that have been used to investigate motion aftereffects. In each case the stimulus can be constructed by modulating either the contrast (top left), size (top right), flicker rate (bottom left), or binocular disparity (bottom right) of the random elements constituting a two-dimensional noise field (carrier) with a drifting, one-dimensional, sinusoidal, or square-wave profile. With the exception of the contrast-modulated image, the carrier is dynamic rather than static (although it is possible to employ a dynamic carrier in a contrast-modulated pattern). The depicted stimuli are members of a class of motion patterns termed "drift-balanced" by Chubb and Sperling (1988) that, in principle, do not contain any net first-order motion energy.

varieties of second-order motion stimuli, including kinetic edges (Anstis, 1980), drifting beat patterns (Derrington and Badcock, 1985), contrast-modulated sinusoidal gratings (Turano and Pantle, 1985; McCarthy, 1993), and contrast-modulated noise (Ledgeway and Smith, 1993), does not produce a discernible MAE when tested with static second-order patterns. However, some second-order motion stimuli such as disparity-defined (cyclopean) gratings (Patterson et al., 1994; Bowd et al., 1996b; see also chapter 4) and contrast-reversing bars (Mather, 1991) do generate measurable MAEs with stationary test patterns, although their magnitudes (quantified in terms of duration) are considerably weaker than those resulting from adaptation to comparable first-order (luminance-defined) motion.

Explanations as to why second-order motion is so ineffective in generating MAEs with stationary test stimuli have tended to focus on either the properties of motion detectors in the visual system or the physical characteristics of the motion stimuli themselves. In terms of the former, it is possible that second-order motion is encoded principally by feature-tracking or feature-matching processes, since adaptation to motion stimuli which are believed to favor such processes does not generate compelling MAEs with stationary patterns (e.g., Banks and Kane, 1972; Anstis and Mather, 1985). Although feature-based strategies may be used, at least some of the time, for the detection of second-order motion (A. T. Smith, 1994a; Lu and Sperling, 1995b), second-order motion patterns support several phenomena which are widely held to preclude explicit feature-encoding strategies (see Cavanagh and Mather, 1989, for a review).

For instance, observers can readily identify the direction of displacement of dense, random-dot patterns in which the dots are defined by contrast variations (e.g., Nishida, 1993) and this suggests that second-order motion, like first-order motion, is likely to be detected most of the time using low-level mechanisms. If second-order motion perception is mediated primarily by low-level mechanisms, as suggested by several current models, then the failure to find compelling MAEs with stationary test stimuli implies that these mechanisms are distinct, and may have different temporal properties, from those that detect first-order motion (Derrington and Badcock, 1985; Badcock and Derrington, 1989; Pantle and Turano, 1992; Derrington, Badcock, et al., 1993; McCarthy, 1993).

However, this proposition is complicated by the finding that when first-order motion stimuli such as luminance gratings are equated for the visual system's relatively poor sensitivity to second-order motion (A. T. Smith, Hess, et al., 1994) or the presence of a salient carrier, MAEs measured with stationary test stimuli are either degraded or absent (A. T. Smith, Musselwhite, et al., 1984; Pantle, Pinkus, et al., 1991; Ledgeway and Smith, unpublished observations cited in A. T. Smith, 1994b; McCarthy,

1993). A stationary carrier may serve to reinforce the immobility of the test stimulus and mask or override weak motion signals derived from differential activation of adapted and unadapted motion detectors (Ledgeway, 1994). In addition, carriers give rise to substantial first-order motion in all second-order motion stimuli (although this may be incoherent or drift in a direction different from that of the second-order information) which may act as a source of external noise during adaptation and degrade signal fidelity in the pathways that encode the direction of second-order motion. These possibilities could account for the finding that cyclopean gratings evoke demonstrable MAEs only when the stationary second-order spatial structure of the test pattern is defined by disparity modulation of a dynamic random-dot carrier, and a relatively long adaptation duration (e.g., 2 minutes) is employed (Patterson et al., 1994; Bowd et al., 1996b). However, an alternative explanation of this phenomenon will be discussed later in the context of MAEs measured with dynamic test patterns.

5.2.3 *Motion Aftereffects Measured with Dynamic, Second-Order Test Patterns*

In contrast to the weak or nonexistent MAEs measured with stationary test patterns, it has been found that adaptation to second-order motion results in substantial aftereffects when dynamic (flickering or drifting) test stimuli are employed. For example, following adaptation to a drifting sinusoidal modulation of the contrast of a random noise field or luminance grating, a directionally ambiguous, second-order test stimulus appears to drift coherently in the direction opposite to adaptation (McCarthy, 1993; Ledgeway and Smith, 1994a). Using a nulling method Ledgeway (1994) found that this MAE could be abolished by manipulating the relative amplitudes of the two oppositely drifting sinusoidal components present in a counterphasing test stimulus such that the amplitude of the component drifting in the same direction as adaptation was approximately twice that of the other component. An MAE of comparable magnitude was found when the adaptation and test stimuli were both first-order, luminance-modulated noise patterns presented at the same multiple of direction threshold as the contrast-modulated stimuli. MAEs measured with dynamic second-order stimuli are not limited to periodic, contrast-defined patterns because adaptation to the stereoscopic motion of disparity-defined random-dot patterns has been found to bias the perceived drift of similar second-order patterns by as much as 20 degrees away from the adaptation direction (Patterson and Becker, 1996). Other manifestations of the MAE have also been reported with second-order motion stimuli. For instance, prolonged exposure to the motion of contrast-modulated noise produces direction-selective increases and decreases in the perceived speeds of drifting test patterns (Ledgeway and Smith, 1997), similar to those reported for luminance gratings (P. Thompson, 1981). Second-order MAEs are not confined to suprathreshold stimuli, since postadaptation detection and motion thresholds for contrast-modulated gratings (Turano, 1991), noise (Ledgeway and Smith, 1992), and beat patterns (Holliday and Anderson, 1994) are elevated relative to those measured in the absence of prior adaptation to motion. These aftereffects exhibit direction selectivity in that thresholds are elevated more for stimuli that drift in the same direction as adaptation than for stimuli that drift in the opposite direction.

An important property of MAEs measured with dynamic test stimuli is that typically they are insensitive to the particular variety of motion presented during adaptation. That is, adaptation to first-order motion affects the perceived direction and speed of second-order motion, and vice versa (e.g., Patterson et al., 1994; Nishida and Sato, 1995; Patterson and Becker, 1996; Ledgeway and Smith, 1997). Indeed, several studies (Turano, 1991; Ledgeway, 1994; Ledgeway and Smith, 1994a) have reported that "cross-adaptation" between first-order and second-order motion patterns produces robust aftereffects of similar magnitude to those found when the adaptation and test stimuli are either both first-order or both second-order motion patterns, particularly when the two varieties of motion are equated for visibility. These phenomena suggest that dynamic test stimuli may provide a more sensitive technique for measuring postadaptation changes in sensitivity to second-order motion than stationary test patterns. Nonetheless, as discussed previously, there is evidence (e.g., Nishida et al., 1994) that aftereffects measured with static and dynamic test stimuli may have qualitatively different bases. For example, Nishida and Sato (1992, 1995) found that following adaptation to a beat pattern in which first-order (luminance-defined) and second-order (contrast-defined) motion drifted simultaneously in opposite directions, a static beat or first-order sinusoidal grating appeared to drift in the direction opposite to the first-order adapting motion. However, the direction of the MAE reversed when the test stimulus was a first-order grating counterphasing at 2 Hz. Thus, it is possible that static and dynamic test stimuli probe the properties of different mechanisms in the pathways that process motion information.

Given the existence of cross-adaptation effects between first-order and second-order motion, great care needs to be taken when investigating conventional MAEs with test patterns that contain static second-order spatial structure in conjunction with a dynamic carrier, such as cyclopean gratings (e.g., Patterson et al., 1994). This is because following adaptation to second-order motion it is possible that any perceived opposite drift of the test stimulus is due entirely, or at least in part, to an aftereffect induced in the dynamic, first-order carrier as a result of cross-adaptation.

Evidence for this possibility comes from the finding (Ledgeway, unpublished observations) that adaptation to a drifting stimulus composed of either contrast-modulated or luminance-modulated dynamic noise produces robust MAEs of comparable magnitude when an unmodulated dynamic noise pattern (carrier) serves as the test stimulus. Specifically, the first-order and second-order adaptation patterns were both presented at approximately 4.5 times direction-identification threshold and the modulation signal in each case was a vertically oriented, 1 cycle/degree sinusoid drifting at 5 Hz. The carrier was spatially two-dimensional and replaced with a new stochastic sample at a rate of 32 Hz to create dynamic noise. Following 2 minutes of adaptation to motion, the modulation signal was removed and the resulting unmodulated dynamic noise field appeared to drift coherently in the direction opposite to adaptation for approximately 5 to 6 seconds, irrespective of whether the adaptation stimulus was a first-order or second-order motion pattern. Thus, attempts to isolate aftereffects exhibited by the second-order structure of a test stimulus in which the carrier is dynamic need to ensure that measures of performance are not contaminated by the presence of MAEs in the first-order carrier itself.

5.2.4 Interpreting Cross-Adaptation Effects Within Models of Motion Processing

The extent to which MAEs measured with dynamic first-order and second-order test stimuli reflect the relative contributions of high-level and low-level motion processes is at present largely unresolved. However, as we will see later in this chapter, in the context of first-order motion there is evidence that high-level, attention-based, feature-tracking processes may mediate, or at least exert a strong modulatory influence upon, some manifestations of the MAE observed with dynamic test patterns (e.g., Culham and Cavanagh, 1994) and it is possible that similar processes also operate within the domain of second-order motion. Nevertheless, it seems doubtful that MAEs measured with dynamic stimuli can be attributed exclusively to the operation of high-level motion-detecting processes, because under a condition believed to selectively favor feature-based motion detection (i.e., the introduction of an interstimulus-interval [ISI] of 60 to 90 msc between successive updates of the spatial position of the adaptation stimulus), the MAE measured with a directionally ambiguous, first-order or second-order test pattern is severely degraded (A. T. Smith and Ledgeway, 1994). This implies that low-level, motion-detecting mechanisms play a direct role in producing MAEs with dynamic first-order and second-order patterns. In terms of current models of motion detection, cross-adaptation effects between first-order and second-order motion appear, at least superficially, strongly to favor models employing a common mechanism for detecting both varieties of motion (e.g., Johnston et al., 1992). However, it is also possible to accommodate cross-adaptation effects within models incorporating separate detection mechanisms for first-order and second-order motion. If the outputs of distinct first-order and second-order motion detectors are subsequently pooled to compute the resultant direction (and speed) of image motion (e.g., Wilson et al. 1992), then adaptation of motion-sensitive mechanisms either prior to or at the stage at which motion signals are integrated will bias the perceived direction (and speed) of subsequently presented dynamic test patterns.

Although cross-adaptation effects considered in isolation do not allow differentiation between current motion models, some adaptation phenomena may be difficult to reconcile with models that utilize a common mechanism to encode both first-order and second-order motion. For example, Hammett, Ledgeway, et al. (1993) found that observers consistently reported transparency (simultaneous movement in opposite directions) when presented with a beat pattern in which first-order (luminance-defined) and second-order (contrast-defined) motion drifted in opposite directions. Following adaptation to a first-order sinusoidal grating that periodically reversed its drift direction, the percept of transparency was typically abolished and the beat pattern appeared to drift in the direction of the second-order motion. These results clearly demonstrate that adaptation to first-order motion may, under some circumstances, selectively desensitize mechanisms responsive to first-order motion but not second-order motion.

Similarly, Nishida and Sato's (1995) finding that adaptation to a beat pattern, analogous to that used by Hammett et al. (1993), can produce MAEs in opposite directions is commensurate with simultaneous adaptation of separate first-order and second-order motion-detecting mechanisms. A recent study by Nishida et al. (1997c) also has a bearing on this issue. These authors directly compared the spatial-frequency selectivity of first-order and second-order MAEs by measuring direction thresholds for sinusoidal luminance gratings and contrast-modulated noise both prior to and following adaptation to motion. Adaptation to either first-order or second-order motion, of comparable visibility, elevated thresholds for detecting the same variety of motion in a manner that was both direction-selective and spatial frequency–selective. That is, band-limited losses in sensitivity were found that were maximal when the adaptation and test stimuli had the same drift direction and spatial frequency. Importantly, although cross-adaptation effects were sometimes observed, these failed to exhibit spatial-frequency selectivity. These results clearly support the notion that, at least initially, first-order and second-order motion are detected by separate but qualitatively similar mechanisms in the visual system that are each selectively sensitive to a limited range of spatial frequencies. Moreover, convergent evidence from a diverse range of psychophysical (e.g., Dosher, Landy, et al., 1989; Landy, Dosher, et al., 1991; L. R. Harris and Smith, 1992; Mather and West, 1993; Ledgeway and Smith, 1994b; Edwards and Badcock, 1995; Nishida et al., 1997b; A. T. Smith and Ledgeway, 1997), electrophysiologic (Zhou and Baker, 1993, 1994, 1996), and neuropsychological (Vaina, Le May, et al., 1993) studies is also consistent with the existence of separate mechanisms for encoding each variety of motion. Thus, given the current balance of evidence, cross-adaptation effects are likely to reflect integration of first-order and second-order motion signals at relatively late stages of motion processing, as suggested by some motion models (Wilson et al., 1992; Zhou and Baker, 1993; Nishida and Sato, 1995).

In summary, adaptation studies have provided valuable insights into the functional architecture of the mechanisms that encode first-order and second-order motion, and many adaptation phenomena can be readily interpreted using current theoretical models of motion processing (a topic that is addressed in detail in chapter 7). However, there remain many issues concerning adaptation and second-order motion that warrant further investigation. For instance, little is known about the precise mechanisms by which carriers influence the quality and magnitude of aftereffects, or about the relationships and possible interactions between high-level, cognitive strategies and low-level processes in the generation and control of MAEs evoked with dynamic, second-order test patterns.

5.3 Attentional Influences on Motion Aftereffects

Since Wohlgemuth (1911), the MAE has traditionally been thought to be a "preattentive" phenomenon; that is, it has been presumed to result from early and automatic motion processes which do not depend on the observer's state of attention. However, growing evidence is emerging to challenge this view. First, a number of investigators have discovered that the perceived duration, direction, and strength of MAEs may indeed be affected by the degree of attention allocated to the adapting stimulus. Second, newer dynamic tests have revealed MAEs for higher-order stimuli which may be processed through an attention-based motion process. Here we review the evidence for attentional modulation of MAEs and consider the possibility that attentional shifts themselves may lead to MAEs which are qualitatively different from the classic MAE. Further, we consider possible neural substrates for the MAE and its attentional influences.

5.3.1 Attentional Modulation of Motion Aftereffects
Initial investigations by Wohlgemuth (1911) suggested that a subject's attentional state had no effect on the MAE. He found no diminution of

the static MAE when subjects listened to reading, added numbers read aloud, or rapidly read or added numbers presented in the center of the adapting display. More recently, however, Chaudhuri (1990) reported marked reductions in the duration of the MAE using a similar paradigm. Chaudhuri found that MAE duration was reduced by 70 percent when observers performed a foveal attention-distracting task (monitoring a letter stream for the occurrence of digits) on a moving textured background. The foveal attention task had only minor effects on subjects' eye movements, which did not appear to account for the drastic reduction in the MAE. No shortening of MAE duration was found when the task required attention to a diffuse area encompassing the moving stimulus, suggesting that attention must be allocated to a different location for a reduction to occur. Although it is not clear why these two sets of experiments differ, a number of other preliminary reports have corroborated Chaudhuri's report of attentional effects on MAEs (Zhou and Chen, 1994; Boutet, Rivest, et al., 1996; Georgiades and Harris, 1996).

A number of recent experiments have also shown that attention to one of two moving components can bias subsequent judgments of motion. Shulman (1993) replicated Chaudhuri's attentional distraction result using a more powerful opponent technique that involved comparing the perceived direction of the MAE following attention to one direction of motion vs. the opposite direction. In his display, two sets of four grating patches were arranged concentrically and rotated in opposite directions while subjects attended to one set vs. the other. Afterward, an ambiguously rotating test set positioned midway between the two adaptation sets was more likely to be seen rotating opposite to the attended direction. Note that like flicker MAE, the test was directionally ambiguous, suggesting that dynamic MAEs are also modulated by attention.

Attention can affect the MAE not only when it is allocated to different regions of space but also when it is allocated selectively within a single region. Lankheet and Verstraten (1995) presented subjects with two superimposed and transparent random-dot patterns moving in opposite directions and asked subjects to attend to one of the two directions. Following attention to one direction, subjects were more likely to see a dynamic noise pattern moving in the opposite direction, an effect that was quite strong when quantified using a signal/noise nulling procedure. Further, Boutet et al. (1996) found that static MAE strength was enhanced when subjects made attentionally demanding judgments of the motion of the adaptation pattern relative to when they made similar judgments about its luminance or color.

One further study suggests that attention may also modulate MAEs for rotation in depth. Shulman (1991) used his opponent paradigm to demonstrate that attention to one of two squares rotating in depth biased the percept of a square in parallel projection which ambiguously rotated in depth.

Thus it appears that attention can enhance the processing of motion for an attended region of motion or even for the attended direction of motion within a region. In addition to this attentional modulation of MAEs, a second intriguing possibility is the attentional mediation of MAEs.

5.3.2 Attentional Mediation of Motion Aftereffects

In addition to attentional enhancement of MAEs for attended regions, attributes, or directions, recent reports suggest that MAEs may also result from prolonged attentional shifts in the same direction. That is, attention to visual features may also produce a reversal in perceived direction of ambiguous stimuli. One key question is whether these attentional after-effects result from attentional shifts per se, or simply from effects similar to the attentional modulations described above. Originally, stimuli in discontinuous apparent motion were said not to generate MAEs (Anstis and Mather, 1985; Mather, Cavanagh, et al., 1985) and this was considered one of the criteria for distinguishing short- and long-range motion systems (Anstis, 1980). However, this distinction was questioned when von Grünau (1986) reexamined MAEs from long-range motion using an ambiguous test stimulus, and did indeed find MAEs. In von Grünau's paradigm, subjects adapted to the discontinuous apparent motion of a large grating patch that was repeatedly displaced from one side of the display to another.

Subsequently, observers viewed a counterphasing test grating. Adaptation produced a bias such that observers often reported that the test grating appeared to move opposite to the direction of adaptation, though the effect was somewhat weaker for adaptation to discontinuous motion than to smooth drifting motion. This flicker MAE from discontinuous motion survived dichoptic presentation of the stimuli, indicating that short-range motion mechanisms (known to be disrupted by dichoptic presentation; see Anstis, 1980; Braddick, 1974) were unlikely to be responsible. Furthermore, the MAE occurred even using test locations that did not overlap with the successive positions in which the discontinuous adapting grating was presented—a result that was surprising at the time, because static MAEs are typically location-specific.

Von Grünau's demonstration of MAEs from apparent motion was initially attributed to the greater sensitivity of directionally ambiguous tests, compared to traditional static tests (Cavanagh and Mather, 1989; von Grünau and Dubé, 1992). In retrospect, given that dynamic MAE tests have different properties than static tests and may involve later stages of motion processing, it may instead be that dynamic tests are susceptible to higher-order factors such as attention that have little or no influence on the static MAE.

Culham and Cavanagh (1994, 1995) have proposed that the flicker MAE, but not the static MAE, can be triggered by shifts in attention that are used to keep track of a moving target's position. This high-level attentive tracking process is said to form the basis of a second motion system distinct from early detector-based motion processes, and to be implicated in the perception of "long-range" or apparent motion (Wertheimer, 1912; Cavanagh and Mather, 1989; Cavanagh, 1991, 1992; Lu and Sperling, 1995a).

Culham and Cavanagh (1994) investigated the effect of attentive tracking on static and flicker MAEs. In order to generate attentive tracking in the absence of net low-level motion signals, they presented a radial grating in counterphase (equal motion energy in opposite directions). Observers used attention to track the bars of the grating in one direction, clockwise or counterclockwise, while fixating on a central bull's-eye. Thus the stimulus was the same for both conditions; only the subjects' instructions differed. Subsequently, static and flicker MAEs were measured using a nulling technique. Attentive tracking of the counterphase grating produced a flicker MAE but not a static MAE. Furthermore, flicker MAEs following attentive tracking were relatively independent of the adapting contrast of the grating, suggesting that any stimulus visible enough to be tracked would produce a flicker MAE. In comparison, passive viewing of smooth motion produced both MAEs which were highly dependent on the adapting contrast.

In a subsequent experiment, Culham and Cavanagh (1995) investigated the retinotopic specificity of MAEs from smooth motion and attentive tracking. Although von Grünau and Dubé (1992) found flicker MAEs even for unadapted test locations, this experiment further investigated whether MAEs were specific to the global direction of rotation or the local direction of motion components. In the display, shown in figure 5.3A, a radial adapting grating was presented in a central ring and the test ring was presented in the periphery to produce a region of overlap. This configuration yielded two possible outcomes for the direction of MAEs: first, "local MAEs" to adaptation could result if linear motion detectors within the region of overlap led to a locally opposite MAE (e.g., for counterclockwise adaptation, local downward motion in the overlap would produce an upward MAE, biasing the observer to see rotation in the same direction as adaptation, counterclockwise); second, "global MAEs" could result from the adaptation of rotation-selective mechanisms (e.g., counterclockwise adaptation would produce a clockwise MAE). As shown in figure 5.3B, attentive tracking produced flicker MAEs opposite

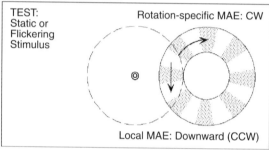

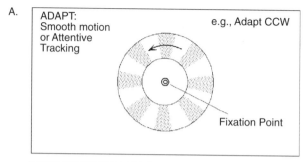

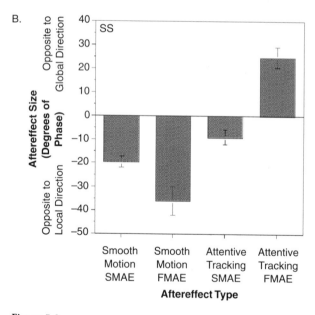

Figure 5.3
Stimulus used to examine retinotopic specificity of attentional aftereffects. Subjects either passively viewed smooth motion or attentively tracked a counterphase grating. The test stimulus was displaced from the adapt to produce a region of overlap which yields two

to the global rotation of the tracked bars. In comparison, attentive tracking led to a negligible static MAE in the local direction. Adapting to
smooth motion produced large local effects for both static and flicker
MAE tests. This interaction suggests that attentive tracking acts at a relatively high level of motion perception in which the analysis can be
rotation-specific, independent of position, and selective to tracked targets
as opposed to physical motion (which was balanced in the counterphasing adapting stimulus).

One possibility raised by these results is that attentive tracking of visible features, rather than low-level motion energy, may be responsible for
flicker MAEs observed with a variety of stimuli, including apparent
motion (von Grünau, 1986) and possibly second-order motion (Nishida
and Sato, 1995). For example, the results of Nishida and Sato, showing
that second-order motion patterns (e.g., defined by texture or depth) generate flicker MAEs, may indicate that these attributes are processed by
higher-order detectors which affect only late stages of motion processing
tapped by the flicker test. Alternatively, subjects may be attentively
tracking the form-defined bars of the adapting patterns, in which case
attention alone could produce a flicker MAE. This is not to say these
results are necessarily attention-based, though further evidence is required
to distinguish the two possible accounts. It may also be that not all second-
order patterns are processed the same way, with some types, such as texture patterns, processed by detector-based systems, and other types, such
as depth-defined or motion-defined patterns, processed by attention-based
systems (Cavanagh, 1995).

Whether or not attention is primarily responsible, it appears to have
a strong influence on flicker MAE results using higher-order stimuli. For
example, two groups have examined flicker MAEs following adaptation
to missing fundamental patterns (Bex, Brady, et al., 1995) or to second-
order beat patterns (Ashida and Osaka, 1995a), both of which include two
opposing motion components—low-level motion energy in one direction
and feature displacement in the other. Bex et al. reported that when no ISI
is present, the flicker MAE appears opposite to motion energy; but when
an ISI is used, the MAE appears opposite to feature motion. Ashida and
Osaka (1995a) reported similar findings, but noted that when an ISI is

Figure 5.3 (continued)
potential outcomes for motion aftereffects (MAEs): local MAEs opposite to the linear motion
within the region of overlap, or global MAEs opposite to the overall direction of rotation.
The phase shifts necessary to null the MAEs are shown for one observer in panel B. Positive
values indicate outcomes consistent with the global MAE; negative values indicate a local
MAE. Vertical bars represent ±1 SE. CCW, counterclockwise; CW, clockwise; SMAE, *Static*
MAE; FMAE, Flicker MAE.

used the MAE was observed only if subjects had to make a judgment about the perceived direction of the adaptation pattern, suggesting that attention was necessary to produce the high-level effect.

5.3.3 Neural Correlates of Attentional Effects on Motion Aftereffects

Attentional influences on the MAE may provide clues as to the neural basis of interactions between attention and motion processing. One very likely candidate for attentional modulation of MAEs in humans is area MT (middle temporal visual area). Specifically, Tootell and his colleagues (1995) have shown that the time course of the functional magnetic resonance imaging (fMRI) signal in the region around "greater MT" (possibly including the medial superior temporal area, or MST) is closely correlated with the subjective strength of the MAE as it decays (see chapter 6). While other motion areas also produced an enhanced magnetic resonance (MR) signal during the MAE, the time course of the response did not match that of the MAE percept (Dale, Reppas, et al., 1996). Furthermore, two other neuroimaging studies have demonstrated stronger activation in greater MT when subjects made judgments of motion than when they made judgments of form or color (Corbetta, Miezen, et al., 1990, 1991), or when they attended to moving dots rather than superimposed stationary dots (O'Craven, Rosen, et al., 1997). A number of physiologic studies have suggested that MST rather than MT is susceptible to "top-down" influences (Wurtz, Richmond, et al., 1984; Newsome, Wurtz, et al., 1988; Ferrera, Rudolph, et al., 1994). However, one elegant study by Treue and Maunsell (1996) demonstrated attentional influences in both areas depending on the nature of the task. Both regions had cells which showed modulation when monkeys attended to a moving dot within vs. outside their receptive fields. One additional possibility is that the locus of attentional modulation depends on the particular motion task. Based on fMRI experiments, Watanabe and Miyauchi (in press) have proposed that area V1 is modulated by attention to motion components, while MT is modulated by attention to integrated motion.

As for the locus of attentional mediation of MAEs, a number of interesting possible neural substrates exist. Given the evidence that attentive tracking leads to global rather than local effects (Culham and Cavanagh, 1995), one possibility is that attentive tracking acts at a level such as MST, which has cells selective to rotation direction and is susceptible to extraretinal influences. However, an intriguing alternative is that attentive tracking and the phenomena that it governs, such as apparent motion and its aftereffects, reflect the activity of higher motion-processing stages. Here, the most likely candidate is the posterior parietal lobe, which has cells responsive to the inferred motion of occluded stimuli (Assad and Maunsell, 1995), has many of the properties necessary for apparent motion correspondence (see Dawson, 1991, for a review), and has been demonstrated to be active while viewing attentive tracking displays (Culham, Cavanagh, et al., 1997). Although further research is required to investigate such a suggestion, this case illustrates that not only may attentional factors be used to understand MAEs but, conversely, MAEs may be used to investigate other higher-order processing such as visual attention.

5.4 Motion Aftereffects from Multivectorial Motion

In previous sections we have dealt with MAEs from simple stimuli, mostly sinusoidal gratings defined by first- or second-order attributes. However, a brief reflection on everyday instances of visual motion suggests that we commonly experience complex interactions between motions. For example, real-world stimuli contain diverse spatiotemporal components, and multiple sets of items can move transparently through each other, sometimes at different depths, as when one looks through falling rain to notice trees bending in a storm. Furthermore, physiologic studies find that neurons in various direction-selective regions show different responses to complex motion stimuli. Thus, restricting our study to simple univectorial motion would neglect the important interactions which can occur between components comprising complex motions. In this section, the study of multivectorial motion is reviewed to investigate not only the neural basis of MAEs but also the levels at which moving components become integrated.

Multivectorial motion refers to the situation in which a given spatial location contains motion in more than one direction. For the most part, investigations of multivectorial motion have been restricted to two motion directions, although in principle more directions could be used. Thus, in discussing multivectorial motion, we will be primarily talking about bivectorial motion. As with other kinds of motion, adaptation to multivectorial motion will produce an MAE. Curiously, however, MAEs induced by adaptation to multivectorial motion are generally not themselves multivectorial. That is, adaptation to multivectorial motion usually generates a univectorial MAE with a direction approximately opposed to the vector sum of the adapting motions. This is the case for bivectorial motion when the two adapting directions are presented in temporal alternation (e.g., Riggs and Day, 1980) or simultaneously (e.g., Mather, 1980; Movshon, Adelson, et al., 1985), and occurs irrespective of whether the adapting motions are perceived to move coherently (as may occur when superimposed gratings form a coherent plaid) or transparently (as occurs when two sheets of random dots are superimposed). Given the unitary nature of MAEs produced by adaptation to this kind of motion, terming them "multivectorial MAEs" is potentially misleading. In the discussion that follows, the term "MAE of multivectorial motion" is used in preference.

5.4.1 Motion of Aftereffects of Transparent Motion

It is surprising indeed that the MAEs of multivectorial motion are uni-directional even in the case of adaptation to completely transparent motion—even though two clearly different directions are perceived during adaptation, the MAE is opposite to a direction that has never been perceived, while the perceived directions apparently produce no MAEs. What happens to the MAEs presumably generated by the component motions?

This question has recently been investigated in a series of studies by Verstraten and colleagues. They used moving random pixel arrays (RPAs—two-dimensional arrays of dots in which each pixel is randomly assigned to be black or white and the pixels are shifted to generate motion). Two RPAs with directions 90 degrees apart were combined and formed a transparent display in which the individual RPA motions were visible. MAE direction was measured on static RPAs for various speed combinations of the two motions. For unequal speeds, MAE direction could be predicted by the vector sum of the components weighted by a measure of sensitivity to the individual components, such as MAE duration and directional sensitivity. Since MAE direction did not change over time, even when one component would be expected to elicit only a brief MAE, Verstraten and colleagues suggested that the MAE is not determined for each component and then combined, but created only at or after an integration stage, perhaps at MT or later (Verstraten et al., 1994a).

A further study (Verstraten et al., 1994b) found that adaptation to uni-directional motion is stored and used in combination with adaptation to subsequent orthogonal motion. The earlier stimulus had a longer influence on the direction of the combined MAE than would be expected from its MAE when measured in isolation, providing additional evidence that the MAE is formed at or after the site where components become integrated. The region over which the component motions influence the integrated MAE appears to be substantially larger than that of the spatial integration area involved in perceiving coherent motion, again suggesting that MAE generation is at a higher level (van Wezel, Lankheet, et al., 1996). Furthermore, the direction of the MAE to transparent motion also depends on the test stimulus type (static noise vs. dynamic noise of various temporal frequencies). One account of these results (Verstraten, 1994) is that they reflect interactions between spatiotemporal filters that are located before the site at which MAEs are generated. This explanation is consistent with the results of physiologic studies that fail to show fatiguing effects at early visual levels that last long enough to support the durations of MAEs observed psychophysically (Barlow and Hill, 1963; Hammond, Mouat, et al., 1986, 1988; Hammond, Pomfrett, et al., 1989). This account is not incompatible with the idea that MAEs are generated at different levels of processing (e.g., Nishida and Sato, 1995), but states only that the relevant levels may be relatively late in the sequence of processing.

5.4.2 Motion Aftereffects of Coherent Motion

A novel kind of multivectorial stimulus known as a plaid was introduced by Adelson and Movshon in 1982 (but see also Exner, 1887, and Borschke and Hescheles, 1902, cited in chapter 1). Plaids are stimuli constructed from superimposed sinusoidal or rectangular grating components drifting in different directions (see figure 5.4). Unlike multivectorial stimuli composed of random-dot patterns, coherent motion is often observed with plaid stimuli (Kim and Wilson, 1993)—the motions of the two component gratings are no longer perceived as independent and a new entity, the plaid pattern, is seen to move rigidly in a third direction. With noncoherent plaids, the component gratings are seen clearly to slide transparently over each other. Movshon et al. (1985) proposed a two-stage model to account for these observations based on their neurophysiologic observations that two kinds of direction-selective cells exist in area MT. The first kind, termed component-selective, responded maximally to the motion of the plaid's components in a manner similar to V1 cells, whereas a minority of cells (approximately 25 percent) were found to be pattern-selective and responded maximally to the coherent motion of the plaid pattern itself. In the first stage of their model, direction-selective units in V1 detect the motion of the component gratings and feed their signals to area MT where, if coherence conditions are met, the component motions are integrated into a coherently moving plaid.

Movshon et al. (1985) proposed that the perceived direction of coherent plaids is determined by the intersection of constraints (IOC) solution, a geometric solution to the inherent directional ambiguity of the plaid's one-dimensional (1-D) components (Adelson and Movshon, 1982; Fennema and Thompson, 1979). Consistent with this model, plaids are usually seen to move in a direction corresponding to that predicted by the IOC (figure 5.4, left side). Plaids in which the component motion vectors both lie to the same side of the resultant vector do not obey this rule (these are so-called type II plaids; figure 5.4, right side; see also Fererra and Wilson, 1987, 1990). Perceived direction in type II plaids is biased toward the component directions and away from the IOC prediction (see figure 5.4, right side). Nonetheless, the MAE is again unitary and is seen to move in the direction opposite to the perceived plaid direction for both

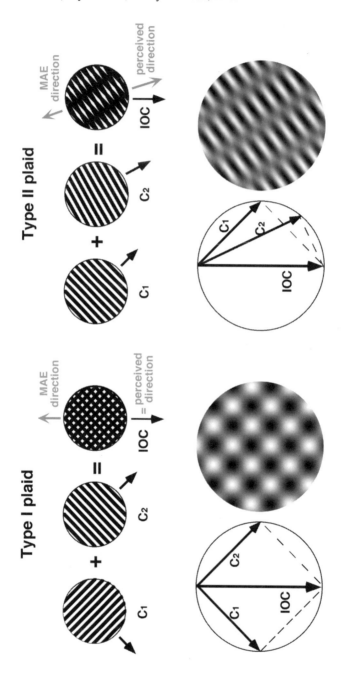

Figure 5.4

Plaid stimuli are formed by the addition of two independently moving gratings (C1 and C2). Following Ferrera and Wilson's (1987) classification, examples are shown of type I plaids (for which component vectors lie on each side of the intersection of constraints [IOC] resultant) and type II plaids (for which both component vectors lie to one side of the IOC resultant). The lower rows show the plaid types as vector diagrams (left) and as the sum of sine-wave components (right). The aperture problem renders each component motion directionally ambiguous so that any vector terminating on the dashed "constraint" line would produce identical percepts; however, the intersection of constraint lines uniquely solves plaid direction. Adelson and Movshon (1982) proposed a neural implementation of this solution to account for perceived plaid direction. Alternatively, the "blob" features produced by grating luminance summation could determine perceived plaid motion, as their motion is identical to the IOC resultant. Neither proposal predicts the bias toward component directions in perceived direction of type II plaids. Another feature produced by summation of grating luminances, more evident in type II plaids, are second-order (contrast-defined) contours. These are the oblique gray contours seen in the figure which would move down and to the right. Plaid motion aftereffects (MAEs) reflect the adaptation of both component motions and both kinds of pattern feature. For both type I and type II plaids, the direction of the MAE is opposite to the perceived direction of motion.

type I and II plaids (Alais, Wenderoth, et al., 1994, 1997). Von Grünau and Dubé (1992) measured the strength of the MAE generated by plaids as a function of the difference in direction between the adapting plaid and the test stimulus (a counterphasing grating in which the relative contrast of the two opposing components could be adjusted to cancel the MAE). The tuning curves of MAEs obtained using plaid and grating adaptation stimuli were very similar. However, there was no evidence for stronger MAEs at test directions opposite to the plaid's component directions, further supporting the conclusion that MAEs (at least those measured with counterphasing test stimuli) might reflect adaptation at extrastriate locations.

5.4.3 The Effect of Blobs
When two drifting gratings with different orientations are superimposed to form a plaid, an array of bloblike features is formed by luminance summation at the intersections. These features always move in the true plaid direction because they are part of the plaid pattern itself, so detection of their motion would provide an alternative to the proposed IOC solution to plaid direction. Such a mechanism was originally rejected by Adelson and Movshon (1982) because 1-D dynamic noise disrupted coherence most when it masked the component directions rather than the plaid direction. Neither IOCs nor blobs can explain the component bias in the perceived direction of type II plaids (Ferrera and Wilson, 1990). Nevertheless, a good deal of evidence suggests that a mechanism sensitive to the motion of blob features does contribute to perceived plaid direction (Alais et al., 1997; Derrington and Badcock, 1992; Gorea and Lorenceau, 1991). Burke and Wenderoth (1993a), investigating earlier data from Wenderoth et al. (1988), compared plaid MAEs produced by grating components presented simultaneously with those produced by grating components presented in alternation (the latter condition precludes the formation of blobs). They suggested that the longer MAE duration obtained after simultaneous presentation could be due to the participation of a blob-tracking mechanism. In interocular transfer conditions (adapt using one eye and test using the other), the duration of the MAE following simultaneous adaptation fell to the same duration as the MAE following alternate adaptation (Burke and Wenderoth, 1993a, using type I plaids; Alais et al., 1994, using type II plaids). This result suggests that the blob-tracking mechanism is monocular. Importantly, MAE direction was more nearly opposite to the true direction of plaid motion in the simultaneous adaptation condition than in the alternating condition, as would be expected if the blob-tracking mechanism provided a veridical input to perceived plaid direction.

Alais et al. (1994) showed that the effectiveness of blobs depends on the spatiotemporal properties of the stimulus. Blobs formed by component gratings of high spatial frequency, low temporal frequency, and high contrast maximized the difference between alternately and simultaneously adapted MAEs, suggesting that these conditions optimally activate the mechanism responsive to the motion of the blobs. The inverse conditions minimized this difference. Using type II plaids, Alais et al. (1994) compared perceived direction for optimal and nonoptimal plaids, and found large differences in perceived direction: optimal blob plaids were perceived more veridically (by nearly 20 degrees) than nonoptimal blob plaids, largely overcoming the component bias known to occur with type II plaids (Ferrera and Wilson, 1990). Alais et al. (1997) further showed that simply increasing the spatial frequency of a type II plaid's components to about 6 cycles/degree progressively reduces the component bias. As would be expected if the blob-tracking mechanism were contributing substantially to perceived plaid direction, it slowly adapts during extended exposure to a drifting plaid, such that perceived direction is most veridical during the initial seconds of presentation (Wenderoth, Alais, et al., 1994).

This effect was examined more closely by Alais, Burke, et al. (1996a), who measured the perceived direction of type II plaids before and after monocular adaptation to the plaid's motion. When tested using the same eye, perceived direction differed significantly from perceived direction before adaptation, and was less veridical by an average of 7 degrees, showing more of the component bias. This difference was not found under interocular transfer conditions, suggesting the involvement of a low-level, monocular mechanism rather than a highly binocular structure such as area MT. The MAEs resulting from this period of adaptation appeared to move opposite to the postadaptation apparent direction, rather than the more veridical initial judgments of perceived plaid direction. The change in perceived plaid direction during a 30-second adaptation period reported by Alais et al. (1996) is in the opposite direction to that reported by Yo and Wilson (1992), who found that, over much briefer periods (on the order of 100 ms) after the onset of motion, plaids become *more* veridically perceived, moving from the component-biased (vector-sum) direction to the predicted IOC direction.

Overall, considerable evidence suggests that a monocular motion mechanism sensitive to the motion of a plaid's so-called blob features is involved in the perceived direction of plaids and their MAEs. In addition, adaptation studies have revealed that this same mechanism largely determines plaid coherence (Burke, Alais, et al., 1994; Alais, van der Smagt, et al., 1996b). Most of this evidence has emerged quite recently, and is interesting in light of the early history of plaid stimuli. It was generally acknowledged at the time that the ambiguous low-level input to the motion system (the well-known aperture problem) posed a considerable challenge to models of motion perception, and seemed to require higher-level processes in order for object motion to be recovered. Plaid stimuli seemed to be the ideal tool for probing these higher-level motion processes since they are perceived to move rigidly (when coherence conditions are met) with an unambiguous direction despite being composed of directionally ambiguous components. However, it eventually became clear that the summation of component luminances produces second-order motion components and moving blob features which also make contributions to plaid motion perception. It is ironic that the mechanism detecting the motion of these features seems to be a low-level and monocular one, given that plaids were intended to probe higher-level motion processes. The importance of blobs is not surprising in view of their subjective salience when viewing a coherently drifting plaid. Component-related factors such as differences in component contrast (Adelson and Movshon, 1982), spatial frequency (A. T. Smith, 1992), and color (Krauskopf and Farell, 1990) also influence plaid coherence, but they may act as segmentation cues, with larger component differences along these dimensions increasing the likelihood that the components will be coded as independent.

5.4.4 Motion Aftereffects for Motion Components Separated in Depth

Verstraten et al. (1994d) demonstrated that under some circumstances, MAEs of bidirectional motion can indeed be bidirectional. Two simultaneous MAEs in different directions were sometimes observed with bivectorial adapting patterns, where the two random-dot patterns were located at crossed and uncrossed disparities, and with stationary test patterns also located at the same disparities. Oppositely moving adaptation stimuli showed significantly more instances of bivectorial MAE than orthogonally moving adaptation stimuli, where a unidirectional MAE was only seen in about 50 percent of the trials. These studies show that integration of motion directions prior to MAE generation is a very powerful mechanism which can persist even when adaptation and test stimuli are presented at different depth planes. On the other hand, the fact that bivectorial MAEs occur when tied to different disparities, but not when tied to color, for instance, speaks to the close interrelationship between channels responsible for direction analysis and for depth segregation (Kwas, von Grünau, et al., 1995, submitted; Trueswell and Hayhoe, 1993; Vallortigara and Bressan, 1991; see also chapter 4).

5.4.5 Attention and Bidirectional Motion Aftereffects

Given that attention to one component of a bidirectional random-dot pattern yields MAEs in the opposite direction (Lankheet and Verstraten,

1995), we may also wonder what would occur with attention to one of the two components forming a transparent plaid stimulus. Bertone, von Grünau, et al. (1997) had subjects adapt to a plaid, either while passively viewing it or while attending to one of the two components. MAEs were tested with counterphase flickering gratings as well as a stationary test plaid. When subjects attended to one of the transparent component gratings during adaptation, they perceived it as in front and dominant for 80 percent of the time. Relative to passive viewing, the strength of the flicker MAE increased when the test orientation matched the attended component and decreased when it matched the unattended component, as shown in figure 5.5A. The facilitatory and inhibitory effects were similar in size. With a stationary test plaid (figure 5.5B), illusory motion was usually perceived in the direction opposite to the adaptation plaid direction. When attention was directed toward one of the transparent component gratings during adaptation, the test plaid appeared to move opposite to the attended direction for a short time. As shown in figure 5.5B, this decayed rapidly and was replaced by motion opposite to the plaid direction. The overall MAE duration was not affected. Watanabe (1995) has also shown that when subjects attended to one edge of a series of translating pie-shaped wedges, tuning curves for static MAEs were shifted toward the orientation of the attended edge. Similar attentional influences have been observed with a bivectorial stimulus that could be seen as first-order motion in one direction or second-order motion in another (Iordanova, Riscaldino, et al., 1996). Again, flicker MAEs were stronger for the attended direction and weaker for the unattended direction, when compared to passive viewing. Taken together, the results of these studies indicate that attention both facilitates and inhibits motion mechanisms at or before the level of the MAE. The effects of attention on the MAEs of bivectorial motion suggest that component MAEs do exist and can be made "visible," but that without this attentional boost the bivectorial MAE is unidirectional.

In conclusion, MAEs to bivectorial motion do not appear bivectorial, even though the existence of the component MAEs can be demonstrated under conditions of selective attention or when direction is disparity-contingent. Most of the evidence suggests that the bivectorial MAE is produced only after the integration of the component motions. It is not clear, however, whether the same mechanisms contribute similarly to the formation of the integrated motion direction and the formation of the MAE direction.

5.5 Effects of Motion Adaptation on Global Motion Sensitivity

We now diverge from studies of the MAE to look at the effects of adaptation on global motion sensitivity, in order to compare the results

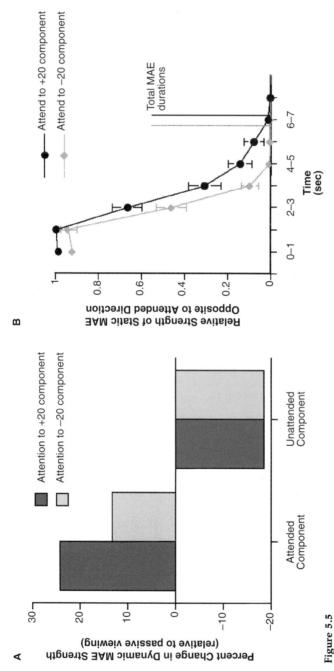

Figure 5.5
Attentional modulation of motion aftereffect (MAE) to a transparent plaid stimulus. A, Test stimuli were phase-reversing gratings with the same orientation as either the attended or unattended component of a moving plaid viewed during adaptation. For the attended orientation, MAE strength increased relative to a passive viewing baseline. For the unattended orientation, it decreased by a similar amount. B, At the beginning of a test period with a stationary plaid, the MAE was characterized by illusory motion opposite to the attended direction. The decay of this percept for successive 1-second intervals is indicated for one observer. Vertical bars represent ± 1 SE.

obtained using the two paradigms. Raymond and her colleagues conducted a series of experiments in which the adapting and test patterns were moving random-dot kinematograms (RDKs)—short-range apparent motion sequences consisting of successive presentations of random-dot displays in which a percentage of dots were displaced by a constant amount and in a single direction (signal dots) while remaining (noise) dots were displaced in random directions. In most of these experiments, the adaptation stimulus was 100 percent coherent and the percent coherence in the test was varied from trial to trial. Sensitivity to global motion in the test was assessed by determining the minimum percentage of signal dots needed for just accurate identification of signal direction. This measure is called the motion coherence threshold. We assume that the perception of global coherence is mediated by high-level motion-sensitive cells, probably in area MT, that integrate local motion signals over larger regions of space and are able to "smooth" across local differences in motion information to yield global signals of direction and velocity.

In the alert monkey, cells in area MT vary their response rates depending on the percentage of signal dots in RDK displays, and the motion coherence threshold of these monkeys can be manipulated by stimulation of these neurons (Salzman, Britten, et al., 1990b). Monkeys with lesions in area MT (Newsome and Paré, 1988) or humans with lesions in V5 (Zeki, 1993), an area homologous to MT (e.g., Baker, Hess, et al., 1991; Barton, Sharpe, et al., 1995), cannot perform motion coherence tasks normally. Raymond (1993b) asked observers to view a rightward moving 100 percent coherent RDK for 90 seconds and then alternated brief (196 ms) test stimuli with 5-second duration "top-up" intervals of 100 percent coherent motion to maintain adaptation. The task was to judge the global test direction from four possibilities: upward, downward, leftward, or rightward. A control condition in which subjects viewed a stationary dot display was used to determine the unadapted baseline threshold. Motion adaptation elevated motion coherence threshold when the test direction matched that of the adaptation stimulus. Group mean coherence threshold for five observers was elevated from a mean baseline 16 percent to 63 percent. This loss in global sensitivity was directionally selective because coherence thresholds for test stimuli with movement orthogonal or opposite to the adapting direction remained unchanged from baseline levels. Raymond (1993b) reported that the loss in sensitivity decreased as the difference in direction between adapt and test increased. The desensitization effect reached half its maximum when the directions differed by +35 degrees, thus describing the directional tuning of global analyzers.

This result is consistent with tuning functions found for MT cells in monkey (Dubner and Zeki, 1971; Felleman and Kaas, 1984) and is notably broader than the +20-degree bandwidth of tuning functions for V1

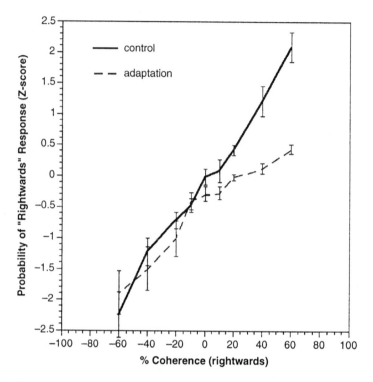

Figure 5.6
The group mean (N = 5) probability of a "rightward" response as a function of the percent coherence of rightward motion in the test stimulus after adaptation to rightward motion (dashed line) or to a static dot display (solid line). Negative percent coherence indicates leftward motion. Vertical bars represent ±1 SE.

direction-selective cells (DeValois, Yund, et al., 1982; Schiller, Finlay, et al., 1976). The effect also showed broad speed selectivity (Raymond, 1994). Raymond and Braddick (1996) conducted a two-alternative forced choice ("rightward" vs. "leftward") experiment in which the psychometric function relating probability of a "rightward" response to percent coherence (varying coherence from 100 percent leftward through 0 to 100 percent rightward) was measured with and without prior adaptation to rightward motion. After adaptation, the slope of the function for rightward motion was flattened (figure 5.6) but the function for leftward motion remained unchanged, indicating that the mechanism mediating leftward detection was unaffected by rightward adaptation. These data suggest that adaptation measured in terms of changes in global motion thresholds affects high-level motion processing after a stage at which opponent interactions might occur (see chapter 7). Consistent with this interpretation was the observation that if the adaptation stimulus consisted of 50 percent leftward and 50 percent rightward dots, that is, a bivectorial transparent display, coherence thresholds for test stimuli moving either leftward or rightward were elevated by an equal amount, while thresholds for the orthogonal directions were unaffected (Raymond, 1993b).

Many adaptation effects, including the MAE (e.g., Keck et al., 1976), increase in size as the duration or strength of the adapting stimulus is increased, and are not seen with brief or weak adapting stimuli. Raymond and Isaak (1998) tested whether the loss in the ability to see coherent motion in partially coherent displays reflected such a process. Long adaptation intervals and top-up intervals were replaced by discrete trials, each consisting of a successive adapt-test pair, with a long intertrial interval. The adaptation stimulus was either 100 percent coherent, rightward or leftward, or 0 percent coherent (i.e., motion noise). Test coherence thresholds were obtained for rightward and leftward motion. The remarkable result was that if the adapting stimulus was even as brief as 200 ms, test thresholds were significantly elevated when the adapt and test directions were the same. When the duration of the adaptation was varied from 200 to 2000 ms, the magnitude of threshold elevation increased modestly, reaching levels consistent with those found in the long adaptation experiment. Even with extremely brief adapting stimuli, motion coherence thresholds were elevated to nearly the same levels as found with much longer adaptation, suggesting that the neural processes leading to the adaptation effect occur very quickly and do not require prolonged exposure. In another experiment the coherence of the adapting stimulus was varied from 100 percent down to thresholds levels. As with stimulus duration, there was a modest increase in threshold elevation with increasing coherence, but even so, minimally suprathreshold coherence in the adapting stimulus raised thresholds significantly. These findings are inconsistent with an account of adaptation in terms of the gradual buildup of neural fatigue (theories of adaptation are discussed further in chapter 7).

Raymond, O'Donnell, et al. (1997) devised an experiment that was modeled after an attentional effect known as negative priming (e.g., Tipper and Cranston, 1985), but used the same stimuli as in the successive motion experiments described above. Results indicated clearly that selective attention modulates visual global motion perception. Attention to one direction caused a loss in sensitivity to that direction in a subsequent event, whereas actively ignoring a direction primed sensitivity for that direction. These effects are opposite in direction to more typical negative priming effects (where ignoring an item causes reduced subsequent processing). However, if we consider that changes in motion are more salient than continuation along a trajectory, mechanisms to reduce sensitivity to already coded information make sense. Another study, by Raymond and

O'Donnell (1996), further suggests that sensitivity reductions may only occur when motion stimuli are perceived as distinct objects. The authors first demonstrated threshold elevation effects when a brief (160 ms) passively viewed unidirectional RDK preceded a test RDK after an ISI (256 ms). In a second condition, the two motion stimuli were linked by a global object motion as the overall shape of the RDK changed between presentations ("morphing motion"; Tse and Cavanagh, in press). Rather than seeing the prime and test as discrete items, subjects perceived them as belonging to the same changing surface. Remarkably, threshold elevation effects disappeared. Given that the low-level stimulus properties were similar between the two conditions, these results suggest that motion adaptation effects depend on the perception of two different "objects."

In sum, the evidence reviewed here suggests that MAEs are but one instance of successive stimulus interactions which display a range of high-level properties. These experiments have indicated that much of the effect of motion adaptation on high-level motion perception does not depend on prolonged adaptation and is unlikely to be due solely to neural fatigue, as has been previously thought. By modifying classic psychophysical adaptation procedures to match widely used attentional negative-priming procedures, it has been demonstrated that successive stimulus interactions in motion perception are modulated by attention.

5.6 Conclusions

The past decade of research on the MAE has generated a new interest in a variety of higher-order effects that influence the illusion and has produced a number of surprising results. In particular, these new directions question the assumption that the MAE is a unitary preattentive effect generated by passive viewing of only unidirectional motion energy. Rather, it now appears that MAEs may be influenced by processing which spans a range of levels, both anatomically and functionally, and that MAE phenomena are the result of complex interactions between stimuli and tasks.

These complex interactions within MAE phenomena provide a rich domain for exploring motion processing and its interactions with other perceptual and cognitive processes. As we have observed, complex stimuli and tasks can be used to probe the MAE. For example, interocular transfer studies and higher-order motion stimuli have suggested that static MAEs may occur at earlier stages than dynamic MAEs. However, not only can complex factors be used to understand the MAE but the MAE can also be used to examine higher-order aspects of stimulus coding and the attentional state. Examples include the use of MAEs to probe the stages of motion integration (for both plaid components and random dot stimuli) and the interactions between attention, priming, and motion processing.

From this recent literature, three primary themes and future research directions emerge. The first concerns the issue of whether static and dynamic test patterns reflect common underlying mechanisms or tap separate levels of motion processing. The list of differences between static and dynamic stimuli is certainly large and growing (see table 5.1), and is difficult to reconcile with a single mechanism. However, a number of studies suggest similarities in the properties of the two test types (e.g., Nishida et al., 1997a) or provide models which can account for some of the data without the need for distinct mechanisms (Wainwright and Cavanagh, 1997). Nevertheless, other properties, such as the differences in interocular transfer, pose difficulties for a single-mechanism account. One possible resolution is that there is a continuum of properties which are differentially tapped by the temporal frequency ranges typically used for static and flicker tests. A second possibility is that multiple factors may account for the properties of flicker MAE tests—a low-level motion adaptation factor which is not fully binocular but is dominant in peripheral vision, and a second high-level factor which is closely linked with attention, contributes to apparent motion correspondence matches, and is more dominant in central vision.

Second, the MAE depends on more than just the first-order motion components making up a stimulus. Second-order motion displays and attentional shifts can also generate MAEs, at least for dynamic tests. Further research will be useful in clarifying interactions between first-order, second-order, and "third-order" (i.e., attention-based) motion systems. Furthermore, even within first-order motion, MAEs are specific to the integrated direction of multiple components rather than the directions of the components themselves (with one intriguing exception in the case of components separated in depth). This research has provided evidence both for low-level monocular mechanisms involved in "blob-tracking" and for higher-level, possibly extrastriate, integration of components before the site where the MAE is generated. Again, these results raise interesting issues concerning the relationships between these mechanisms, and their physiologic substrates.

Third, the MAE may be much more susceptible to cognitive factors, particularly attention, than previously believed. Many recent studies show that responses to motion stimuli and their components can be enhanced or suppressed depending on whether they are attended and selected or not. Furthermore, attention may act in multiple ways, both modulating the strength of motion signals and possibly mediating correspondences in a motion system capable of producing distinct aftereffects. Finally, motion sensitivity measures suggest that only brief, suprathreshold motion instances may be necessary to produce "adaptation" effects and that such effects may be related to other cognitive interactions between successive stimuli such as priming.

In sum, the main theme that emerges from this chapter is that there may not be a single unitary MAE measured by all studies which address it. Rather, the properties of the MAE may depend substantially on the type of adaptation stimulus employed (first- or second-order, components or integrated patterns), the type of test stimulus used (static or dynamic), and the subject's state during adaptation (including attentional and response selection factors). Many of these data are preliminary, the theories are sometimes speculative, and, as might be obvious from some of the earlier chapters in this book, a number of different interpretations are available. Nonetheless, these different theories and speculations provide an excellent impetus for further research into higher-order factors in the MAE.

Chapter 6
The Physiologic Substrate of Motion Aftereffects

Michael Niedeggen and Eugene R. Wist

In this chapter we seek answers to the following questions: (1) What clues concerning the physiologic basis of motion aftereffects (MAEs) can we gain from experimental studies of single-unit activity in the cat and monkey, and human evoked potential studies? (2) Which physiologic models based on such data seem best suited at this stage of research to account for the psychophysical data? (3) Must the seminal model of Barlow and Hill (1963) be revised in the light of current research? In the first part, the cerebral neuronal mechanisms involved in visual motion perception are briefly reviewed. In the second part, single-unit studies of adaptation in visual motion-sensitive neurons are reviewed and evaluated. In the final section, studies of human evoked potentials and functional magnetic resonance imaging (fMRI) are evaluated in terms of their potential for providing a bridge between single-unit and psychophysical studies of MAEs.

6.1 Cerebral Neuronal Mechanisms of Visual Motion Perception

The following brief outline of some of the functional characteristics of motion-sensitive neurons within the visual cortex is intended to provide a context in which the experimental findings reported later can be better understood. Although several important studies discussed in the next section were carried out on rabbits (Barlow and Hill, 1963) and cats (Hammond, Mouat, et al., 1985), the remainder of this review is concentrated on the primate cortex. More extensive treatments can be found in Grüsser and Landis (1991) or Maunsell and Newsome (1987).

6.1.1 Precortical Motion Processing
Selectivity for the quality "motion" can be found already within the afferent input to the visual cortex: achromatic α-ganglion cells respond to high-contrast, light-dark borders, and flicker stimuli, whereas a subclass of γ-ganglion cells respond selectively to slow movement (Grüsser and Grüsser-Cornehls, 1976). These ganglion cells project to the lateral

geniculate nucleus (LGN), where selective response to slow movement has paradoxically not been reported until recently. The findings of K. G. Thompson, Zhou, et al. (1994) in cats do suggest some directional selectivity in the LGN. Magnocellular on-center and off-center neurons in the LGN appear to be sensitive to stimuli moving at higher speeds (Grüsser and Grüsser-Cornehls, 1973).

6.1.2 Motion Processing in Striate Cortex
Motion and direction selectivity can be reliably found in neurons of the primary visual cortex (V1) (figure 6.1). Most motion-sensitive neurons here respond best to a contrast border oriented perpendicular to its preferred motion direction. Some segregation of movement-selective neurons can also be observed within area V1: strongest direction sensitivity is found in a class of neurons located in layer IVB, which receive their input from simple and complex neurons in layer 4Cα. Both layers are part of the magnocellular system projecting from the magnocellular layers of the LGN (see DeYoe and van Essen, 1988, for a review). The neurons within this pathway are characterized predominantly by insensitivity to color, poor response to stationary contours, but rapid, transient responses to moving stimuli.

6.1.3 Motion Processing in Area MT
The motion direction–sensitive neurons of layer IVB project either directly or via V2 to area MT (middle temporal visual area, or V5 of Zeki, 1974), where 80 to 90 percent of neurons exhibit clear motion sensitivity (Albright, 1984). In addition to this cortical pathway, the retina projects via the superior colliculi to the pulvinar and from there to MT. The importance of this retino-tecto-pulvinar pathway for motion perception is still not clear. The central role of area MT in visual motion perception has been demonstrated by several experimental lesion studies. Dürsteler and Wurtz (1988) observed a serious impairment of visual pursuit movement and Newsome and Paré (1988) found a significant reduction in motion direction discrimination after lesions in area MT. Furthermore, neurologic case studies suggest that lesions involving area MT can cause selective motion blindness (Zihl et al., 1983; Vaina, Lemay, et al., 1990). In experiments in which the coherence of motion direction in dynamic random-dot patterns was varied, Newsome, Britten, et al. (1989a) demonstrated a high correlation between neuronal activity in area MT and psychophysical sensitivity to motion direction. This finding, as well as data from lesion studies (Newsome and Paré, 1988) indicates that area MT is necessary for discrimination of *motion direction*. The functional properties of area MT neurons have been investigated intensively during the last decade. A good review can be found in Newsome, Shadlen, et al. (1995).

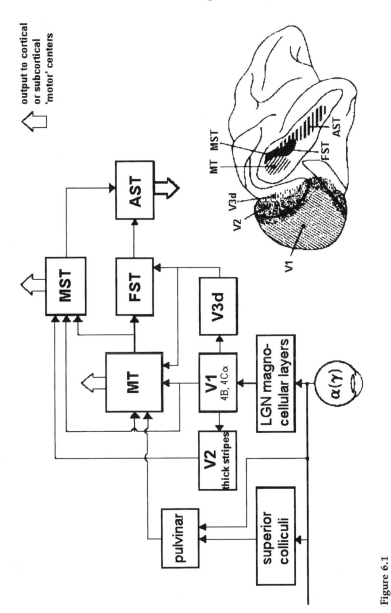

Figure 6.1
Processing streams of the movement-sensitive areas in the visual cortex of primates. Retinal information projects to the highly complex neurons in the superior temporal sulcus (MT, MST, FST, and AST) via the magnocellular layers of the lateral geniculate nucleus (LGN) or via pulvinar (Adapted from Grüsser and Landis, 1991.)

6.1.4 Motion Processing Beyond MT

Area MT projects to area MST (medial superior temporal area), where receptive field sizes are considerably larger than in area MT, and where responsiveness to complex motion patterns is characteristic. Some neurons in area MST respond selectively to radial and circular motion (Duffy and Wurtz, 1991). Further projections have been found from MT and MST to other motion-sensitive areas along the upper bank of the superior temporal sulcus of the monkey brain. It has been suggested that these higher-order visual movement areas are involved in the integration of afferent with efferent visual motion signals in the form of efference copies (Grüsser and Landis, 1991).

6.2 Single-Unit Recordings: A "Neuronal Motion Aftereffect"?

6.2.1 The First Physiologic Correlates of Motion Adaptation

Sutherland (1961) seems to have been the first to offer a hypothesis concerning the neuronal basis of MAEs (see chapter 7). He suggested that

> The direction in which something is seen to move might depend upon the ratios of firing in cells sensitive to movement in different directions, and after prolonged movement in one direction a stationary image would produce less firing in the cells which had just been stimulated than normally, hence apparent movement in the opposite direction would be seen to occur. (p. 227)

Barlow and Hill (1963) were the first to offer empirical evidence for the physiologic basis of the MAE in the form of discharge characteristics of single neurons in the visual system. They recorded the firing rate of motion-sensitive ganglion cells in the rabbit retina during and following prolonged stimulation with a rotating random-dot pattern. When the retina was exposed to the stimulus, the ganglion cell's firing rate was initially brisk, but gradually declined over the first 15 to 20 seconds. When motion stopped, the firing rate fell below its spontaneous level, recovering gradually over 30 seconds. A rebound effect would have been expected on the basis of an inhibition model, but none was found. Spontaneous activity did not change following continuous motion in the null direction (figure 6.2), though an inhibition model would have predicted an increase in response (due to adaptation of inhibitory neurons). Barlow and Hill regarded the transient reduction in spontaneous activity as the substrate of the MAE. Nevertheless, they noted that "it seems unlikely that similar effects occur at a retinal level in man" (p. 1346). Furthermore, psychophysical studies of interocular transfer (Wade, 1976) in normal and stereoblind subjects, as well as those involving complex plaid patterns

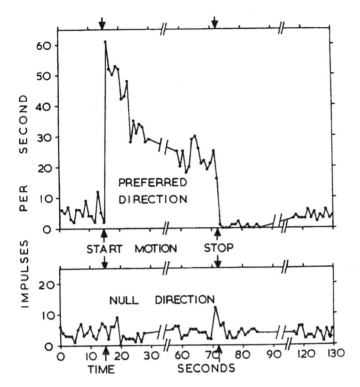

Figure 6.2
Activity of a ganglion cell in the rabbit's retina as a function of prolonged motion stimulation (rotating random-dot disk). As shown in the upper graph, motion in the preferred
direction led to an exponential decline in firing rate. When motion stopped, discharge frequency dropped abruptly to zero. In contrast, motion adaptation in the null direction (lower
graph) resulted in no change in the discharge rate, either during stimulus motion or during
the static phase. (From Barlow and Hill, 1963.)

(Wenderoth et al., 1988), suggest that the adaptation of neurons in the
striate and extrastriate cortex is involved in the generation of MAEs.
More recent research on adaptation in single units, briefly reviewed
below, has concentrated mainly on neurons in the striate cortex of cats
and monkeys.

Barlow and Hill's data implicate a change in the spontaneous activity of
adapted neurons as the substrate of the MAE. In order to evaluate this
explanation as it applies to cortical cells, at least three basic questions
must be considered:

1. What actually happens to the discharge rate of neurons during motion
adaptation? According to the findings of Barlow and Hill, the response of

neurons sensitive to the adapting direction should decline gradually during continuous motion stimulation. This effect can be compared to the buildup of MAEs measured psychophysically.

2. How does previous adaptation affect the driven activity of neurons sensitive to the adapting direction and its opposite? This question addresses the direction specificity of motion adaptation. According to Barlow and Hill, firing rates of neurons sensitive to the adapting direction should be below baseline at first, but should recover gradually. In contrast, the discharge rates of neurons that prefer the opposite direction should not be affected.

3. How does previous adaptation in the preferred direction affect spontaneous activity? In psychophysical experiments, MAEs are observed once the adapting pattern stops. According to Barlow and Hill's findings, a reduction of spontaneous activity in the adapted direction-selective neurons during this stationary phase constitutes the neural basis of the aftereffect. Neurons tuned to other motion directions should show unchanged spontaneous activity both during and after adaptation.

We shall now review and evaluate modern research on adaptation in single cortical neurons for their ability to answer these questions.

6.2.2 Motion Adaptation in Cat Striate Cortex: Early Findings

The answers to these three questions provided by the literature are conflicting, in part owing to the fact that different methods, species, and adapting or test stimuli have been employed. Studies were selected for review here on the basis of their historical importance as well as their ability to resolve conflicts. One of the first studies measuring the effect of motion adaptation on neurons in the visual cortex was reported by Maffei, Fiorentini, et al. (1973). They presented cats with a drifting high-contrast grating for 1 minute, followed by the presentation of a slowly drifting low-contrast grating moving in the same direction. During the adaptation period, the firing rate of simple cells fell from around 60 to 20 spikes/second. The firing rate was also clearly reduced in response to the low-contrast test stimulus. The time course for complete recovery from adaptation depended on cell type. Simple cells recovered normally within 30 seconds to 2 minutes, whereas complex cells either recovered very fast (within about 10 seconds) or did not show any appreciable adaptation effect. Furthermore, the adaptation effect on simple cells was highly selective for orientation and spatial frequency: Maffei et al. (1973) noted that when the orientation and spatial frequency of the adapting grating fell outside the cell's tuning curve, a reduction in discharge rate during adaptation did not occur. In agreement with psychophysical findings, they also reported interocular transfer, which was taken as indicating the cortical origin of the adaptation effect. A reduction in discharge rate after adaptation was found both when the right eye was adapted and the left eye tested, and vice versa (figure 6.3).

6.2.3 Enhanced Neural Activity Following Motion Adaptation?

Von der Heydt, Hänny, et al. (1978) also measured the activity of simple and complex direction-selective cells within the cat's visual cortex. They examined the effect of moving the adapting grating in the preferred as well as in the nonpreferred direction (for 1 minute) on subsequent response to a test grating that was switched on and off at 0.5-second intervals. For simple cells, response during adaptation in the null direction firing rate remained unchanged from that generated by a stationary stimulus, but responses in the test phase were slightly enhanced. Adaptation to a stimulus moving in the preferred direction was characterized by a vigorous initial response, which declined rapidly. Responses to the test pattern were depressed for nearly 20 seconds, and recovered gradually (figure 6.4). It is notable that changes in spontaneous activity following adaptation were not found using blank fields. Spigel (1962a) reported reduced MAE strength in the absence of contours during the test phase. The findings of von der Heydt et al. also support an imbalance model of MAEs but, in striking contrast to Barlow and Hill (1963), they suggested that this imbalance is not due to a reduction in spontaneous activity such as occurs in rabbit gangion cells. The authors described the adaptation effect "as a modulation, or gain setting, of the evoked response, rather than subtraction or addition of activity" (p. 253). It is important to note that von der Heydt et al. (1978) found reduced responses after preferred-direction adaptation, and enhanced responses after null-direction adaptation, only for simple cells and not for complex cells (see figure 6.4). These data are consistent with the Maffei et al. (1973) finding that motion adaptation differentially affects the responses of simple and complex cells.

6.2.4 The Time Course of Motion Adaptation

The findings of Vautin and Berkley (1977) are consistent with those of von der Heydt et al. (1978) and Maffei et al. (1973). During continuous motion of a grating or slit in one direction, they found that the firing rate of motion-sensitive neurons in the cat's striate cortex gradually declined to asymptote. But in contrast to Maffei et al. (1973), no differences in the time course of decay between simple and complex cells were found. Time constants ranging from 1.92 seconds to 12.45 seconds were found depending on stimulus type. Time constants were higher for adaptation to gratings (4.92 to 12.45 seconds) than for adaptation to spatially discrete

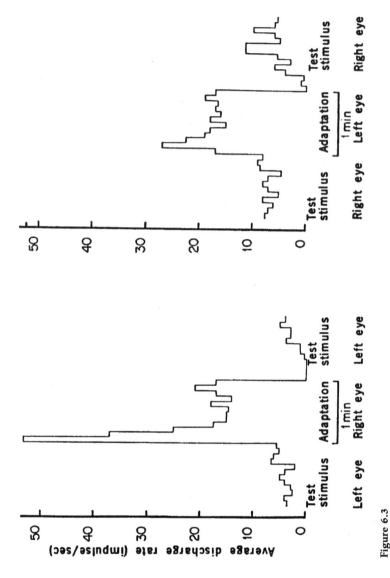

Figure 6.3
Neuronal correlate of interocular transfer of adaptation in a simple cell in the cat striate cortex. In both conditions, one eye was exposed to a drifting high-contrast grating. After adaptation, a low-contast grating was exposed to the other eye. Reduction in discharge rate during adaptation, as well as a slow recovery post adaptation, was found in both conditions. (From Maffei et al. 1973.)

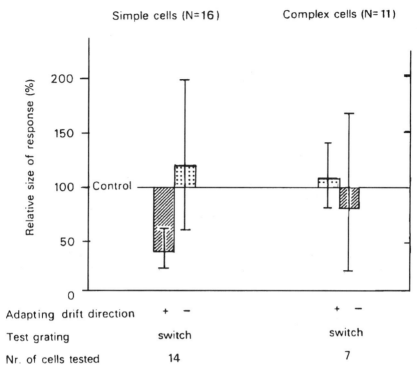

Figure 6.4
Postadaptation changes in firing rate in simple and complex cells in response to a stationary test pattern. Change in mean firing rate is related to a baseline value. Reduced response after preferred direction drift, and a slight enhancement after nonpreferred direction drift, can be observed in simple but not in complex cells. (Adapted from von der Heydt et al., 1978).

stimuli, for example, slits (1.92 to 8.55 seconds). Vautin and Berkley noted that the rate of decline in response during adaptation parallels the time course of adaptation to phase-reversed grating stimuli measured psychophysically (Blakemore and Campbell, 1969; figure 6.5). Following adaptation, they reported a brief silent period in adapted neurons, which recovered completely within 5 to 35 seconds. Prolonged stimulation in the nonpreferred direction also resulted in a moderate reduction in subsequent spontaneous activity, but this effect could not be observed consistently for different neurons. Vautin and Berkley (1977) attribute these changes to a nonspecific fatigue effect.

6.2.5 Hammond and Colleagues' Cat Studies
Hammond and co-workers have examined correlates of the MAE in simple and complex cortical cells in the cat (Hammond and Mouat, 1988;

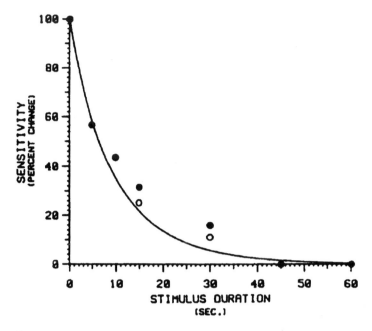

Figure 6.5
Decline in response during motion adaptation in the visual cortex of the cat. The curve reflects the mean percentage decrement in firing for five simple cells during adaptation in the preferred direction with a grating pattern. An exponential fit to these data has a time constant of 9.5 seconds. For comparision, psychophysical data are also shown from Blakemore and Campbell (1969) on the time course of adaptation to a phase-reversed grating (closed circles: high contrast; open circles: low contrast), and exhibit a similar time course. (From Vautin and Berkley, 1977.)

Hammond, Mouat, et al., 1985, 1986, 1988; Hammond et al., 1989). Their studies concentrated on the effects of pattern type (gratings vs. textured fields), interocular transfer, and orientation specificity. Their basic findings concerning the effect of adaptation are contained in Hammond et al. (1988). During adaptation a square-wave grating or textured field drifted continuously (1 minute), either in the preferred or in the nonpreferred direction of a given cell. Subsequent testing of the time course of recovery was done by sweeping the adapting stimulus alternately in each direction for 1 second. Activity was compared with the cell's response to a uniform field of the same mean luminance following adaptation. During adaptation the firing rate declined exponentially within 30 seconds. Adaptation was manifested primarily as a transient depression of response to motion in the preferred direction immediately following the adaptation period. For bidirectional neurons, adaptation to one direction did not alter responsiveness to test stimuli moving in the opposite direction. For complex cells, only a tendency for enhanced firing following adaptation in the null direction was observed. A clear enhancement in neuronal discharge following adaptation in the opposite direction was not found for complex cells.

The time course of neuronal recovery after adaptation—normally within 30 to 60 seconds—clearly depends on stimulus characteristics such as drift velocity and spatial frequency. For example, both Ohzawa, Sclar, et al. (1985) and Hammond et al. (1985) found stronger adaptation for high- than for low-contrast gratings. Surprisingly, after motion adaptation, the spontaneous activity of the cells did not change when either a blank field or the stationary adapting pattern was presented, although these conditions correspond to those eliciting MAEs in psychophysical studies (Hammond et al., 1988). Marginal effects can only be found for special complex cells, responding to short contours. Differences between the cell types were restricted to the onset and subsequent time course of recovery, which was more rapid in simple than in complex cells.

In two papers, Hammond and co-workers described the effect of adaptation to contourless, that is, textured, stimuli (Hammond et al., 1986, 1988). Qualitatively, adaptation to gratings and textured patterns had comparable effects, in that the firing rate decreased gradually during adaptation and response was temporally reduced during the following test phase. The strength of this "neuronal MAE" depended on drift velocity and motion direction for both patterns, but, consistent with the results of psychophysical studies (A. T. Smith and Hammond ,1985), quantitative differences were found. Adaptation effects from textured patterns were invariably weak in strength compared with those evoked by gratings.

Neuronal correlates of interocular transfer (IOT), first described by Maffei et al. (1973), were also observed by Hammond and Mouat (1988). In a monocular viewing condition, strongly binocular neurons were adapted to square-wave gratings or randomly textured fields drifting either in the preferred or in the nonpreferred direction. In the IOT condition, the dominant eye was adapted by continuous motion, whereas the nondominant eye viewed the stationary pattern during the test phase. The nonadapted or nontested eye viewed a uniform background pattern throughout. A positive IOT effect was found for all binocularly driven simple and complex neurons. This adaptation effect was comparable in its direction specificity and time course to that for monocular adaptation of the dominant or nondominant eye alone, although its strength was always much weaker. This finding contrasts with that of Maffei, Beradi, et al. (1986), who examined IOT in split-chiasm cats and found a small number of simple cells in area 17 that responded only to input from the ipsilateral eye, but which nonetheless showed IOT.

In a more recent study, Hammond et al. (1989) examined the interaction of motion direction and orientation on adaptation to moving gratings in the cat. Neurons were adapted with gratings drifting in a nonoptimal direction followed by a test pattern of optimal orientation and vice versa. Depression of the firing rate of simple, standard complex and intermediate complex neurons was greatest when adaptation and test orientation were matched and optimal, and progressively decreased as the relative difference in orientation between adaptation and test stimuli increased. Taken together, the findings of Hammond and his co-workers (1988, 1989) make clear some important properties of neurons in area 17 involved in neural MAEs. The direction and orientation specificity of adaptation of these neurons, as well as IOT effects, cannot easily be explained by the properties of precortical neurons.

6.2.6 Functional Differences Between Simple and Complex Cells

Marlin, Hasan, et al. (1988) examined the selectivity of adaptation in the cat striate cortex to unidirectional motion of a high-contrast grating, drifting either in the preferred or in the nonpreferred direction. Immediately following adaptation, the stimulus was swept through the receptive field once in each direction. Nearly all neurons displayed strong adaptation effects. A decreased response was evident as early as 3 seconds into the adaptation period, with most units reaching an asymptotic level at about 40 seconds. Most of the simple cells, but relatively few complex cells, showed significant direction-specific adaptation effects, expressed as a proportionally larger decrease in preferred direction response compared with nonpreferred direction response. It was found that adaptation to the nonpreferred direction, which typically did not result in vigorous changes in response during adaptation, did produce changes in response and in direction specificity after adaptation. The authors suggest "that the adaptation may not be simply proportional to the amount of activity in the neuron under study, but may result from the adaptation of pools of afferent neurons" (p 1326). The authors also observed modified spontaneous activity both to blank fields and to a stationary grating after adaptation. Adaptation in the preferred direction decreased spontaneous activity, whereas adaptation in the nonpreferred direction resulted in a slight increase in spontaneous activity. Because of the generally low spontaneous activity of neurons in V1, the changes in spontaneous activity were small in relation to changes in response to moving test stimuli. Perhaps the most striking finding here is that simple and complex cells differ in the selectivity of adaptation. In contrast to simple cells, a large proportion of complex cells actually increased their direction specificity because of relatively large decreases in their nonpreferred direction responses. According to Marlin et al. (1988), differences between these neuron types could be due to a different organization of the inputs to simple and complex cells. While interaction between neurons is primarily inhibitory in simple cells, in complex cells a combination of inhibitory and excitatory interactions exists (figure 6.6)

6.2.7 Separation of "Figural" and "Kinetic" Phases in Motion Aftereffects

In a more recent study, Giaschi, Douglas, et al. (1993) noted that the only consistent finding of the last two decades of research is that prolonged motion stimulation decreases the reponsiveness of cortical neurons. The issues of direction specificity and of differences in the properties of simple and complex neurons are still controversial. These authors suggested that inconsistencies in findings could be explained by several factors, including (1) methodological differences in the measurement and comparison of spontaneous activity and driven activity; (2) the failure to record the responsive of neurons to the nonstimulated direction during adaptation; (3) differences in the type of pattern used during adaptation and test phases; and (4) selection artifacts, since the response characteristics in some types of neurons showed large variability.

Giaschi et al. (1993) went on to examine the time course of changes in the response of simple and complex cells in the cat during adaptation and recovery, using a sophisticated design intended to counter the failings of previous designs. After a 2-second baseline measure of the neuron's response to preferred and nonpreferred directions, the neuron was adapted to a high-contrast drifting grating for 120 seconds. Every 8 seconds during this phase, brief recordings were made of the neuron's response to the nonadapted direction. During the recovery period that followed, the grating was again presented once every 8 seconds over a period of 120 seconds, moving either in the adapted or nonadapted direction. During adaptation in the preferred direction a large number of neurons showed reduced responses to both the adapted and the nonadapted directions (figure 6.7). During adaptation to the nonpreferred direction, these effects were less pronounced. In most neurons a reduced response was observed, while in others it was facilitated. Particularly interesting was the finding that two different processes—at least in simple cells— could be differentiated: the time course of adaptation could be described by an initial fast exponential decay with a time constant of about 8 seconds, followed by a slow exponential decay with a time constant of about 88 seconds. This observation held for the recovery phase as well. The authors suggest that the different time constants may reflect the distinction between "kinetic" and "figural" phases of the MAE (Bonnet and Pouthas, 1972), with the former restricted to the activity of the movement-analyzing system and the latter to the figural system.

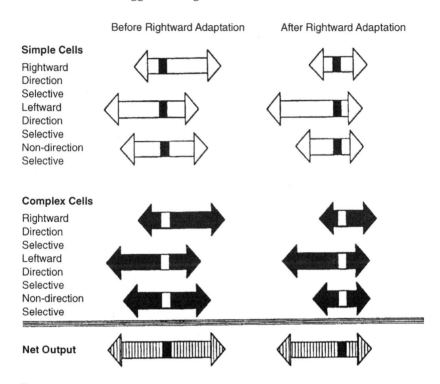

Figure 6.6
Neural imbalance following rightward motion adaptation, based on the findings of Marlin et al. (1988). Baseline response of simple and complex cells with different direction preferences is shown at the left of the figure, while changes in response after rightward adaptation are shown at the right. Response to rightward motion decreases in all simple cells independently of their direction selectivity. The same decrease can be observed in complex cells, with the exception of those preferring leftward motion. Furthermore, spontaneous activity is decreased in all cells preferring rightward motion. Response to leftward motion is increased in simple cells preferring leftward motion. For both simple and complex non–direction–selective cells, overall response declined, with a selective loss of rightward response among simple cells. The net output of motion-detecting neurons produces a motion aftereffect (MAE) opposite in direction to that of the adapting stimulus. (Adapted from Marlin et al., 1988.)

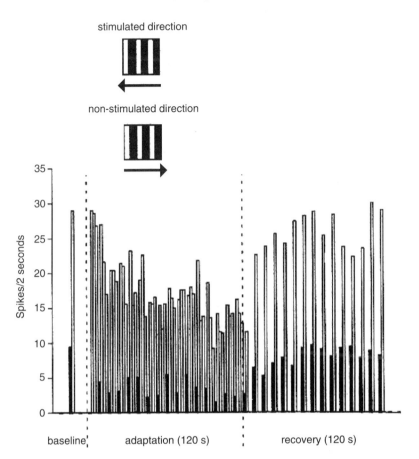

Figure 6.7
Typical response to stimulated (open bars) and nonstimulated directions (black bars) in a single simple cell in the cat striate cortex during and after adaptation in the preferred direction. During adaptation, the cell showed reduced firing rate in the stimulated direction as well as in the nonstimulated direction. In such cells, the reduction in firing rate for the stimulated direction is greater than that for the nonstimulated direction, which indicates direction selectivity of motion adaptation in these cells. (Adapted from Giaschi et al., 1993).

6.2.8 Effects of Motion Adaptation in Area MT

All studies described to this point restricted themselves to the activity of neurons in the cat primary visual cortex. Since it has been shown by Newsome et al. (1989a,b) and by others (e.g., DeYoe and van Essen, 1988; Albright, 1984) that direction selectivity is greater in areas of the extrastriate cortex such as MT and MST, it makes sense to seek electrophysiologic correlates of MAEs in these areas. It seems more likely that a relationship between neural activity and conscious motion perception can be found in the motion-sensitive neurons of area MT rather than in those of V1 (Newsome and Paré, 1988).

To the best of our knowledge, only Petersen et al. (1985) have systematically examined the responsiveness of direction-specific extrastriate neurons during motion adaptation. Cells in area MT of the owl monkey were adapted for 20 seconds to large-field random visual noise which either moved in the preferred direction, moved in the null (i.e., opposite) direction, or was stationary. Following a 5-second delay after adaptation, a bar was swept through the receptive field in the preferred or in the null direction. The authors' central finding was that adaptation to in the preferred direction suppressed responses to motion in the preferred direction, while adaptation to the null direction enhanced responses to motion in the preferred direction (figure 6.8). Petersen et al. explained the enhancement of MT cell response following adaptation to the nonpreferred direction in terms of the habituation of an inhibitory input tuned to the direction opposite to the preferred direction. These findings are comparable with psychophysical models in which direction-specific channels tuned to opposing motion directions are postulated (e.g., Moulden and Mather, 1978; Mather, 1980). Locating the site of adaptation effects at the level of MT did not seem plausible to Petersen et al., since the adaptation stimuli (random-dot kinematograms) rarely elicited high initial firing rates in MT cells.

The conclusion of Petersen et al. was seriously questioned by Wenderoth et al.(1988), who pointed out that vigorous responses by MT cells to drifting dot fields have been reported by Newsome et al. (1989). Further, Wenderoth et al. (1988) noted that the use by Petersen et al. (1985) of different stimuli for the adaptation (random-dot kinematogram) and test (a single bar) phases is not optimal for the production of MAEs. Also less than optimal was their use of large-field random dot patterns, which elicit low firing rates before adaptation. This lack of excitability is possibly due to the fact that many MT cells have inhibitory surrounds. Consequently, enhanced responsiveness following adaptation in the nonpreferred direction may also be explained by adaptation of the inhibitory surrounds.

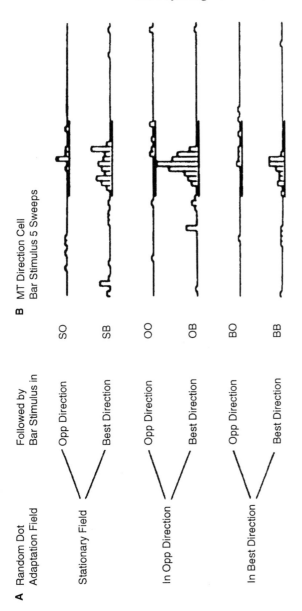

Figure 6.8
Adaptation effects in area MT of the owl monkey. A, Neurons were adapted to stationary or moving noise either in the preferred or opposite direction. B, Postadaptation responses were evoked by a bar stimulus either moving in the preferred or opposite direction. Compared to the neuronal discharge following stationary adaptation, response to movement in the preferred direction is clearly reduced when preceded by adaptation in the same direction, but enhanced when preceded by adaptation in the opposite direction. The first letter of the code refers to the direction of motion during adaptation (S, stationary field; O, adaptation in the neuron's null or opposite direction; B, adaptation in the neuron's preferred direction), while the second letter indicates motion direction during the test phase. (Adapted from Petersen et al., 1985.)

Further single-unit recordings in extrastriate cortex are necessary in order to examine the effects of adaptation on these neurons. Available fMRI studies in humans (see next section) do indicate that strong MAE effects might be localized in area MT.

6.2.9 *Summary of Single-Cell Findings*

In summary, the results of single-unit recordings in cat and monkey visual cortex cannot, as yet, be readily unified to provide a consistent account of MAEs. For one thing, the neuronal mechanisms leading to an imbalance in the activity of direction-specific units are still controversial. An important consideration here is that in most studies the imbalance is restricted to the driven activity of neurons after adaptation, that is, moving test stimuli. This is entirely different from the traditional psychophysical paradigms used for the elicitation of MAEs, where the presentation of a stationary target follows a period of adaptation. Furthermore, single-unit studies have not been able to clearly define the neural site or sites involved in MAEs. Direction specificity would be a requirement for potential sites, but the degree of direction specificity varies considerably between motion-sensitive areas in the visual cortex (DeYoe and van Essen, 1988). Further studies are required to answer the question of whether the higher directional sensitivity of neurons in the extrastriate cortex (MT, MST) is also associated with a greater imbalance in discharge rate following adaptation. In the event that this is found to be true, neurons with such properties would be good candidates for a physiologic substrate of MAEs. Support for a cortical origin of the MAE is provided by studies demonstrating "neuronal" IOT effects (e.g., Maffei et al., 1973; Hammond and Mouat, 1988).

In the light of the above considerations, only partial answers to the three basic questions raised at the beginning of this section can be given:

1. What actually happens to the discharge rates of motion-adapted neurons? The only consistent finding appears to be that prolonged motion stimulation in one direction gradually decreases the responsiveness of neurons. The time constants of this decrease, estimated between 5 and 13 seconds, may differ between simple and complex cells (Giaschi et al., 1993). Moreover, the direction selectivity of this adaptation process seems to be restricted, since responsiveness in the nonstimulated direction can be reduced as well (Giaschi et al., 1993).

2. How does preceding adaptation affect the postadaptation driven activity of neurons sensitive to the same and to the opposite direction? The reduction in driven activity after adaptation appears to differ for different neuron types: Some findings indicate that complex cells do not adapt or

recover very rapidly (Maffei et al., 1973; von der Heydt et al., 1978). However, these results could not be replicated by Vautin and Berkley (1977). Also still controversial are the effects of adaptation in the preferred and nonpreferred directions, as well as the direction specificity of adaptation effects. The findings of Giaschi et al. (1993) questioned the direction specificity of cells in the striate cortex. They found that adaptation in the preferred direction reduced the responsiveness of neurons for both the preferred and the nonpreferred direction. Not only are more single-unit studies required here, analogous psychophysical studies involving moving rather than stationary test stimuli are also required.

3. How does preceding adaptation affect spontaneous activity? This is probably the most important question with regard to the perception of MAEs. In most reported studies, the effects of adaptation on spontaneous activity were negligible in comparision to the effects evoked by driven activity (Hammond et al., 1988; Marlin et al., 1988). A slight reduction in driven activity was observed by Vautin and Berkley (1977). Furthermore, using a stationary on/off pattern as a test stimulus, von der Heydt et al. (1977) were able to find a clear reduction in neuronal activity following adaptation in the preferred direction, as well as an enhancement in activity following null-direction adaptation. This kind of neural response pattern would seem to parallel the perceptual phenomenon most closely. It should be noted that most neurons in V1 have very low spontaneous activity levels, which complicates statistical comparisons between baseline and postadaptation activity.

6.3 Human Electrophysiologic studies: Visual Evoked Potentials (VEPs)

In contrast to single-unit recordings in animals, there are only a small number of MAE studies with human subjects that take advantage of the noninvasive technique of recording VEPs to motion stimuli. By averaging electroencephalographic (EEG) epochs time-locked to the onset or offset of motion stimuli, characteristics of the averaged potentials can be related to psychophysical measures (see Regan, 1989, for an extensive review of this method and experimental findings). The transient negative and positive potentials occurring within the first 200 ms after stimulus onset, obtained at occipital electrode sites, have been related to visual information processing within different areas of the visual cortex (Maier, Dagnelie, et al., 1987; Ossenblok and Spekreijse, 1991). The analysis of sustained cortical activity after stimulation, which requires dc recordings, has been applied rarely in visual studies (Patzwahl, Zanker, et al., 1994), although prolonged motion stimulation as well as its aftereffects could be reflected in slow waves. In most studies, transient components within the VEP have been related to cortical processing of motion onset.

6.3.1 N2: The Motion-Specific Response of the Visual Cortex

The question of which component of the VEP reflects activation in motion-sensitive areas has been controversial. Spekreijse, Dagnelie, et al. (1985) considered that a single positive peak occurring at about 120 ms (P_1) is correlated with the processing of motion onset, whereas a negative peak at about 200 ms (N2) was favored by Göpfert, Müller, et al. (1983), Kuba and Kubova (1992), and Wist et al. (1994). Recent studies (Bach and Ullrich, 1994; Kubova, Kuba, et al., 1995) have shown that differences in these findings can be explained primarily by differences in the relation of motion to stationary phases in the stimulus displays employed. Motion onset can be primarily related to the N2 complex, whereas the positive peak seems to be related to pattern rather than motion offset. The dependency of P1 on luminance contrast, in comparison to the contrast independence of N2, supports this interpretation. A comparison of pattern reversal and motion onset VEPs from a study by Kubova et al. (1995) is shown in figure 6.9.

6.3.2 N2 Amplitude Reflects Motion Adaptation

If N2 is the prominent motion-sensitive component within the VEP, its characteristics should be affected by motion adaptation. To our knowledge, the first study on this question was reported by Göpfert et al. (1983). They adapted subjects to a horizontally moving grating for 10 seconds. After a short stationary phase, the N2 amplitude evoked by a renewed motion onset was clearly reduced compared to the N2 amplitude evoked in the control condition (no adaptation). Results were interpreted in terms of the Barlow model. The reduction in N2 amplitude after motion adaptation was attributed to reduced sensitivity in motion-sensitive neurons.

In a more recent study, Bach and Ullrich (1994) also analyzed the sensitivity of N2 to motion adaptation. Subjects adapted to a moving grating pattern for 20 seconds, after which evoked potentials to motion onset were recorded in cycles consisting of three successive trials followed by 9 seconds of readaptation. Compared to baseline, N2 amplitude clearly fell after adaptation, whereas the preceding P1 complex clearly increased in amplitude. Although the latter effect could not be easily explained in terms of the Barlow and Hill (1963) model, the N2 effect seemed to be consistent with the imbalance theory. The authors also explained the reduction of N2 amplitude with increasing adaptation time in terms of a linear decay over time. The prediction of a model based on a push-pull

Pattern - reversal

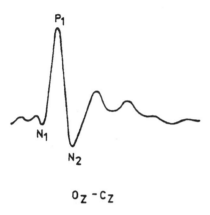

$$O_Z - C_Z$$

Motion - onset

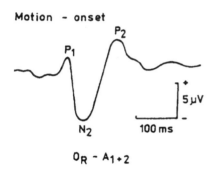

$$O_R - A_{1+2}$$

Figure 6.9
Example of a typical pattern-reversal and motion-onset visual evoked potential. Pattern reversal is associated with a prominent positive potential (P_1) at the medial occipital electrode position (O_z) occurring at about 100 ms, which depends on stimulus contrast. Motion onset generates a prominent negative potential (N_2) at about 200 ms, which is more pronounced at lateral occipital positions. (Adapted from Kubova et al., 1995.)

arrangment of motion detectors would be that a test stimulus moving in the direction opposite to the adaptation stimuli will evoke an enhanced N2 amplitude.

6.3.3 N2 Amplitude Reduction Lacks Direction Specificity
If N2 is the motion-specific component, direction-specific adaptation should be found. Bach, Hoffmann, et al. (1996) showed that this prediction does not hold. After adaptation to a moving grating, N2 amplitude to motion onset of the test pattern drifting in the adapted direction was reduced by nearly 40 percent. Surprisingly, the reduction of N2 amplitude

is nearly as great if the test pattern is moved in the opposite, nonadapted direction (figure 6.10). However, direction-specific adaptation effects can be found using random-dot kinematograms (RDKs) with motion characteristics as defined by Newsome and Paré (1988). Adaptation to 50 percent coherent motion direction (i.e., 50 percent of the pixels moving in random directions, while the remaining 50 percent move in the same direction) led to a 50 percent reduction in N2 amplitude, when the identical test pattern was moved in the adapted direction. When this test pattern was moved in the direction opposite to that of adaptation, the reduction in N2 amplitude was negligible. Consequently, it appears that direction-specific adaptation can only be tested with pure motion stimuli such as RDKs, which contain no orientation information. Taken together, the findings of Bach et al. (1996) and Newsome and Paré (1988) are consistent with those of Hammond et al. (1988), who showed that the VEP can reflect adaptation to motion direction as well as local pattern characteristics (e.g., orientation).

Wist et al. (1994) also found that the reduction in N2 amplitude after adaptation was independent of the motion direction of the test stimulus. Subjects were adapted for 1.4, 5.6, or 17.5 seconds to a form-from-motion checkerboard pattern in which the individual checks consisted of alternating stationary or horizontally moving random dot patterns. During a short (1 second) stationary phase following adaptation, the presence or absence of MAEs was recorded (figure 6.11). Reported MAEs decreased as expected with increasing adaptation duration. During test trials, motion-onset potentials were recorded to the adapting stimulus moving briefly in the same or opposite direction. N2 amplitudes were reduced for both test directions, relative to a nonadapted control condition. The maximum N2 amplitude reduction occurred after only 5.6 seconds of adaptation. The relative lack of direction specificity is consistent with the hypothesis that the N2 amplitude following motion onset is influenced by nonmotion variables such as orientation.

6.3.4 N2 Amplitude and the Time Course of Motion Adaptation
Dorn, Hoffmann, et al. (1997) suggested that the time course of motion adaptation as well as of recovery should be reflected in the N2 component. They manipulated adaptation "depth" by varying the duty cycle (time moving/time total) of a moving random-dot pattern. N2 amplitude decreased with increasing adaptation depth with a time constant of approximately 2.5 seconds. It is noteworthy that N2 amplitude diminished exponentially within an adaptation period of almost 20 seconds, but did not fall to zero. This is in contrast to the results of animal studies in which a "silent period" in firing rate occurs after adaptation. Thus N2 amplitude cannot be regarded as a direct analogue of diminished firing

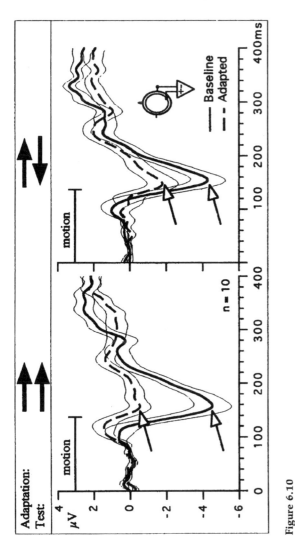

Figure 6.10
Effect of motion adaptation on N2 amplitude. Relative to a baseline measure, the negative visual evoked potential (VEP) amplitude related to motion onset is clearly reduced following prolonged motion stimulation. Since reduced amplitudes can be found for both test and adapting stimuli moving in the same and opposite directions, direction specificity of the VEP correlate of adaptation is not clear. (Adapted from Hoffmann, Bach, et al. 1996.)

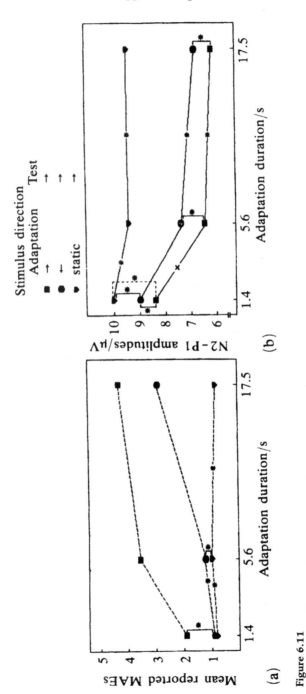

Figure 6.11

(a) Mean reported motion aftereffects (MAEs) as a function of adaptation duration and adaptation stimulus. The direction of MAEs was always opposite to previous adaptation. (b) Mean N2-P1 amplitudes obtained simultaneously for the conditions shown in (a). Statistically nonsignificant differences are marked with an asterisk. (Adapted from Wist et al., 1994.)

rate in single neurons in animal studies. During the recovery period N2 amplitude increased exponentially with a time constant of 10.2 seconds. Both of these time characteristics fit in well with those found in single-cell recordings (Giaschi et al., 1993). In contrast, the relationship between N2 amplitude reduction and adaptation depth found by Dorn et al. (1997) is quantitatively not comparable to that found by Wist et al. (1994). Their result would predict a lower time constant. Differences between the results of these studies probably reflect differences in the stimuli employed.

6.3.5 Motion-Onset and Motion-Offset N2 Potentials and Motion Aftereffects

Although the motion onset–related VEPs summarized to this point are relevant to the question of what happens during motion adaptation, they can provide only indirect evidence for the neural activity underlying the MAE. Since the MAE occurs after adaptation has ended, the brain activity during this static offset phase might be directly linked to the perception of MAEs. The recording of VEPs in this phase has been largely neglected. The robust and reliable motion N2 component is clearly related to motion onset , but has rarely been related to motion offset. Since motion offset following effective adaptation is associated with the illusory motion onset of the pattern in the opposite direction, "motion onset"–like potentials may occur in the offset phase. In order to examine motion offset–related brain activity, Niedeggen, Müller, et al. (1992) adapted their subjects to a spiral pattern. The pattern rotated either clockwise, ("expanding") or counterclockwise ("contracting"). Following a 5-second adaptation period resulting in a clear MAE, a clearly defined negative potential was recorded (N2-off response), occurring at about 170 ms. Its amplitude was up to 70 percent greater after 5.0 seconds of adaptation than after 2.5 seconds (figure 6.12). An N2-on response was also recorded with characteristics comparable to those found by Göpfert et al. (1983) and by Bach and Ullrich (1994). With an adaptation period of 5.0 seconds its amplitude was reduced by up to 40 percent compared to the 2.5-second adaptation condition. Furthermore, a slow negative shift was observed after 5.0 seconds of adaptation, during the period in which the subjects reported seeing the MAE most clearly.

    Motion onset–like N2-off potentials following the offset of a prolonged motion stimulus were also found for "decomposed" patterns: a windmill pattern and one consisting of concentric rings in radial motion. A comparable N2-off response was not found using a pattern consisting of a random-dot checkerboard pattern (as in Wist et al., 1994) in which motion was either leftward or rightward. The N2-off response appears to be identifiable only in spiral-like patterns, not in random-dot checkerboard patterns, whereas the N2-on response can be observed in both types of

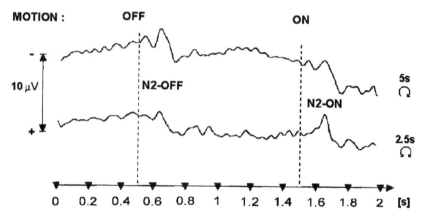

Figure 6.12
Grand-average potentials related to motion offset and onset. The upper trace represents the
course visual evoked potential for motion adaptation with a spiral pattern for 5.0 seconds.
The lower trace was recorded after adaptation with the same pattern when motion direction
reversed every 2.5 seconds. The negative potentials (upward deflections) elicited by motion
offset are nearly twice as great in amplitude in the former than in the latter condition. At
motion onset (right side of figure) this effect was reversed. (Adapted from Niedeggen et al.,
1992.)

pattern. If we can assume that the N2 response is associated with the activation of motion-sensitive neurons located in extrastriate cortex (Probst,
Plendl, et al., 1993), then the offset effect can be related to an increase in
activity of the nonadapted direction-specific neurons. This interpretation
parallels that of Petersen et al. (1985) for area MT in the owl monkey
cited earlier.

In an unpublished experiment, Niedeggen and Wist (1995) were able
to relate the gradual decrease of the MAE strength after adaptation to
the VEP on-and-off responses using the spiral pattern described above
(Niedeggen et al., 1992). After a motion adaptation period of 5 seconds
(clockwise rotation and contraction), five short static test phases (duration:
1 second) were introduced, separated by five short dynamic phases (duration: 0.7 second; direction: same as adaptation phase). The subjects had to
decide whether an MAE occurred in the static test phase. The probability
of an MAE decreased over the successive test phases, as can be seen
in figure 6.13. The simultaneously recorded N2-off response parallels this
finding: its amplitude decreased progressively while the N2-on response
increased gradually, reflecting recovery from adaptation.

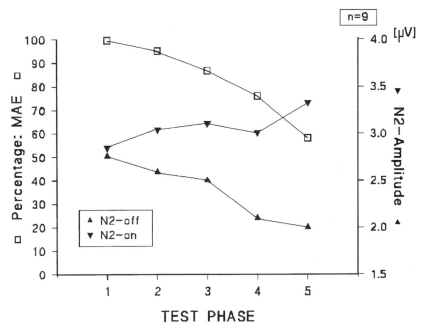

Figure 6.13
Comparison between the psychophysically measured motion aftereffect (MAE) and N2 amplitude following motion adaptation (10 seconds, spiral pattern). During testing, the spiral pattern was presented stationary for 1 second, followed by a 1-second movement in the adapted direction. This cycle was repeated five times. The probability of reporting an MAE in the stationary phase decreased monotonically from 100 percent to 58 percent over the five test phases. The amplitude of the simultaneously recorded N2-off responses also decreased. In contrast, the amplitude of the N2, elicited by motion onset, increased slightly over the test series. (Adapted from Niedeggen and Wist, 1995.)

Our hypothesis concerning the increase in N2-off response amplitude during the stationary period associated with the clear perception of an MAE is that it is probably related to an enhancement in activation of the nonadapted neurons. To our knowledge, none of the single-cell recordings of cortical neurons in V1 have found a comparable increase in spontaneous activity during a stationary postadaptation period. Radial or circular motion direction is primarily processed by highly selective extrastriate neurons, such as MT and MST (Duffy and Wurtz, 1991), whereas coherent, frontoparallel motion is sufficiently processed by motion analyzers in V1. One might speculate that a tonic, reciprocal direction-specific inhibition between neurons is more expressed in extrastriatal compared to striatal cortical sites (Lagae, Gulyas, et al., 1989). Furthermore, the findings of Petersen et al. (1985) indicate the existence of an inhibitory mechanism at the level of area MT.

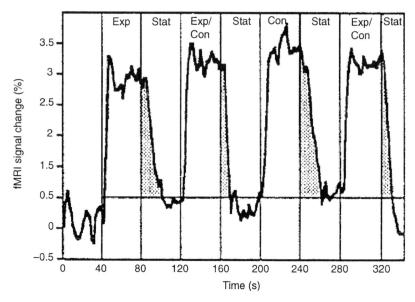

Figure 6.14
Averaged magnetic resonance imaging (MRI) time course recorded during stimulation with expanding, contracting, or stationary concentric rings. Following continuous expansion (Exp: 40 seconds) or contraction (Con: 40 seconds) a clear motion aftereffect occurred in the subsequent stationary epoch, which was associated with prolongation of the MRI signal amplitude (shaded areas). This prolongation of the MRI signal appears to reflect direction-specific adaptation, since direction reversals during motion adaptation (Exp/Con) did not elevate the MRI signal. (Adapted from Tootell et al., 1995.)

6.4 Locating the Motion Aftereffect in the Human Brain Using Functional Magnetic Resonance Imaging

Further evidence for cortical activation enhancement is provided by an fMRI resonance study by Tootell et al. (1995; figure 6.14). The poorer temporal resolution of this technique is compensated for by its higher spatial resolution, which facilitates the identification of activated cortical sites. They found that the amplitude of the MRI signal was increased during adaptation to expanding or contracting rings but not to stationary ones. Furthermore, the falloff in signal strength during tests with stationary concentric rings was much slower when preceded by adaptation to either expanding or contracting patterns as compared to patterns which alternately expanded and contracted. Subjects reported MAEs under the first two conditions, but not under the last one. The strongest enhancement in cortical activation during MAEs was found on the lateral surface at the occipitotemporal parietal junction, where area MT is presumably located. Smaller fMRI MAEs were seen in the areas designated as V2 and V3a. For the cortical region within the calcarine fissure—located as V1—no MAE-specific excitation was found. Further analysis confirmed that the prolonged MRI activation is highly associated with the illusory motion perception: simultaneous recording of MAE strength and fMRI signal strength during the stationary test phase resulted in an excellent fit between the time courses of the psychophysical data and MRI activation (best fit exponents: 8.3 seconds and 9.2 seconds, respectively).

6.5 Summary of the Human Studies

In summary, noninvasive electrophysiologic studies and brain imaging in humans can be as promising as single-cell recordings in exploring the physiologic basis of the MAE. The relationship between MAE strength and physiologic measures in humans can be better delineated by the simultaneous recording of psychophysical and electrophysiologic data. These data can be related to inhibitory and excitatory interactions of motion-sensitive neurons at several levels in the visual cortex. Furthermore, functional brain imaging techniques such as fMRI should prove to be extremely helpful in the localization of those areas involved in MAEs.

On the basis of the human electrophysiologic studies the three questions raised earlier may be tentatively answered as follows:

1. What happens during adaptation? Since Dorn et al. (1997) obtained an exponential N2 amplitude reduction during the course of motion adaptation, one might conclude that responsiveness of the adapted neurons decreased gradually on the assumption that N2 amplitude reflects the pooled responses of the activity of the neurons involved.
2. How does adaptation effect postadaptation potentials to motion in the same and opposite directions? When test and adaptation motion direction corresponded, N2-onset amplitude was reduced in all the studies reviewed (Göpfert et al., 1983; Bach et al., 1996; Wist et al., 1994). The directional specificity of the adaptation effect is still questionable. Both Wist et al. (1994) and Bach et al. (1996) found an N2 amplitude reduction independent of the preceding motion adaptation direction. Direction-specific adaptation has been found using "contourless" stimuli such as random-dot kinematograms (Bach et al., 1996). Thus it would appear that local pattern characteristics such as orientation may influence the directional specificity of N2. Lastly, the time constant of recovery of N2 amplitude (Dorn et al. 1997) is in good agreement with both single-unit (Giaschi et al., 1993) and psychophysical data (Taylor, 1963).
3. How does adaptation affect spontaneous activity? Physiologic correlates of motion offset associated with the perception of an MAE have

been found only using complex motion stimuli (expanding and contracting rings, spirals, windmill patterns), which appear to be processed by highly selective motion-sensitive neurons in extrastriate cortex. After prolonged adaptation, a static test stimulus evokes a potential comparable in amplitude to that evoked by motion onset. The amplitude of this motion-off potential has been found to be associated with the strength of the psychophysically measured MAE. During the postadaptation phase both MAE strength and N2 amplitude decrease over time. (Niedeggen and Wist, 1995). A similar effect was found using the fMRI technique (Tootell et al., 1995). Here, the locus of activation during MAE was identified as an extratriate area. In contrast to most single-unit recording studies, these studies taken together are consistent with the functional role of tonic, reciprocal, direction-specific inhibition leading to an enhanced activation of nonadapted neurons.

6.6 General Conclusions

Any attempt to integrate the findings reviewed here into a single coherent model of the physiologic mechanism underlying the MAE would seem doomed to failure at this point. Reasons for the inhomogeneity of experimental results in single-unit studies have been explicitly analyzed by Giaschi et al. (1993), who pointed out several methodological pitfalls, including differences in recording methods, data analysis, and pattern selection.

At least some of these pitfalls are a source of variance in human electrophysiologic studies as well. Adaptation and test patterns differ among studies. The importance of pattern selection was pointed out by Bach et al. (1996), who found a tendency for direction specificity after motion adaptation with RDKs, but not with grating patterns. It should also be noted that N2-off responses which correlated with the occurrence and subjective strength of MAEs (Niedeggen and Wist, 1995) could be observed only following adaptation to complex motion patterns (expanding or contracting spirals).

The relevance of pattern selection in determining the nature of the physiologic response is obvious both in animal single-unit studies (Hammond et al., 1988) and in human VEP studies (Bach et al., 1996), and must be related to the functional characteristics of neurons within the visual cortex. It seems that the basic demand of most MAE theories—direction-specific adaptation of channels tuned for opposing directions (Moulden and Mather, 1978)—can be observed primarily in extrastriate cortex. As we have seen, Petersen et al. (1985) found direction specificity in area MT in the owl monkey. Furthermore, direction specificity in VEP studies can be observed only when using "noisy" RDKs containing direction signals

(Bach et al., 1996). Global motion direction in such stimuli is analyzed by extrastriate MT neurons (Newsome et al., 1989a), whereas the primary visual cortex is involved in the analysis of local motion signals (Movshon, Adelson, et al., 1985). The importance of pattern characteristics is also highlighted by the findings of Niedeggen et al. (1992) and Tootell et al. (1995). VEP-off responses and fMRI signals that are clearly related to the perception of MAEs can be evoked using radial or circular moving patterns which are analyzed by extrastriate area MST (Duffy and Wurtz, 1991).

This last point should not be taken to imply that the neural basis of the MAE is restricted to extrastriate cortex. Direction-specific adaptation can be observed in V1 as well, according to Giaschi et al. (1993) and von der Heydt et al. (1978). The latter authors reported increased activity after adaptation to the cell's nonpreferred direction, as well as decreased activity following adaptation in the preferred direction. One might suggest that neurons in V1 are adapted to motion direction as well as to other pattern characteristics, such as orientation. The findings of Hammond et al. (1989) support this hypothesis.

Perhaps the most general conclusion we can draw at this juncture is as follows. MAEs would seem to be related to the reduced responsiveness of V1 neurons tuned to the adapting direction, with nearly no change in the response of nonadapted neurons, and to repulsion effects (i.e., inhibitory interactions) between neurons in extrastriate areas such as MT. The lack of repulsion in V1 is consistent with the original imbalance theory of Barlow and Hill (1963). Direct evidence for repulsion in extrastriate cortex is provided by the findings of Petersen et al. (1985), who found enhanced activity in nonadapted neurons. More indirect evidence comes from the fMRI findings of Tootell et al.(1995) and Niedeggen and Wist (1995). Such findings fit in well with the psychophysically based model of Mather (1980). Thus the strength of repulsion effects would appear to vary with the neural level of processing, with weak effects at the V1 level and strong ones at the MT level. This conclusion is also in line with Barlow's more recent general treatment of aftereffects in which he formulated a general "law of repulsion" (Barlow, 1990).

Chapter 7
Theoretical Models of the Motion Aftereffect

George Mather and John Harris

In a rather short chapter, Holland (1965) reviewed a number of early theoretical explanations of the motion aftereffect (MAE) from the 1800s up to the 1950s, such as eye movement and blood flow theories, but he did not discuss the new theory that emerged in the early 1960s inspired by cortical cell physiology. This theory placed the MAE in a unique position among perceptual phenomena in terms of the directness of the proposed links between cortical cell activity and perception. It is founded on two psychophysical linking hypotheses: (1) that perception of motion is mediated by some form of comparison between the responses of cells in the visual system sensitive to different directions; and (2) that following adaptation to a moving stimulus there is a change in the responsiveness of these cells, so that cells tuned to motion directions congruent with the adapting stimulus show a reduction in response relative to cells tuned to other directions.

In the spirit of Brindley (1970), we should first confirm the plausibility of these hypotheses by correlating properties of neural events with corresponding properties of perceptual phenomena. This is a straightforward task in the case of motion perception and aftereffects. Data from direct cell recordings show that the middle temporal area (MT) in primates is particularly rich in motion-sensitive cells (see chapter 6). Human brain imaging studies show high activity in a corresponding region of cortex—the occipitotemporal parietal junction—in the presence of MAEs (Tootell et al., 1995), and closed head injuries in the same area of cortex lead to impaired motion perception (Vaina et al., 1990). It is also not difficult to find more specific evidence supporting the involvement of cortical cells in the MAE. For example, classic MAEs are confined to the area of retina exposed to the adapting stimulus, a property that can be related to the restricted receptive field of cortical cells; the perceptual phenomenon is also usually short-lived, in agreement with data on changes in neural responsiveness following adaptation; and the degree of interocular transfer of the aftereffect can be related to the binocularity of cortical cells, and may be used to infer the probable sites of adaptation, as discussed below and in chapter 4. There are exceptions to these clear psychophysical links which are theoretically significant (e.g., von Grünau, 1986; Masland, 1969), but on the basis of a large body of evidence, much of it surveyed in this book, we can accept the two hypotheses as a firm basis for constructing theoretical models. The first section begins by discussing the first, and simplest modern theoretical model of MAE, and then discusses a more complex model that is also able to accommodate other phenomena in motion perception. Section 7.2 examines the functional significance of perceptual adaptation in relation to MAEs.

7.1 Models of Direction Coding

The MAE has both a direction and an apparent speed. However, theoretical models have restricted themselves to explaining the directional properties of the effect. Apparent speed has been used predominantly as a measure of MAE magnitude, since it correlates very well with duration (Pantle, 1974). As there have been no attempts to built explicit assumptions about velocity coding into explanatory models of the MAE, this section deals only with models of direction coding.

7.1.1 Opponent Process Coding

Precisely how do the two hypotheses above permit an explanation of the MAE? Sutherland (1961) proposed the first minimally sufficient model of the MAE—the ratio or "opponent-process" model:

> Hubel and Wiesel (1959) have, however, found cells which respond differentially according to the direction in which a stimulus is moved across the retina. If direction of movement is coded in single cells in human beings, adaptation in these cells might clearly underly [sic] the after-effect of movement. Once again the direction in which something is seen to move might depend upon the ratios of firing in cells sensitive to movement in different directions, and after prolonged movement in one direction a stationary image would produce less firing in the cells which had just been stimulated than normally [sic], hence apparent movement in the opposite direction would be seen to occur. (p. 227)

Sutherland's prediction of adaptation effects in single visual cells was first confirmed by Barlow and Hill (1963), who measured responses in rabbit retinal ganglion cells, and later confirmed by a number of workers recording from cat and monkey cortical cells (see chapter 6). Barlow and Hill (1963) themselves concluded that "the after-effects of motion may result from the temporary imbalance of the maintained discharges of cells responsive to opposite directions" (p. 1346).

There is a subtle difference in wording between Sutherland's and Barlow and Hill's proposals, in that the former deals with comparisons between cells tuned to "different" directions, and the latter deals with comparisons between cells tuned to "opposite" directions. The opponent-process account has become the standard explanation of the MAE. Direction-selective cells tuned to opposite directions provide paired inputs to a comparator cell, one excitatory and the other inhibitory. Perceived direction is said to depend on the difference between the outputs of the oppositely tuned detectors, signaled by the comparators. The sign of the difference in detector output is crucial, of course, since this specifies direction sense. For example, assume that detectors tuned to upward motion provide excitation at the comparator, while detectors tuned to downward motion provide inhibition. Net excitation at the comparator then signifies upward motion, and net inhibition signifies downward motion. However, it is not feasible physiologically for a comparator cell to signal both excitation and inhibition (i.e., signed differences) over a wide dynamic range. The solution to this kind of problem, as we know from studies of retinal ganglion cells that signal intensity differences, is to have separate comparator cells supply the positive and negative portions of the difference signal as positive responses. Some comparators supply the positive half of the response (i.e., are excited by upward motion and inhibited by downward motion) and others provide the negative half of the response (i.e., are inhibited by upward motion and excited by downward motion). This scheme is illustrated in figure 7.1.

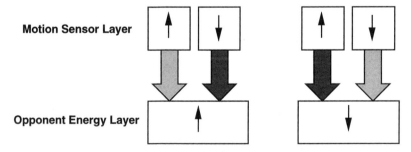

Figure 7.1
Simple opponent-process model of direction coding. Direction-selective motion sensors (upper layer) provide paired inputs to opponent-energy units (lower layer). One input is excitatory (light gray), and the other input is inhibitory (dark gray). On the left, sensors tuned to upward motion provide excitation and sensors tuned to downward motion provide inhibition, so the opponent-energy unit produces a positive response to upward motion. On the right, excitatory and inhibitory inputs are reversed, so that the opponent-energy unit produces a positive response to downward motion.

The model contains two layers of units. Motion sensors in the first layer provide initial measurements of motion energy. Their opposed outputs feed a pair of units in the opponent-energy layer, one of which provides a positive signal to upward motion, while the other provides a positive signal to downward motion. Motion in one direction is perceived when the output of the opponent-energy unit signaling that direction exceeds some internal threshold. The opponent-energy units correspond to those proposed by Adelson and Bergen's (1985), partly on the basis that "adaptation phenomena such as the MAE suggest that motion perception involves the balance between opposing leftward- and rightward-motion signals" (p. 293). Note that responses at the sensor layer of this scheme interact competitively, but responses at the opponent-energy layer do not.

In principle, adaptation could arise at the sensor layer, or at the opponent-energy layer, or at both. What are the predicted effects of adaptation in the two layers? We assume that adaptation in either layer has two consequences for cell activity. First, the resting level of the affected cell is depressed. Second, the amount of stimulation required to reach a particular level of response in the cell is elevated. Figure 7.2 illustrates the pattern of responses in the two layers during an MAE experiment. The upper row of graphs plots the output of units in the sensor layer sensitive to upward and downward motion, and the lower row of graphs plots the output of units in the opponent-energy layer. All responses are shown relative to a resting level of activity (which could also represent the small response to a nondirectional stimulus). As indicated, the response of each unit in the opponent-energy layer is given by the sum of its resting level and the difference between the responses of two sensor units. Responses in this layer that exceed some minimum magnitude, shown by the dashed line at threshold, lead to the perception of motion.

Before adaptation and in the absence of motion (figure 7.2a), the system is in equilibrium, with all units at resting level. During adaptation to upward motion (figure 7.2b), the upward sensor UP_s responds strongly, but the downward sensor $DOWN_s$ remains at resting level. This leads to an above-threshold response from the upward opponent-energy unit UP_o and a suppressed response from the downward opponent-energy unit $DOWNo$. Consider first the result of adaptation that is confined only to the *sensor* layer (figure 7.2c). The resting level of the upward sensor will be depressed, whereas the resting level of the downward sensor will be unaffected. This difference will be reflected in the outputs of the opponent-energy units, with the upward unit showing a depressed response and the downward unit showing an above-threshold response that should lead to perception of an MAE. Now consider the consequences of adaptation that is confined only to the *opponent-energy* layer (figure 7.2d).

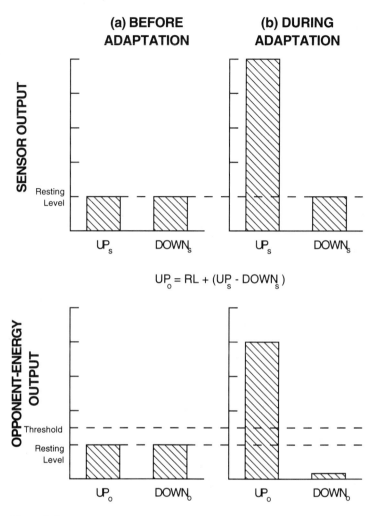

$$UP_o = RL + (UP_s - DOWN_s)$$

Figure 7.2
Explanation of the motion aftereffect (MAE), according to the opponent-process model in figure 7.1. The upper row of graphs shows the output of motion sensors tuned to upward motion (UP_s) and to downward motion ($DOWN_s$) in different stimulus conditions. Sensor output in the absence of motion is shown by the broken line. Each graph in the lower row shows the output of opponent-energy units connected to the sensors depicted in the graph immediately above. Opponent-energy units signaling upward motion (UP_o) receive positive inputs from upward sensors and negative inputs from downward sensors, and vice versa for opponent-energy units signaling downward motion ($DOWN_o$). It is assumed that each opponent-energy unit has a resting level of response, and that motion is seen only when opponent-energy output exceeds a threshold value (broken lines). Different columns show sensor and opponent-energy output (a) before adaptation and in the absence of motion; (b) during adaptation to upward motion; (c) after adaptation and in the absence of motion,

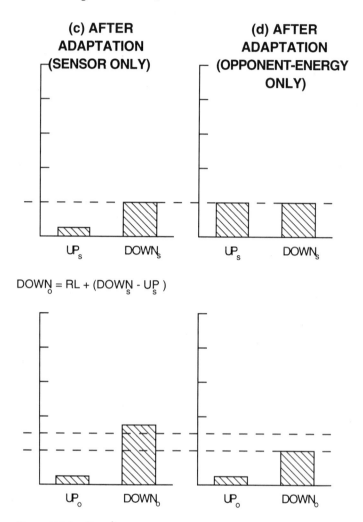

$$DOWN_o = RL + (DOWN_s - UP_s)$$

Figure 7.2 (continued)
assuming that only sensor output is depressed; (d) after adaptation and in the absence of motion, assuming that only opponent-energy output is depressed. The graphs reveal that only sensor adaptation can lead to above-threshold opponent-energy responses in the absence of motion, that is, MAEs. See text for more details.

Following adaptation there will be no imbalance in sensor outputs, but despite this the opponent-energy unit that was active during adaptation will show a suppressed response, whereas the unit that was not active will be unaffected. Neither opponent-energy unit will respond above threshold, so there will be no MAE, but the depressed output in the adapted unit should lead to a loss of sensitivity to the adapted direction, since more stimulation will be required to exceed threshold than before adaptation, perhaps reflected in higher motion detection thresholds. In reality, adaptation may be present in both layers, but the main point is that only adaptation in the sensor layer is associated with an MAE.

The very existence of the MAE points to the presence of adaptation in the sensor layer. Is there any evidence for the presence of adaptation in the opponent-energy layer? Raymond (1993a) measured motion coherence thresholds for motion in the four cardinal directions (up, down, left, right) following adaptation to rightward motion. She found significantly reduced sensitivity to rightward motion, but no significant changes in sensitivity to the other three directions. This result can be explained by the opponent-process model if we assume that the obtained coherence threshold elevation mainly reflected adaptation at the opponent-energy layer in figures 7.1 and 7.2. In a second experiment, Raymond (1993b) found that coherence thresholds for unidirectional motion were raised by approximately 22 percent after bidirectional adaptation, but were raised by 47 percent after unidirectional adaptation. According to the model, unidirectional adaptation should drive units in both layers strongly, whereas bidirectional adaptation should drive only sensors (the opposite sensor signals tend to cancel out at opponent-energy units). The obtained difference between unidirectional and bidirectional adaptation effects may therefore reflect adaptation in opponent-energy units. The effect reported by Raymond and Braddick (1996; see chapter 5, figure 5.6) can also be explained by adaptation at the opponent-energy layer.

7.1.2 Two-Dimensional Models

Despite its success in accounting for some basic properties of the MAE and motion adaptation, the opponent-process model sketched above has serious limitations. First, it cannot accommodate the high-level MAE phenomena already described in chapter 5 (e.g., second-order motion, multivectorial MAEs). Second, it is inherently one-dimensional, since it codes direction only along a single axis, but there are strong grounds, both empirical and theoretical, for believing that human motion perception involves two-dimensional (2-D) analysis (e.g., Adelson and Movshon, 1982). The addition of a third layer to the model permits 2-D interactions between motion signals which can potentially overcome many of these limitations. The model proposed by Wilson et al. (1992)

and Wilson and Kim (1994) contains three layers of units, the first two of which correspond to the sensor and opponent-energy layers sketched in figure 7.1. The third layer contains integrator units which receive both excitatory and inhibitory inputs from opponent-energy units tuned to a wide range of directions, in order to compute global motion direction. Figure 7.3 is a simple illustration of the model. The top row depicts the preferred direction of units in the sensor layer, the middle row depicts units in the opponent-energy layer, and the bottom row depicts units in the integrator layer. Units tuned to directions within ±120 degrees from vertical are shown, with each unit having directional tuning of ±11 degrees.

Thus units in the first two layers correspond to the units depicted in figure 7.1. Each integrator unit in the third layer sums inputs from a range of opponent-energy units signaling directions within a range of ±120 degrees. For illustration, only connections to the integrator tuned to upward motion are shown. Opponent-energy inputs within ±75 degrees are excitatory (light-gray connections), and the remainder are inhibitory (black connections), weighted so that the maximum response in the integrator unit layer will be from a unit tuned to the vector sum direction of the input activity. There are recurrent inhibitory (feedback) connections between integrator units, so that each integrator unit inhibits other units with preferred directions differing by between ±45 degrees and ±120 degrees. The figure illustrates the inhibitory connections feeding back from the upward integrator (black connections). This inhibition generates a form of "winner-take-all" interaction, and the restriction of interactions to ±120 degrees allows for more than one winner to be computed, that is, motion transparency.

Wilson and Kim (1994) proposed that the opponent-energy layer contains both "first-order" and "second-order" units. In first-order stimuli (Cavanagh and Mather, 1989; Chubb and Sperling, 1988) the motion signal is carried by stable differences in intensity (e.g., drifting luminance gratings). In second-order stimuli there are no stable intensity differences correlated with the motion signal. Motion is carried by differences in texture properties (e.g., contrast, spatial scale, temporal modulation).[1] Wilson and Kim tentatively identified the opponent-energy layer of the model with cells in cortical areas V1 and V2, and identified the integrator layer with cells in cortical area MT.

7.1.3 Multiple Sites of Adaptation
Since this model is built from the same sensor and opponent-energy units as those in figure 7.1, it can provide the same explanation for simple MAEs, if we assume that adaptation occurs in the sensor layer (H. R. Wilson, personal communication, 1997). Selective adaptation in this layer

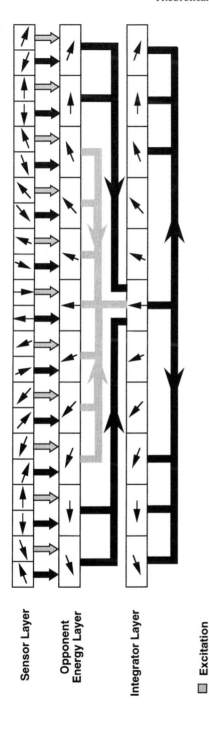

Figure 7.3
Three-layer model of motion processing proposed by Wilson et al. (1992) and Wilson and Kim (1994). The first two layers of the model (sensor and opponent-energy) contain arrays of units that correspond to those described in figure 7.1. Each unit is tuned to a range of directions spanning ±11 degrees. The third layer contains an array of integrator units, each receiving inputs from a range of opponent-energy units spanning directions within ±120 degrees. Opponent-energy inputs within ±75 degrees are excitatory (light-gray connections), and those in the range of 75 to 120 degrees are inhibitory (black connections). In addition, there are recurrent inhibitory connections between integrators, so that each integrator inhibits others tuned to a range of directions spanning ±5 to ±120 degrees. Note that the full array of units in each layer spans all directions around the clockface. For the purposes of illustration the figure only shows those units that provide ascending inputs to the integrator unit tuned to upward motion. This unit also receives recurrent inhibition from other integrators, but these too are not shown.

will be expressed as an imbalance between excitation and inhibition in the opponent-energy layer, leading to an MAE. The presence of integrators in the three-layer model introduces two more potential sources of MAE signals. Recall that in the original opponent-process model selective adaptation in the opponent-energy layer alone could not lead to an MAE. In the three-layer model, selective adaptation in the opponent-energy layer could potentially result in an MAE. For example, upward adaptation would depress the response of the upward opponent-energy unit, but would leave the downward unit unaffected (figure 7.2d). The resulting imbalance between excitation and inhibition arriving from the opponent-energy layer may be sufficient to generate a motion signal at the integrators. Indeed, as far as integrators are concerned, it should not matter whether the imbalance arises from sensor adaptation or from opponent-energy adaptation. MAEs could also arise from adaptation that was confined only to the integrators. In this case the resultant change in the pattern of recurrent inhibition between integrators may be sufficient to generate a motion signal.

Initial results of computational modeling (H. R. Wilson, personal communication) indicate that adaptation of integrator units can certainly explain changes in perceived plaid coherence, and changes in the perceived direction of moving stimuli. There is some psychophysical evidence that integrator adaptation also contributes to MAEs. Verstraten et al. (1994a, p. 356) measured MAEs following adaptation to two transparent motion fields which individually generated MAEs of different duration. They reasoned that if the resulting MAE arose from adaptation of individual responses to each field, then the MAE should change direction as the effect of the weaker adapting component disappeared. No change in direction was reported, so the aftereffect must have been generated at a site after the individual responses had been combined. Van Wezel, Verstraten, et al. (1994b) measured motion discrimination thresholds and MAE durations using a checkerboard pattern in which alternating checkers contained texture drifting in opposite directions. The two measures were differentially affected by checker size, leading the authors to conclude that the adaptation effect occurred at an integration stage which covers a much greater retinal area than that occupied by the receptive fields of individual sensors.

Recall from chapter 5 that consistent differences have been reported between static MAEs and flicker MAEs, leading a number of workers to conclude that they reflect adaptation at different levels of motion analysis (see chapter 5, table 5.1). To take one example, Nishida et al. (1994) measured the relative duration of monocular and interocular MAEs using static and flickering tests. For static tests, interocular MAEs lasted only 30 to 50 percent as long as monocular MAEs, but there was little difference between monocular and interocular conditions for flicker MAEs. Nishida et al. argued that more complete interocular transfer indicates adaptation at higher levels of processing, and on this basis argued that static MAEs reflect adaptation at low-level detectors and flicker MAEs reflect adaptation at high-level integration. They speculatively identified the latter with cells in cortical area MT. A simple application of the authors' interpretation to the three-layer model would identify static MAEs with adaptation at the sensor layer, and flicker MAEs with adaptation at the integrator layer.

The empirical differences between static and flicker MAEs shown in table 5.1 are certainly consistent with this idea. For example, integrator units are likely to have larger receptive fields, show less spatiotemporal specificity, and be more binocular than sensor units. However, this interpretation does beg the following question. Why should static test stimuli favor the contribution of sensor adaptation to the visible MAE, and flickering test stimuli favor the contribution of integrator adaptation? The argument that sensors are sensitive to stationary test patterns and integrators are sensitive only to dynamic patterns (cf. McCarthy, 1993; Nishida and Sato, 1995) is not tenable. Any sensor response that leads to a motion percept must necessarily generate a directional signal in integrators, so anything that sensors "see," integrators must "see" also. It is fair to assume that dynamic test stimuli will drive motion sensors tuned to many directions much more effectively than will static tests. Perhaps differences between the responses of adapted and unadapted units are greatest at relatively low response levels (cf. response normalization in spatial vision), so dynamic tests minimize the contribution of sensor adaptation, and static tests maximize its contribution. There is no clear answer to this question at present, so further research is needed.

We have seen that some MAE phenomena can be attributed to sensor adaptation, and others can be attributed to integrator adaptation. If this is the case, the middle layer of opponent-process units in the model may be superfluous—we could omit the top layer from figure 7.3 and relabel the opponent-energy layer as the sensor layer. Adaptation-induced differences in sensor output would result in imbalances between inhibition and excitation arriving directly at the integrators. However, it is not possible to determine the significance of the opponent-energy layer without detailed computational analysis of the model. In the meantime, the issue remains open. Adaptation-induced changes in global motion thresholds were earlier (section 7.1.1) attributed to the opponent-energy layer, and it is not clear how well the model can account for such effects without this layer.

With these caveats in mind, the general motion-processing scheme outlined in figure 7.4 includes only the sensor and integrator layers of the model in figure 7.3, since these seem the minimum necessary to accommodate much of the MAE data. A few points are worthy of emphasis.

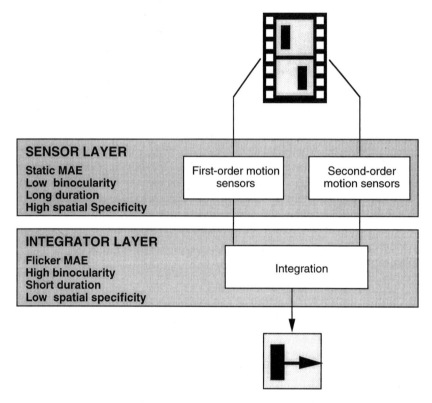

Figure 7.4
Hypothetical architecture for motion processing, incorporating motion aftereffect (MAE) phenomena. Only two of the three layers from the model in figure 7.3 are shown, since these seem the minimum necessary to accommodate the data. Properties associated with adaptation in the two layers are shown inside the boxes.

First, the perceptual manifestation of an MAE must represent the combined effect of adaptation at both sites. Neurons in the two layers are likely to differ in their response properties, such as receptive field size and binocularity (Wilson and his colleagues have speculated that sensors are located in V1, and integrators in MT), so their relative contribution to the resultant MAE should depend on stimulus conditions (i.e., the nature of adapting and test stimuli), leading to the different properties listed in the figure. Second, in the figure, static MAEs are attributed to sensors, and dynamic MAEs are attributed to integrators, but as we have seen there is as yet no coherent account for this division. Third, the difference in duration between sensor and integrator adaptation reflects the conclusion in chapter 3, section 3.1, that there is an association between binocularity, spatial specificity, and duration of MAEs. Fourth, given the empirical properties of adaptation effects from second-order motion (e.g., similarities with dynamic MAE properties; see chapter 5), they may predominantly reflect integrator adaptation.

7.1.4 Summary

The original opponent-process model attributed the MAE to adaptation at a single neural site (motion sensors). This model can no longer offer an adequate account of the phenomenon. Instead, the complex pattern of MAE data implicates a motion-processing system that involves at least two stages of analysis, incorporating 2-D interactions, with the potential for adaptation at both stages. Models of motion perception containing either two or three layers of analysis appear capable of accommodating much of the MAE data, if assumptions about adaptation are included. However, a firm conclusion on the most capable model must await detailed computational research. Important questions remain regarding the explanation of differences between static and dynamic MAEs.

7.2 What is the Functional Role of Selective Adaptation?

As the rest of this book shows, selective adaptation has been one of the most important tools in the study of the early stages of processing in human vision. It has been critical not only in helping to identify the range of stimulus attributes which are independently processed and to characterize the tuning of the underlying mechanisms but also in providing strong links between psychophysic studies on people and physiologic studies on animals. However, despite its undoubted utility in experiments, the phenomenon of adaptation itself remains puzzling. Why should it occur at all?

The reason for the puzzle is as follows. One might suppose that it is important for vision, or any other sensory system, to provide its owner with as veridical a picture of the world as possible. Consequently, any design fault which introduced distortions would be maladaptive and be weeded out by natural selection. However, aftereffects seem to break this rule: they show in a very immediate fashion that the visual system can produce profoundly distorted messages about the world, so that an object that is physically upright may appear to tilt and one that is physically stationary may appear to be moving. On the face of it, this appears to be an example of bad design which should have been removed during evolution.

Nevertheless, the idea that aftereffects result from the "fatigue" or "satiation" of visual neurons has been a pervasive one (Kohler and Wallach, 1944), driven perhaps by an implicit analogy between the supposed effects of continued stimulation on sensory nerves and those of continued exercise on skeletal muscles. Fatigue might reflect, for example, the inability of neurons to continue to produce neurotransmitter at high concentrations for long periods. However, there are several lines of evidence against this idea. First, visual aftereffects can result from very short adapting exposures of 200 ms or less (e.g., Wolfe, 1984; J. P. Harris and Calvert, 1989; Raymond and Isaak, 1998). It is hard to envisage that such brief periods of activity could lead to serious depletion of neurotransmitter stores. Second, there is physiologic evidence that even prolonged activation does not cause a decline in output of some visual neurons. Thus, although cortical neurons in the cat certainly do adapt to motion (Hammond et al., 1985) and to flicker (van de Grind, Grüsser, et al., 1972), retinal and geniculate cells do not (van de Grind et al., 1972). This last result implies that there are some visual neurons which do not fatigue with continued activation, suggesting that fatigue is not the reason for the adaptation of others. Third, the time course of recovery from adaptation does not seem to match that expected from neural fatigue. For example, Stromeyer (1978) reports that some visual aftereffects can be elicited days or even weeks after the end of adaptation. It seems that the adapted neurons would have replenished their stores of neurotransmitter within a shorter time than this. Thus the notion of neural fatigue does not seem to offer a total explanation for visual aftereffects, though it might be one component.

Other suggested answers to the puzzle have had two parts. The first has been to point out that the production of aftereffects requires somewhat unusual circumstances, namely, continuous fixation on the same invariant stimulus. This may be common in the laboratory but is rare in the "real world." The second part has been to postulate some mechanism or process which is normally beneficial to its owner but produces perceptual distortions in these rather special situations. The rest of this section considers various suggestions for what this mechanism might be. There are three related themes underlying these ideas. One is that aftereffects are produced by error-correcting mechanisms within the visual system. The second is that aftereffects reflect the visual system's attempts to optimize its coding of the environment. Visual neurons have a restricted dynamic range because their firing rate will not increase above a certain amount, and so there are limits to the range of stimuli which they can code. Adaptation aims to use this limited dynamic range most effectively, by shifting it around to match the range of stimuli in the current environmental conditions. The third theme is that of calibration: how the brain interprets sensory messsages (or the pattern of firing in sensory neurons). Although most of the studies have not involved the MAE, many of the experiments could be redone in, and the theories extended to, the motion domain.

7.2.1 Error-Correcting Accounts

The central idea behind these accounts is that the design of visual system means that it is prone to errors of various kinds, but that these can be removed by suitable correction processes which rely on consistencies and redundancies in visual signals (Andrews, 1964). Some of these errors may arise in the optical system of the eye. For example, it is known that the lens of the eye must produce chromatic aberrrations in the retinal image. Thus the retinal image of a black-white edge will contain color fringes. Similarly, an astigmatism will produce distortions of relative orientation. Other neural changes may arise as the brain ages, and the blood supply to some neurons becomes restricted so that they work less efficiently. Such constant errors can be detected by sampling the visual input over a sufficiently long period. For example, in the image, the color fringes on a black-white edge reverse direction if the edge is rotated through 180 degrees, and the relative orientation of two lines on the retina in astigmat is in changes as the stimulus configuration is rotated. These consistent changes can be removed by suitable neural tuning, provided some assumptions can be made about the environment. For example, the orientation of edges on the retina is probably detected by somehow pooling the activity of a number of neurons tuned to different orientations. Some of these neurons will be strongly excited, others less excited, by the edge, and perceived orientation may be coded by the distribution of their activity. If the blood supply to neurons coding one end of the distribution is reduced, and their firing rate is reduced, the distribution would be skewed, so that perceived orientation would be altered.

How could this potential problem be overcome ? First, an assumption needs to be made about the likely occurrence of different orientations in the world (most simply, that, over a long enough time interval, they are all equally likely). Second, a monitoring device is required which checks whether the activity of individual orientation-sensitive neurons reflects the assumption (so that their time-averaged activity is equal). Third, a mechanism is needed which alters the activity of individual neurons to restore the equality of neuronal activity to the desired state by altering their response characteristics (increasing or decreasing their firing rate to a particular input pattern). In principle, this mechanism would be like a "graphic equalizer" on a sound system, in which different frequency bands in the input signal are processed by different channels whose gain (volume) can be adjusted manually by the listener, to suit his or her own taste and the acoustics of the room. In the visual system, the gains of individual channels (neurons) would be set automatically by a comparison of actual and ideal time-averaged activity. An arrangement of this type has been suggested by Ullman and Schechtman (1982). In normal circumstances, such a mechanism would act to keep its owner's internal representation of orientation veridical despite unwanted changes (or drift) in individual components of the visual system. However, prolonged viewing of, say, a vertical grating would lead to an excess of activity in vertical neurons, which would be mistaken for a change in their gain, and lead to a reduction in their output. This reduction would manifest itself as a tilt aftereffect (TAE) (e.g., J. P. Harris and Calvert, 1985).

One can give a similar account of the processes underlying contingent aftereffects, such as the McCollough (1965) effect. To obtain this aftereffect, the observer stares for about 10 minutes at a field of vertical black stripes on a red background, alternating every 10 seconds or so with horizontal black stripes on a green background. After this adaptation regimen, black-and-white stripes appear tinged with green when vertical and tinged with pink when horizontal. Anstis (1975) suggests that the system which keeps the coding of, say, color and orientation separate is imperfect, and produces unwanted intermodulation or crosstalk. A possible analogy here might be that of a cable which contains many separate wires, in which activity in one wire (A) can produce spurious activity in a neighboring wire (B). Since this activity in B would always occur when wire A was active, it could be detected and edited out by a suitable filter. During adaptation to colored gratings, then, the brain would treat the correlation in the stimulus between red and vertical as unwanted noise, and turn down the gain of the red mechanism when the vertical mechanism was active. Thus black-and-white vertical edges would produce "anti-red" (or green) activity in the color channels. Such a mechanism would also act to remove the effects of chromatic aberration in the retinal image from the neural image.

Although such accounts clearly explain the basic phenomena of aftereffects, we can ask how well they explain more detailed aspects of the data. They seem to imply that aftereffects should take time to build up and also to decay, since the underlying processes need to sample appropriate aspects of the visual input over time. This fits with Stromeyer's report of the longevity of the McCollough effect, noted above. On the face of it, it does not fit so well with reports of aftereffects from very brief exposures. However, such studies involve a series of short adapting exposures, each followed by presentation of one of a range of test fields in, say, a staircase procedure. Thus, it could be argued that the aftereffects result from the cumulative effect of many short exposures. Error-correcting accounts also imply that recovery from adaptation should not occur simply with the passage of time, but require exposure to a relevant perceptual diet different from that during adaptation. Consistent with this, Spigel (1962a) reported that the MAE can still be obtained if an interval is left between the end of adaptation and presentation of the test field. The MAE still occurs when this interval is longer than the duration of the

MAE when the test field is presented immediately after adaptation. Such "storage" of aftereffects is further evidence against the "neural fatigue" explanation (since presumably neurons would recover from fatigue during the adapt-test interval), but supports an explanation involving sampling of the visual input over time.

7.2.2 Coding Optimization Accounts

7.2.2.1 Redistributing Sensitivity   The central problem in explaining selective adaptation is that at first sight it appears to make perception worse. Several studies have tried to show that in fact adaptation can improve some aspects of perception. Barlow, Macleod, et al. (1976) measured various aspects of detection and discrimination of gratings before and after adaptation to gratings which varied in their similarity to the test grating. They found no improvements for the stimulus variables of contrast, spatial frequency, and orientation. However, it may be that the method and, especially, the relationship between the adapting and test stimuli are critical for such improvements to become apparent. Both De Valois (1977) and Tolhurst and Barfield (1978) report increases in sensitivity in detecting gratings after adaptation. However, this did not occur at the adapting spatial frequency (for which sensitivity was reduced, as found in many other studies), but rather when the test grating differed by about two octaves from the adapting grating. De Valois suggests that improved detection arises because neurons tuned to different spatial frequencies inhibit each other. So, in normal circumstances, when one channel is excited by a stimulus, it will not only pass on that information to the rest of the visual system but actively try to prevent other channels (which may be excited to a lesser extent) from doing so. The effect will be to increase the precision of the neural response of the whole system to any stimulus. However, adapting to one spatial frequency reduces not only the output of the most active channel (so that it is less sensitive to its preferred spatial frequency) but also reduces the inhibition which it exerts on other spatial-frequency channels. Thus the latter become more sensitive.

Greenlee and Heitger (1988) measured how different in contrast two successively presented gratings had to be for an observer to discriminate which had the higher contrast. They found that the just noticeable difference (JND) in contrast rose with the absolute contrast of the gratings. The authors then repeated the experiment, preceding every presentation of these test gratings with a period of adaptation to a high-contrast (0.8) grating. Although they still found a dependency of the JND on absolute contrast, the slope of the graph was much shallower than that without adaptation, and the two graphs crossed over at around the value of the

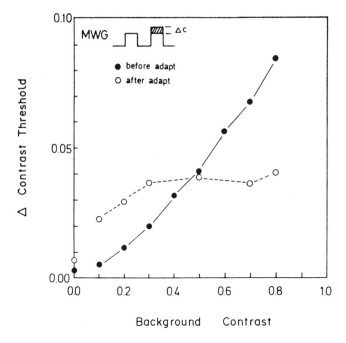

Figure 7.5
Size of the contrast difference (contrast threshold) needed by one subject (MWG) to discriminate which of two gratings had the higher contrast. Values on the abscissa show the background (or standard) contrast on each presentation. Filled symbols show the contrast thresholds before adaptation, open symbols the thresholds after adaptation to a grating of 0.8 contrast. Note that thresholds are lower (discrimination is easier) after adaptation for gratings whose contrast exceeds about 0.5.

adapting contrast (figure 7.5). In other words, for absolute contrasts lower than the adapting contrast, discrimination performance was worse than before adaptation, and for contrasts higher than the adapting contrast, performance was better.

This result was explained as follows. The visual system has a nonlinear response to contrast, so that the plot of perceived or neurally signaled contrast against physical contrast is an S shape rather than a straight line (figure 7.6). At very low or very high contrasts, for which the slope of the graph is very shallow, the change in physical contrast needed to produce a given change in perceived contrast will be large, whereas for medium contrasts (for which the slope of the graph is steeper) this change will be relatively small. Presumably, the JND reflects the size of this change in contrast. Greenlee and Heitger suggest that adaptation to high contrasts shifts the contrast response function, so that some contrasts which previously fell on a steep region now fall on a shallow one, and vice versa.

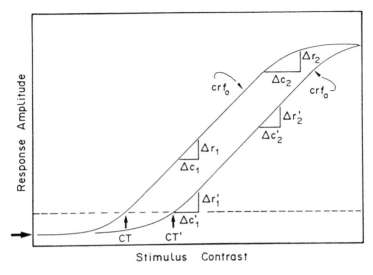

Stimulus Contrast

Figure 7.6
Explanation of the result shown in figure 7.5. It is supposed that the output (response amplitude) of the neural mechanisms responding to stimulus contrast follows that of the S-shaped
functions shown in the graph. Thus at very low, or very high, contrasts, a larger change of
stimulus contrast is needed to produce a given change in response amplitude than at intermediate contrasts. The key idea in the explanation is that adaptation to a high stimulus contrast shifts the response function from position crf_0 to position crf_a. Thus, before adaptation,
the change in stimulus contrast (Δc_2) needed to produce a change in response amplitude (Δr_2)
is larger than that ($\Delta c_2'$) needed to produce the same change in response amplitude ($\Delta r_2'$) after
adaptation. In other words, after adaptation, contrast discrimination thresholds for high-
contrast gratings will be smaller than before adaptation, as the data in figure 7.5 suggest.

This would improve discrimination for some contrasts and impair it for
others, as their data suggest.

One potential problem with this account is the time course over which
the effects operate. One might suppose that the shift in the contrast
response function would need to be fast, since, to be useful, it would presumably need to operate within a single glance as one changes fixation
from a low- to a high-contrast part of the scene. Greenlee and Heitger
provide no evidence that such fast changes can occur, though there is certainly evidence, noted above, that aftereffects can result from a series of
very brief stimulus presentations.

There is a distinction to be made between the models of De Valois and
of Tolhurst and Barfield, on the one hand, and of Greenlee and Heitger,
on the other. The results of all three studies show a redistribution of
sensitivity to a particular stimulus attribute produced by adaptation to
some value of that attribute. Thus, after adaptation, observers are more
sensitive to some value of the attribute and less sensitive to others. For

Greenlee and Heitger, this occurs because adaptation acts to readjust the nonoptimized coding system within a single channel to the presently prevailing visual diet. Although the other authors do not explicitly discuss its functional significance, in their accounts adaptation appears to act by disrupting a system already optimized by mutual inhibition between separate neural channels.

7.2.2.2 Decorrelation   These ideas about aftereffects reflecting mechanisms that optimize neural coding have been extended by Barlow (1990). He suggests that the cortex is a device for detecting the occurrence of novel events, and changes its own organization on the basis of correlations between different features of the environment. Barlow first considers contingent aftereffects, using the example of the aftereffect of color contingent on orientation (the McCollough effect—see above). He explains this effect as follows, with reference to figure 7.7a–d. In figure 7.7a, ψ_A on the vertical axis and ψ_B on the horizontal axis represent two perceptual variables, each capable of discriminating only four values (say blue, green, yellow, red; and horizontal, left oblique, vertical, right oblique), which depend on the values of two physical variables, A and B (color and orientation). The points on the graph show how which combinations of values of the two physical variables have occurred over some period of time. The variables are uncorrelated, so that all colors are about equally likely to have occurred with a particular orientation (and vice versa). Moreover, the combination of perceptual variables represents the combination of physical variables well, since all sixteen regions of the graph have some points in them. In figure 7.7b, the physical variables are correlated, and so particular colors occur only in combination with particular orientations (as they do during McCollough adaptation). In this case, many cells in the graph have no points in them because those combinations of color and orientation never occur, so that the coding of environmental events is inefficient, with only seven out of sixteen regions containing points. The solution is, in effect, to rotate the axes of the graph, so that the perceptual dimensions represent the physical dimensions more efficiently, since all cells now have some points within them, as shown in figure 7.7c. When this "oblique" graph paper is stretched (figure 7.7d), so that the perceptual axes are orthogonal again, the axes for the physical dimensions are now oblique. Thus the physical variable A, which was originally plotted vertically, now has a negative component on the perceptual axis plotted horizontally, giving, say, the negative contingent aftereffect of color found by McCollough.

   Barlow suggests that the lesson to be drawn from such aftereffects is that "perceptions are intended to occur independently, and define independent axes in perceptual space." When stimulus dimensions are

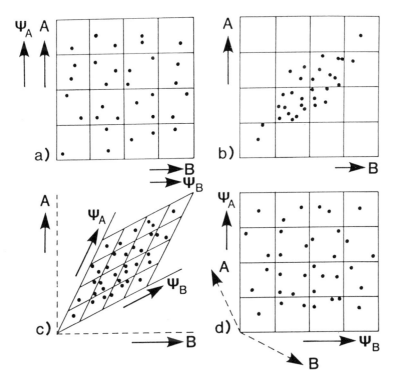

Figure 7.7
Two perceptual variables, Ψ_A and Ψ_B, each capable of discriminating only four levels, depend principally on two physical variables, A and B. In figure 7.7a, the two physical variables are uncorrelated, and the scatter diagram of joint occurrences shows that they fill all the cells in the diagram. In figure 7.7b, on the other hand, the physical variables are correlated. If the perceptual variables were simply proportional to A and B, the coding scheme would be inefficient, because some joint values do not occur and many of the cells are empty. The solution is to rotate the perceptual axes (figure 7.7c), so that the grid fits the joint values of A and B which actually occur, and all sixteen cells of the grid are filled. This can be seen when the grid is replotted with Ψ_A and Ψ_B as orthogonal axes instead of A and B (figure 7.7d). Now the "perceptual surface" is fully covered by the joint values. The rotation of the perceptual axes is thought to be the equivalent of adaptation to McCollough stimuli. In figure 7.7d, the axis of the physical variable A has a backward tilt, implying a negative component on the percept Ψ_A, as would be expected from the occurrence of the McCollough effect.

artificially linked, as in McCollough adaptation, then a repulsive force develops between the perceptions which spreads out the cluster of responses in perceptual space. This "repulsive force" might be mutual inhibition between the neural systems underlying each separate percept. The result of a large number of such repulsive forces, built up by the correlations and redundancies of a particular visual environment, would be a visual system which tended to produce little activation in response to familar combinations of stimulus attributes, but a lot of activation to novel stimuli.

Although this idea, that aftereffects reflect mechanisms which "decorrelate" different stimulus attributes, applies most obviously to contingent aftereffects, Barlow extends it to simple aftereffects, such as the MAE. He argues that these occur because adapting stimuli are large enough to cover the receptive fields of many neurons. During continuous motion, many neurons will be active simultaneously, and so will inhibit each others' activity. When a stationary test field is viewed, the inhibition will be sustained and so the appearance of reversed motion will be produced. On this view, aftereffects result because the adapting stimuli produce correlated activity in a group of neurons, rather than activity in single neurons.

Some physiologic evidence in support of this idea has been provided by Carandini, Barlow, et al. (1997). They measured the responses of cells in the primary visual cortex of the monkey to each of two gratings, oriented at 90 degrees to each other, and to the compound stimulus (or plaid) formed by presenting the gratings simultaneously. One of the gratings (G1) was oriented in the preferred orientation of the cortical cell, while the other (G2) was oriented at right angles to G1. The authors varied the contrast of the gratings and of the plaid, and measured the responses to a range of stimulus contrasts, after continuous stimulation of the cell by (or adaptation to) high-contrast versions of these stimuli. An important aspect of the findings was as follows. The responses of the cells to G2 (always orthogonal to the cell's preferred orientation) were negligible. Thus, if it were simply the physical characteristics of the stimulus which governed the adaptation of the cell, adapting to G1 alone should have the same effect on tests of G1 alone and G1 + G2 as adapting to G1 + G2. However, this was not so. Adaptation affects were much larger when the adapting and test stimuli, whether plaid or grating, were the same than when they were different. In other words, although G2 itself was an ineffective adaptor, the compound G1 + G2 had adapting effects for a G1 + G2 test which were greater than the effects for adapting to G1 alone. This result is consistent with the authors' suggestion that the cells were adapting to the contingent occurrence of G1 and G2, and is physiologic support for Barlow's ideas about the role of selective adaptation.

7.2.3 Recalibration

A central problem for the brain must be the interpretation of sensory activity. Unlike the laboratory scientist, who can measure with a ruler, for example, how many centimeters a lever must be moved to produce a given change of voltage in some apparatus, the brain has no metric of the external world which is independent of its own activity. Calibration of sensory messages can only be done on the basis of assumptions about the nature of the world. Examples of such assumptions might be that, averaged over a long enough time period, all orientations or directions of motion are equally likely to occur in any region of the retinal image. These ideas were touched on earlier in discussing error-correcting devices. Like Andrews, J. J. Gibson (1937) noted that the brain has a potential problem in keeping the physical and phenomenological worlds in correspondence. He pointed out that many sensory dimensions have a norm or null point. For example, stationarity (or absence of motion) can be thought of as a null or midpoint on a continuum running from, say, fast motion to the left through to fast motion to the right (or as the midpoint of a two-dimensional space). Gibson's account essentially suggests that this null point, or norm, is somehow calculated by the brain from the stream of sensory information about that particular stimulus dimension. As he put it, there is "a tendency for sensory activity to become normal, standard or neutral" (Gibson, 1937, p. 226). Put another way, his view is that the value of the null point of a sensory dimension is not wired into the brain, but represents, say, the average activity on that dimension over the recent past. Adaptation biases that activity, and so shifts the null point. This means that after adaptation to, say, movement to the left, stimuli which fall on the old null point (stationary) now no longer do so, but appear to move to the right. This idea suggests that the brain must continually recalibrate its inputs to optimize the correspondence between the external world and its internal visual representation.

If this view of perception is correct, then interpreting sensory messages must involve a comparison of the present sensory state with some longer-term measure of sensory activity, since the latter provides the only reliable reference. In their discussions of the functions of the processes underlying the McCollough effect and related contingent aftereffects, both Dodwell and Humphrey (1990) and Durgin and Proffitt (1996) point out that this idea is essentially that behind Helson's (1948, 1964) adaptation level theory. In Dodwell and Humphrey's words, "The most important idea in adaptation level theory is that the 'neutral point' (adaptation level), in some sense the 'center' of psychophysical judgements, is a weighted average of the set of stimuli so far presented" (p. 79).

For moving stimuli in the real world, then, stationarity (lack of retinal motion, or the neutral point of the "motion scale") would be the time-averaged activity of motion-sensitive neurons. The brain would not have to make strong assumptions about the consistency and reliability of its own internal machinery, but rather assume that the world was consistent, and that this consistency provides a potentially reliable reference. There have been various suggestions about what the brain does with this reference once it has been extracted. Dodwell and Humphrey suggest that an error-correcting device (like that of Andrews) operates to change the values ascribed to particular patterns of sensory activity, in order to maintain a correspondence between the world and its internal representation. Durgin and Proffitt prefer the ideas underlying Barlow's model: the reference can be used in a system giving efficient sensory coding, while at the same time highlighting novel sensory events.

The problem with a system which relies on long-term statistical properties of the input is its vulnerability to atypical short- and medium-term changes. Inevitably, these will bias the reference and so change the way in which subsequent sensory events are interpreted, as initially suggested by Gibson.

All the above accounts have in common that they discuss relatively local processes, confined to adapted areas of the retina. However, some types of adaptation can produce more global changes in perception in which the subject's entire frame of reference may be altered. Much of Gibson's experimental work on adaptation concerned the TAE (Gibson and Radner, 1937). One important aspect of this work was the demonstration that the vertical and horizontal axes of visual space could be linked in some way. So, after adapting to a line slightly off vertical, a small aftereffect was found on a horizontal test line. Gibson called this the "indirect" effect, to distinguish it from the "direct" effect on a vertical test line. This indirect effect implies that adaptation to a line close to vertical can distort the whole visual frame of reference, rather than simply affect the perception of stimuli which are similar to the adapting stimuli. Morant and Harris (1965) showed that in addition to this "global" effect on the visual frame of reference, there is also a "local" effect, which is confined to test stimuli similar to the adapting stimuli. Presumably, the local and global effects of adaptation to tilt (and by implication to motion also) reflect processing at different levels of visual analysis.

As noted earlier, adaptation is known to occur at several cortical sites, and the local and more global effects of adaptation may be the perceptual correlates of activity in these different anatomical sites. Wenderoth (e.g., Wenderoth and Johnstone, 1987) has suggested that different effects originate in different cortical areas, local effects perhaps in V1, more global effects in extrastriate cortical areas, such as V4 or MT. For example, MT may be involved in the perception of the speed and direction of a drifting plaid (and the MAE which results from it), whereas mechanisms in

V1 may respond to the component gratings of which the plaid is formed or the "blobs" of luminance where the gratings cross (see, e.g., Wenderoth et al., 1994; and chapter 5). A similar account can be given for the direct and indirect components of the tilt illusion (Wenderoth and Johnstone, 1987). More recently, Wiesenfelder and Blake (1992) have reported evidence for multiple sites of adaptation in the MAE, based on the use of binocular rivalry, in which a stimulus presented to one eye can suppress the information from the other eye. It had already been shown that the strength of monocular MAEs from adaptation of the same eye is unaffected by the presence of a rivalrous stimulus seen by the other eye, which suppressed the perception of adapting motion (Lehmkuhle and Fox, 1975). This suggests that the MAE is generated before the site at which visual information is blocked by binocular rivalry suppression. When, however, Wiesenfelder and Blake looked at the effect of a binocularly suppressed test field on storage of the MAE, they found a different picture. If, after monocular adaptation, the presentation of the test field to the adapted eye is delayed until the MAE obtained with immediate presentation of the test field would have decayed away, an MAE can still be obtained. It turns out that rivalrous suppression of an immediately presented test field permits this storage of the MAE, just as physically removing the test field would. This suggests that storage and decay of the MAE must be mediated at least in part by processes which lie after the site of rivalry suppression. It is tempting to attribute the presuppression adaptation stage to changes in motion sensors, and the postsuppression storage stage to activity in the integrator or higher levels.

MAEs do not store perfectly, in the sense that stored MAEs are weaker than MAEs measured immediately after the same adaptation regimen, as noted by Wiesenfelder and Blake, as well as by other workers. Thus some decay of the MAE occurs even in the absence of any test field.Wolfe and O'Connell (1986) measured the TAEs produced by varying periods of adaptation. They found that the TAE from 2 minutes of adaptation decayed away within 4 minutes, whereas the TAE from 4 minutes of adaptation could still be measured after 2 weeks, even though, at the end of adaptation, the TAEs from the two periods of adaptation were of similar magnitude. The authors suggested that the fast-decaying component of adaptation occurs in "broadly-tuned channels," and perhaps reflects neurotransmitter depletion (arguably, neural fatigue). On the other hand, the longer-lasting component was thought to reflect a change in the activity of "labelled-lines," which detect ratios of activity between the broadly tuned channels. Although Wolfe and O'Connell invoke neural fatigue in their explanation of the TAE, the data do not force such an explanation upon us. The best evidence for neural fatigue seems to be the apparent decay of the MAE in storage experiments in the absence of a

test field. However, the walls of an experimental laboratory or the sur-
faces of experimental apparatus have a microtexture, as well as the dark
field produced by closing the eyes. Thus the visual system is being presented during the storage interval with information about stationary patterns, as would be required by accounts such as recalibration.

Although some of the detail seems open to dispute, this suggestion of
multiple sites of adaptation seems to fit well with the data from the binocular rivalry experiments. Thus imperfections of storage of MAEs would
result from changes in presuppression opponent-energy sensors, whereas
the stored component of MAEs would reflect changes of integration.

So far, it has been suggested that visual calibration takes place relative
to the statistical properties, over time, of the retinal image alone. However, there are other sources of information which could, in principle,
affect the interpretation of visual activity, namely, vestibular and proprio-
ceptive (and perhaps auditory) information, and the corollary discharges
associated with motor activity. L. R. Harris et al. (1981) suggested that
the MAE might result from a process which calibrates the relationships
between different sensory inputs. They pointed out that the most common cause of retinal motion is not motion of the environment but motion
of the observer. Thus, for example, the expanding optical flow on the
retina produced by forward locomotion is normally accompanied by
correlated signals from the vestibular system. To check the idea that
the MAE might result from an unusual mismatch between vestibular and
retinal signals, they placed the adapting display, and in some conditions
the observer, on a movable trolley. Sinusoidal-to-and-fro motion of the
trolley was converted via the voltage across a potentiometer into expansion and contraction of a field of dots on an oscilloscope screen. The
authors found a strong contracting MAE , from retinal expansion without
observer motion, but this was markedly reduced when the observer
moved with the display, as the intersensory recalibration hypothesis suggests. However, one might have expected a similar reduction in strength
of the MAE resulting from retinal expansion due to backward motion, and
this was not found: the expansion MAE was only slightly reduced when
the observer moved backward with the display. Nor was the MAE
enhanced when the direction of motion on the retina and the direction of
observer motion were put into conflict.

Despite these apparent discrepancies within their experiment, however,
there is other evidence for the kind of intersensory recalibration suggested by these authors. An experiment complementary to that of L. R.
Harris et al. (again changing the usual relationship between retinal and
vestibular signals) would be to have the observer move during adaptation, but to keep the retinal image motionless. After jogging on a tread-

mill for 10 minutes, subjects report a sensation, when walking normally on solid ground, of moving at an accelerated rate (Pelah and Barlow, 1996). The authors, who describe other related illusions, conclude that disturbing the normal relationship between self-induced motion and expected sensory input leads to a recalibration of the relationship between optic flow, vestibular signals, and movements of the legs. One way to describe this illusion is as an MAE produced by the absence of visual motion where such motion would normally occur.

It is not yet certain whether the site of these intersensory MAEs is the integration level described in the previous section. If so, they should show the same patterns of binocularity and spatial tuning as other MAEs which are thought to reside there. Such experiments have yet to be done, though Pelah and Barlow note that, after adaptation with a textured wall on one side, their effect was stronger when walking with a wall on that side rather than the other. Without such evidence, it is not clear whether one needs to postulate a third, higher, level of motion adaptation, at which visual and nonvisual information is integrated. Whatever the answer, it seems that the mechanisms underlying these global (integrator) effects may save the same functions as those underlying the local (sensor) effects. That is, drift or optical errors mean that, say, the perceived vertical or the perceived stationarity of the whole visual field needs to be continuously recalibrated; or the range of possible orientations or directions of motion need to be redistributed across the available mechanisms to suit particular visual environments.

7.2.4 Which Account Is Best?

One difficulty in deciding between error-correcting, coding optimization, and recalibration accounts of motion adaptation is that they appear to make very similar predictions. They allinvolve monitoring activity in visual mechanisms over time, suggesting that aftereffects should build up relatively slowly, and also decay slowly, since the visual system needs time to take account of the change of visual (or other perceptual) diet between adaptation and testing. They all appear to predict storage of aftereffects between adaptation and presentation of the test field, since it is an alteration of visual or other input, not simply the passage of time, which is needed to readjust the underlying mechanisms. However, there are situations in which the three accounts seem to make different predictions. For example, the error-correcting account implies that MAEs should be stronger the more characteristics are shared by the adapting and test fields, since it is a subset of motion-sensitive mechanisms which would be affected by the test field. On the recalibration account, however, evidence of, for example, absence of movement could come from a test field with spatial charateristics very different from those of the adapting field.

Although the error-correcting, optimization, and recalibration accounts have been presented as alternatives, they do not exclude one another. The same kind of mechanism or process within the visual system could fulfill all these roles. To illustrate this point, consider the human nose. Although one can ask whether the function of the nose concerns respiration or olfaction, the answer is clearly "both." Indeed, it is just because breathing through the nose produces a regular flow of air over the nasal membranes that it is a prime site for olfactory receptors. Thus it may be that "self-tuning" devices of the kind outlined here can fulfill all these "housekeeping" functions in vision. One possibility is that adaptation in opponent-energy sensors is best thought of as error correction, whereas that in higher-order integrators reflects optimization and calibration processes.

7.2.5 Conclusions

Early views that selective adaptation reflects neural satiation or fatigue are probably inadequate, since they are not consistent with evidence on the buildup and decay of aftereffects, or the evidence that some visual neurons do not fatigue with continuous stimulation. Alternative accounts (error correction, coding optimization, and recalibration) fit the evidence better, and present evidence does not decisively favor one of these over the others. They are not mutually exclusive, and all may be correct.

Adaptation occurs at several cortical sites, and this may be reflected in a range of motion, tilt, and other aftereffects. For example, there seem to be two types of TAE, one to do with local orientation processing, the other with the more global frame of reference ("perceived vertical"). There seem to be analogous MAEs.

MAEs can result from the interaction of visual and nonvisual signals. It is not yet clear at which level of motion analysis this interaction occurs.

7.3 General Conclusions

A strong theme to emerge from section 7.1 was the need for models of motion analysis containing several layers of processing, with adaptation arising at each layer. Without computational modeling, it is not clear just how well such models can account for the detailed properties of many MAE phenomena reported in this book. However, the recent emergence of new stimulus paradigms in MAE research has provided new data against which to test computational models, so the way is open for significant theoretical advances in the near future. New ideas on the significance of adaptation, described in section 7.2, hint at the functional logic behind multiple adaptation sites in motion processing. Short-term imbalances between excitation and inhibition are highly significant, because they indicate directional bias in the image, either locally if they arise from sensor responses, or globally if they arise from recurrent connections between integrators. Selective adaptation may serve to ensure that, over a longer time scale, excitation and inhibition in different layers tend to balance out.

Note

1. Second-order motion sensors can be constructed using the same sequence of processing as used by first-order motion sensors, with one additional operation: a nonlinear transformation (e.g., rectification) is applied to the signal before it is subjected to motion-energy analysis, to convert texture modulation into "intensity" modulation in the neural image. There is good evidence for the existence of both kinds of detector, and Wilson and Kim (1994) accordingly assumed that both first-order and second-order opponent-energy responses sum their responses in the pattern layer of the model.

Epilogue

The MAE presents perhaps the clearest example in modern neuroscience of the link between neural events and perceptual experience. There can be little doubt that there is an intimate relationship between the aftereffect and changes in cortical cell response. To take one example from the many findings reported earlier, the time course of changes in cell response during and after adaptation to motion mirrors very closely the time course of changes in perceptual experience. Modern theories of motion perception (and, arguably, the rest of perception) really began with Sutherland's and Barlow and Hill's descriptions of the ratio model of the MAE. The power of the model lies in the very direct link it proposed between changes in neural response and alterations in perceived movement. As is true for many phenomena, in the intervening years motion research on several fronts has served to highlight the shortcomings of the original ratio model. Electrophysiologic research has uncovered several populations of cells in the visual system, located in different visual areas, which all respond selectively to motion, and also show adaptation effects, making it difficult to attribute the MAE to changes in the response of a single population of cells. Psychophysical research has confirmed that the observed properties of the MAE are too complex and diverse to admit explanation by a single process. For example, variations in retinal specificity and interocular transfer with stimulus conditions are difficult to explain on the basis of a single homogeneous population of simple motion-detecting cells. Computational research has revealed the complexity of the problem facing the visual system during motion analysis. The solution to the aperture problem, for example, requires a degree of analysis that is well beyond the propositions contained in the ratio model, which now appears capable of explaining the MAE, but not much else.

The main consequence of this complexity, as all of the chapters in this book conclude, is that there can be no single explanation of the MAE. The phenomenon is actually an expression of at least two sources of adaptation at different sites in the visual system. Since the different sites are connected so that they function as parts of a motion-processing system, they necessarily interact to determine perceptual experience. The outcome of this interaction is dependent on the nature of the visual stimulus at the time of adaptation and testing.

The modern successor to the ratio model is thus a multistage system incorporating both local and global stages of analysis, with adaptation occurring at all stages. Such a model is consistent with the known physiology, and should be capable of solving the aperture problem and accommodating the diverse properties of the MAE. The problem now is that, although very able computational models of this kind are already available (reviewed in Wilson, 1994), none seem to have adaptation built in explicitly to accommodate MAE data. Consequently we do not yet know how well such models will be able to deal with the diverse properties of the MAE once appropriate propositions are added. This is a major issue for future research.

In 12 years' time, according to current trends (see Preface, figure P. 1), we will have seen about another 400 papers on the MAE published. It is to be hoped that they bring renewed order and simplicity to our understanding of the phenomenon. For encouragement we need only glance into an adjacent field—color research—which was in a chaotic state 40 years ago (see Osgood, 1953, for a textbook treatment of color vision as it was then understood, or misunderstood). Since then, a two-pronged attack by psychophysicists and physiologists has led to the state of relative clarity that we enjoy today (see Kaiser and Boynton, 1996). The field of motion research has already experienced rapid growth in recent years, and the time is ripe for significant new advances.

References

Addams, R. (1834). An account of a peculiar optical phænomenon seen after having looked at a moving body. *London and Edinburgh Philosophical Magazine and Journal of Science* 5: 373–374.

Addams, R. (1835). Optische Täuschung nach Betrachtung eines in Bewegung begriffenen Körpers. *Annalen der Physik und Chemie* 34: 348.

Adelson, E. H. and J. R. Bergen (1985). Spatiotemporal energy models for the perception of motion. *Journal of the Optical Society of America A* 2: 284–299.

Adelson, E. H. and J. A. Movshon (1982). Phenomenal coherence of moving visual patterns. *Nature* 300: 523–525.

Aitken, J. (1878). On a new variety of ocular spectrum. *Proceedings of the Royal Society of Edinburgh* 10: 40–44.

Alais, D., D. Burke, et al. (1996a). Further evidence for monocular determinants of perceived plaid direction. *Vision Research* 36: 1247–1253.

Alais, D., M. J. van der Smagt, et al. (1996b). Monocular mechanisms determine plaid motion coherence. *Visual Neuroscience* 13: 615–626.

Alais, D., P. Wenderoth, et al. (1994). The contribution of one-dimensional motion mechanisms to the perceived direction of drifting plaids and their aftereffects. *Vision Research* 34: 1823–1834.

Alais, D., P. Wenderoth, et al. (1997). The size and number of plaid blobs mediate the misperception of type II plaid direction. *Vision Research* 37: 143–150.

Albright, T. D. (1984). Direction and orientation selectivity of neurons in visual area MT of the macaque. *Journal of Neurophysiology* 52: 1106–1130.

Andrews, D. P. (1964). Error-correcting perceptual mechanisms. *Quarterly Journal of Experimental Psychology* 16: 104–115.

Anstis, S. (1990). Motion aftereffects from a motionless stimulus. *Perception* 19: 301–306.

Anstis, S. M. (1975). What does visual perception tell us about visual coding? In *Handbook of Psychobiology*. Ed. M. Gazzinaga and C. Blakemore. New York, Academic Press, p. 269–323.

Anstis, S. M. (1978). Apparent movement. In *Handbook of Sensory Physiology*, Vol. 8. Ed. R. Held, H. W. Leibowitz and H.-L. Teuber. New York, Springer-Verlag, 655–673.

Anstis, S. M. (1980). The perception of apparent movement. *Philosophical Transactions of the Royal Society of London. Series B. Biological Sciences* 290: 153–168.

Anstis, S. M. (1986). Motion perception in the frontal plane: Sensory aspects. In *Handbook of Perception and Human Performance* Vol 1 Ed. K. R. Boff, L. Kaufman et al. New York, Wiley, pp. 16-1–16-27.

Anstis, S. M. and K. Duncan (1983). Separate motion aftereffects from each eye and from both eyes. *Vision Research* 23: 161–169.

Anstis, S. M. and R. L. Gregory (1965). The after-effect of seen motion: The role of retinal stimulation and of eye movements. *Quarterly Journal of Experimental Psychology* 17: 173–174.

Anstis, S. M. and J. P. Harris (1974). Movement aftereffects contingent on binocular disparity. *Perception* 3: 153–168.

Anstis, S. M. and G. Mather (1985). Effects of luminance and contrast on the direction of ambiguous apparent motion. *Perception* 14: 167–179.

Anstis, S. M. and B. P. Moulden (1970). Aftereffect of seen movement: Evidence for peripheral and central components. *Quarterly Journal of Experimental Psychology* 22: 222–229.

Anstis, S. M. and A. H. Reinhardt-Rutland (1976). Interactions between motion aftereffects and induced movement. *Vision Research* 16: 1391–1394.

Aristotle (1955). *Parva Naturalia*. Revised text with introduction and commentary by W. D. Ross. Oxford, U.K., Oxford University Press.

Ashida, H. and N. Osaka (1994). Difference of spatial frequency selectivity between static and flicker motion aftereffects. *Perception* 23: 1313–1320.

Ashida, H. and N. Osaka (1995a). Effects of direction judgment on motion aftereffect induced by second-order motion. *Perception* 24: 103.

Ashida, H. and N. Osaka (1995b). Motion aftereffect with flickering test stimuli depends on adapting velocity. *Vision Research* 35: 1825–1834.

Ashida, H., K. Susami, et al. (1996). Re-evaluation of local adaptation for motion aftereffect. *Perception* 25: 1065–1072.

Ashida, H. and K. Susami (1997). Linear motion aftereffect induced by pure relative motion. *Perception* 26: 7–16.

Ashida, H., F. A. J. Verstraten, et al. (1997). What is the transition point between static and dynamic motion aftereffects? *Perception* 26 (Suppl.): 86.

Assad, J. A. and J. H. R. Maunsell (1995). Neuronal correlates of inferred motion in primate posterior parietal cortex. *Nature* 373: 518–521.

Aubert, H. (1886). Die Bewegungsempfindungen. *Archiv für die gesammte Physiologie des Menschen und der Thiere* 39: 347–370.

Bach, M., M. Hoffmann, et al. (1996). Motion-onset VEP: Missing direction-specifity of adaptation? *Investigative Ophthalmology and Visual Science* 37 (Suppl.): 446.

Bach, M. and D. Ullrich (1994). Motion adaptation governs the shape of motion-evoked cortical potentials. *Vision Research* 34: 1541–1547.

Badcock, D. R. and A. M. Derrington (1989). Detecting the displacement of spatial beats: No role for distortion products? *Vision Research* 29: 731–739.

Baker, C. L., R. F. Hess, et al. (1991). Residual motion perception in a "motion-blind" patient, assessed with limited-lifetime random dot stimuli. *Journal of Neuroscience* 11: 454–461.

Banks, W. P. and D. A. Kane (1972). Discontinuity of seen motion reduces the visual motion aftereffect. *Perception and Psychophysics* 123: 69–72.

Barlow, H. B. (1953). Summation and inhibition in the frog's retina. *Journal of Physiology (London)* 119: 69–88.

Barlow, H. B. (1990). A theory about the functional role and synaptic mechanism of visual after-effects. In *Coding and Efficiency*. Ed. C. Blackmore. Cambridge, U.K., Cambridge University Press, 363–375.

Barlow, H. B. and G. S. Brindley (1963). Inter-ocular transfer of movement aftereffects during pressure blinding of the stimulated eye. *Nature* 200: 1347.

Barlow, H. B. and R. M. Hill (1963). Evidence for a physiological explanation for the waterfall phenomenon and figural aftereffects. *Nature* 200: 1345–1347.

Barlow, H. B., D. I. A. Macleod, et al. (1976). Adaptation to gratings: No compensatory advantages found. *Vision Research* 16: 1043–1045.

Barton, J. J. S., J. A. Sharpe, et al. (1995). Retinotopic and directional defects in motion discrimination in humans with cerebral lesions. *Annals of Neurology* 37: 665–675.

Basler, A. (1909). Über das Sehen von Bewegungen. III. Mitteilung. Der Ablauf des Bewegungsnachbildes. *Archiv für die gesammte Physiologie des Menschen und der Thiere* 128: 145–176.

Basler, A. (1910). Über das Sehen von Bewegungen. V. Mitteilung. Untersuchungen über die simultane Scheinbewegung. *Archiv für die gesammte Physiologie des Menschen und der Thiere* 132: 31–142.

Basler, A. (1911). Über das Sehen von Bewegungen. VI. Mitteilung. Der Beginn des Bewegungsnachbildes. *Archiv für die gesammte Physiologie des Menschen und der Thiere* 139: 611–622.

Beattie, W. (1838). *Caledonia Illustrated in a Series of Views Taken Expressly for the Work of W. H. Bartlett, T. Allom, and Others*. London, Virtue.

Bertone, A., M. W. von Grünau, et al. (1997). The effect of selective attention on the motion aftereffect of a transparent plaid. *Investigative Ophthalmology and Visual Science* 38: 370.

Bex, P. J., N. Brady, et al. (1995). A motion aftereffect to correspondence-based stimuli. *Perception* (Suppl.) 24: 107.

Bex, P. J., F. A. J. Verstraten, et al. (1996). Temporal and spatial frequency tuning of the flicker motion aftereffect. *Vision Research* 36: 2721–2727.

Blake, R. and R. Fox (1973). The psychophysical inquiry into binocular summation. *Perception and Psychophysics* 14: 161–185.

Blake, R. and R. O'Shea (1987). "Abnormal fusion" of stereopsis and binocular rivalry. *Psychological Review* 95: 151–154.

Blake, R. and E. Hiris (1993). Another means for measuring the motion aftereffect. *Vision Research* 33: 1589–1592.

Blake, R., R. Overton, et al. (1981a). Interocular transfer of visual aftereffects. *Journal of Experimental Psychology* 7: 367–381.

Blake, R., M. Sloane, et al. (1981b). Further developments in binocular summation. *Perception and Psychophysics* 30: 266–276.

Blakemore, C. and F. W. Campbell (1969). On the existence of neurones in the human visual system selectively sensitive to the orientation and size of the retinal images. *Journal of Physiology (London)* 203: 237–260.

Blakemore, C. B., J. Nachmias, et al. (1970). The perceived spatial frequency shift: Evidence for frequency-selective neurones in the human brain. *Journal of Physiology (London)* 210: 727–750.

Blakemore, C. and P. Sutton (1969). Size adaptation: A new aftereffect. *Science* 166: 245–247.

Bonnet, C. and V. Pouthas (1972). Interactions between spatial and kinetic dimensions in movement aftereffect. *Perception and Psychophysics* 12: 193–200.

Borschke, A. and L. Hescheles (1902). Über Bewegungsnachbilder. *Zeitschrift für Psychologie und Physiologie der Sinnesorgane* 27: 387–398.

Boutet, I., J. Rivest, et al. (1996). The role of attention on motion, color and luminance aftereffects. *Investigative Ophthalmology and Visual Science* 37 (Suppl.): 528.

Bowd, C., M. Donnelly, et al. (1996a). Coherent plaid motion and the barberpole illusion perceived with cyclopean (stereoscopic) components. *Investigative Ophthalmology and Visual Science* 37 (Suppl.): 738.

Bowd, C., D. Rose, et al. (1996b). Enduring stereoscopic motion aftereffects induced by prolonged adaptation. *Vision Research* 36: 3655–3660.

Bowditch, H. P. and G. S. Hall (1881). Optical illusions of motion. *Journal of Physiology (London)* 3: 297–307.

Braddick, O. J. (1974). A short-range process in apparent movement. *Vision Research* 14: 519–527.

Braddick, O. J. (1980). Low-level and high-level processes in apparent motion. *Philosophical Transactions of the Royal Society of London. Series B. Biological Sciences* 290: 137–151.

Brewster, D. (1845). Notice of two new properties of the retina. *Report of the British Association for the Advancement of Science Transactions of the Sections* 9–10.

Brigner, W. L. (1982). Spatial frequency selectivity of spiral aftereffect. *Perceptual and Motor Skills* 55: 1129–1130.

Brindley, G. S. (1970). *Physiology of the Retina and Visual Pathway*. Baltimore, Williams & Wilkins.

Broerse, J., P. Dodwell, et al. (1992). Anomalous spiral aftereffects: A new twist to the perception of rotating spirals. *Perception* 21: 195–199.

Broerse, J., P. C. Dodwell, et al. (1994). Experiments on the afterimages of stimulus change (Dvorak 1870): A translation with commentary. *Perception* 23: 1135–1144.

Budde, E. (1884). Über metakinetische Scheinbewegungen und über die Wahrnemung von Bewegungen. *Archiv für Anatomie und Physiologie* 20: 127–152.

Burke, D., D. Alais, et al. (1994). A role for a low-level mechanism in determining plaid coherence. *Vision Research* 34: 3189–3196.

Burke, D. and P. Wenderoth (1989). Cyclopean tilt aftereffects can be incuded monocularly: Is there a purely binocular process? *Perception* 18: 471–482.

Burke, D. and P. Wenderoth (1993). Determinants of two-dimensional motion aftereffects induced by simultaneously- and alternately-presented plaid components. *Vision Research* 33: 351–359.

Cameron, E. L., C. L. J. Baker, et al. (1992). Spatial frequency selective mechanisms underlying the motion aftereffect. *Vision Research* 32: 561–568.

Campbell, F. W., G. F. Cooper, et al. (1969). The spatial selectivity of the visual cells of the cat. *Journal of Physiology (London)* 203: 223–235.

Carandini, M., H. B. Barlow, et al. (1997). Adaptation to contingencies in macaque primary visual cortex. *Philosophical transactions of the Royal Society of London Series. B. Biological Sciences* 1149–1154.

Carlson, V. R. (1962). Adaptation in the perception of visual velocity. *Journal of Experimental Psychology* 64: 192–197.

Carney, T. and M. N. Shadlen (1993). Dichoptic activation of the early motion system. *Vision Research* 33: 1977–1995.

Carpenter, R. H. S. (1988). *Movements of the Eyes*. London, Pion.

Cavanagh, P. (1991). Short-range vs. long-range motion: Not a valid distinction. *Spatial Vision* 5: 303–309.

Cavanagh, P. (1992). Attention-based motion perception. *Science* 257: 1563–1565.

Cavanagh, P. (1995). Is there low-level motion processing for non–luminance-based stimuli? In *Early Vision and Beyond*. Ed. T. V. Papathomas, C. Chubb, et al. Cambridge, Mass., MIT Press.

Cavanagh, P. and O. E. Favreau (1985). Color and luminance share a common motion pathway. *Vision Research* 25: 1595–1601.

Cavanagh, P. and G. Mather (1989). Motion: The long and short of it. *Spatial Vision* 4: 103–129.

Chaudhuri, A. (1990). Modulation of the motion aftereffect by selective attention. *Nature* 344: 60–62.

Chaudhuri, A. (1991). Eye movements and the motion aftereffect: Alternatives to the induced movement hypothesis. *Vision Research* 31: 1639–1645.

Chubb, C. and G. Sperling (1988). Drift-balanced random stimuli: A general basis for studying non-Fourier motion perception. *Journal of the Optical Society of America A* 5: 1986–2007.

Chubb, C. and G. Sperling (1989a). Second-order motion perception: Space/time separable mechanisms. In *IEEE Workshop on Visual Motion*. Washington, D.C., IEEE Computer Society Press, 126–138.

Chubb, C. and G. Sperling (1989b). Two motion perception mechanisms revealed through distance-driven reversal of apparent motion. *Proceedings of the National Academy of Sciences U S A* 86: 2985–2989.

Classen, A. (1863). *Über das Schlussverfahren des Sehaktes*. Rostock, Leopold's Universitätsbuchhandlung.

Clymer, A. B. (1973). *The Effect of Seen Motion on the Apparent Speed of Subsequent Test Velocities: Speed Tuning of Movement Aftereffects*. PhD thesis, Columbia University.

Coltheart, M. (1971). Visual feature-analysers and after-effects of tilt and curvature. *Psychological Review* 78: 114–121.

Corbetta, M., F. M. Miezin, et al. (1990). Attentional modulation of neural processing of shape, color, and velocity in humans. *Science* 248: 1556–1559.

Corbetta, M., F. M. Miezen, et al. (1991). Selective and divided attention during visual discriminations of shape color, and speed: Functional anatomy by positron emission tomography. *Journal of Neuroscience* 11: 2383–2402.

Cords, R. and E. von Brücke (1907). Über die Geschwindigkeit des Bewegunsnachbildes. *Archiv für die gesammte Physiologie des Menschen und der Thiere* 119: 54–76.

Cornsweet, T. N. (1970). *Visual Perception*. Orlando, Fla., Academic Press.

Culham, J. C. and P. Cavanagh (1994). Attentive tracking of a counterphase grating produces a motion aftereffect. *Investigative Ophthalmology and Visual Science* 35 (Suppl.): 1622.

Culham, J. C. and P. Cavanagh (1995). Motion aftereffects of attentive tracking are rotation-specific but independent of position. *Investigative Ophthalmology and Visual Science* 36 (Suppl.): 857.

Culham, J. C., P. Cavanagh, et al. (1997). Attentive tracking of moving targets produces parietal activation revealed by functional magnetic resonance imaging. *Investigative Ophthalmology and Visual Science* 38 (Suppl.): 1174.

Dale, A. M., J. B. Reppas, et al. (1996). The representation of image motion in human visual cortex. Unpublished manuscript.

Dawson, M. R. W. (1991). The how and why of what went where in apparent motion: Modeling solutions to the motion correspondence problem. *Psychological Review* 98: 569–603.

Day, R. H. and E. Strelow (1971). Reduction or disappearance of visual aftereffect of movement in the absence of patterned surround. *Nature* 230: 55–56.

Dember, W. N. (1964). *Visual Perception: The Nineteenth Century*. New York, Wiley.

Derrington, A. M. and D. R. Badcock (1985). Separate detectors for simple and complex patterns? *Vision Research* 25: 1869–1878.

Derrington, A. M. and D. R. Badcock (1986). Detection of spatial beats: Non-linearity or contrast increment detection? *Vision Research* 26: 343–348.

Derrington, A. M. and D. R. Badcock (1992). Two-stage analysis of the motion of 2-dimensional patterns: Which is the first stage? *Vision Research* 32: 691–698.

Derrington, A. M., D. R. Badcock, et al. (1993). Discriminating the direction of second-order motion at short stimulus durations. *Vision Research* 33: 1785–1794.

De Solla Price, D. J. (1963). *Little Science, Big Science*. New York, Columbia University Press.

De Valois, K. K. (1977). Spatial frequency adaptation can enhance contrast sensitivity. *Vision Research* 17: 1057–1065.

De Valois, R. L., E. N. Yund, et al. (1982). The orientation and direction selectivity of cells in macaque visual cortex. *Vision Research* 22: 531–544.

DeYoe, E. A. and D. C. van Essen (1988). Concurrent processing streams in monkey visual cortex. *Trends in Neurosciences* 11: 219–226.

Dierig, S. (1994). Extending the neuron doctrine: Carl Ludwig Schleich (1859–1922) and his reflections on neuroglia at the inception of the neural-network concept in 1894. *Trends in Neurosciences* 17: 449–452.

Dodwell, P. C. and G. K. Humphrey (1990). A functional theory of the McCollough effect. *Psychological Review* 97: 78–89.

Donnelly, M., C. Bowd, et al. (1996). Bandwidth of directionally-selective mechanisms for cyclopean (stereoscopic) motion. *Investigative Ophthalmology and Visual Science* 37 (Suppl.): 285.

Donnelly, M., C. Bowd, et al. (1997). Direction discrimination of cyclopean (stereoscopic) and luminance motion. *Vision Research* 37: 2041–2046.

Dorn, T. J., M. Hoffmann, et al. (1997). Motion adaptation time constants of the motion-onset VEP. *Investigative Ophthalmology and Visual Science* 38 (Suppl.): 992.

Dosher, B. A., M. S. Landy, et al. (1989). Kinetic depth effect and optic flow—I. 3D shape from Fourier motion. *Vision Research* 29: 1789–1813.

Drysdale, A. E. (1975). The movement after-effect and eye movements. *Vision Research* 15: 1171.

Dubner, R. and S. M. Zeki (1971). Response properties and receptive fields of cells in an anatomically defined region of the superior temporal sulcus in the monkey. *Brain Research* 35: 528–532.

Duffy, C. J. and R. H. Wurtz (1991). Sensitivity of MST neurons to optic flow stimuli. I. A continuum of response selectivity to large-field stimuli. *Journal of Neurophysiology* 65: 1329–1345.

Dureman, I. (1962). Factors influencing the the apparent velocity of the visual movement aftereffect. *Scandinavian Journal of Psychology* 3: 132–136.

Durgin, F. H. and D. R. Proffitt (1996). Visual learning in the perception of texture: Simple and contingent effects of texture density. *Spatial Vision* 9: 423–474.

Dürsteler, M. R. and R. H. Wurtz (1988). Pursuit and optokinetic deficits following chemical lesions of cortical areas MT and MST. *Journal of Neurophysiology* 60: 940–965.

Durup, G. (1928). Le problème des impressions de mouvement consécutives d'ordre visuel. *L'Année Psychologiques* 29: 1–56.

Dvorak, V. (1870). Versuche über die Nachbilder von Reizveränderungen. *Sitzungsberichte der Wiener Akademie der Wissenschaften* 61: 257–262.

Edwards, M. and D. R. Badcock (1995). Global motion perception: No interaction between the first- and second-order pathways. *Vision Research* 35: 2589–2602.

Exner, S. (1887). Einige Beobachtungen über Bewegungsnachbilde. *Centralblatt für Physiologie* 1: 135–140.

Exner, S. (1888). Über optische Bewegungsempfindungen. *Biologisches Centralblatt* 8: 437–448.

Exner, S. (1894). Entwurf zu einer physiologischen Erklärung der psychischen Erscheinungen. Vienna, Deuticke.

Favreau, O. E. (1976). Motion aftereffects: Evidence for parallel processing in motion perception. *Vision Research* 16: 181–186.

Favreau, O. E., V. Emerson, et al. (1972). Motion perception: A color contingent aftereffect. *Science* 176: 78–79.

Felleman, D. and J. H. Kaas (1984). Receptive field properties of neurons in middle temporal (MT) visual area of owl monkeys. *Journal of Neurophysiology* 52: 488–513.

Fennema, C. L. and W. B. Thompson (1979). Velocity determination in scenes containing several moving objects. *Computer Graphics and Image Processing* 9: 301–315.

Ferrera, V. P., K. K. Rudolph, et al. (1994). Responses of neurons in the parietal and temporal visual pathways during a motion task. *Journal of Neuroscience* 14: 6171–6186.

Ferrera, V. P. and H. R. Wilson (1987). Direction specific masking and the analysis of motion in two dimensions. *Vision Research* 27: 1783–1796.

Ferrera, V. P. and H. R. Wilson (1990). Perceived direction of moving two-dimensional patterns. *Vision Research* 30: 273–287.

Fleet, D. J. and K. Langley (1994). Computational analysis of non-Fourier motion. *Vision Research* 34: 3057–3079.

Fox, R., R. Patterson, et al. (1982). Effect of depth position on the motion aftereffect. *Investigative Ophthalmology and Visual Science* 22 (Suppl.): 144.

Frisby, J. P. (1979). *Seeing. Illusion, Brain and Mind.* Oxford, U.K., Oxford University Press.

Gates, L. W. (1934). The after-effect of visually observed movement. *American Journal of Psychology* 46: 34–46.

Georgiades, M. S. and J. P. Harris (1996). Diverting attention reduces motion aftereffect velocity as well as motion aftereffect duration. *Perception* 25 (Suppl.): 124.

Giaschi, D., R. Douglas, et al. (1993). The time course of direction-selective adaptation im simple and complex cells in cat striate cortex. *Journal of Neurophysiology* 70: 2024–2034.

Gibson, J. J. (1937). Adaptation with negative aftereffect. *Psychological Review* 44: 222–244.

Gibson, J. J. and M. Radner (1937). Adaptation and contrast in the perception of tilted lines. 1. Quantitative studies. *Journal of Experimental Psychology* 20: 453–467.

Glickstein, M. (1988). The discovery of the visual cortex. *Scientific American* 259(3): 84–91.

Gogel, W. C. (1990). A theory of phenomenal geometry and its applications. *Perception and Psychophysics* 48: 105–123.

Goldstein, A. G. (1959). Judgments of visual velocity as a function of length of observation. *Journal of Experimental Psychology* 54: 457–461.

Göpfert, E. R., R. Müller, et al. (1983). Visuell evozierte Potentiale bei Musterbewegung. *Zeitschrift für EEG-EMG* 14: 47–51.

Gorea, A. and J. Lorenceau (1991). Directional performances with moving plaids: Component-related and plaid-related processing modes coexist. *Spatial Vision* 5: 231–252.

Granit, R. (1928). On inhibition in the aftereffect of seen movement. *British Journal of Psychology* 19: 147.

Green, M., M. Chilcoat, et al. (1983). Rapid motion aftereffect seen within uniform flickering test fields. *Nature* 304: 61–62.

Greenlee, M. W., M. A. Georgeson, et al. (1991). The time course of adaptation to spatial contrast. *Vision Research* 31: 223–236.

Greenlee, M. W. and F. Heitger (1988). The functional role of contrast adaptation. *Vision Research* 28: 791–797.

Grindley, G. C. and R. T. Wilkinson (1953). The aftereffect of seen movement on a plain field. *Quarterly Journal of Experimental Psychology* 5: 183–184.

Grunewald, A. and M. J. M. Lankheet (1996). Orthogonal motion after-effect illusion predicted by a model of cortical motion processing. *Nature* 384: 358–360.

Grüsser, O.-J. and U. Grüsser-Cornehls (1973). Neuronal mechanisms of visual motion perception and some psychophysical and behavioral correlations. In *Handbook of Sensory Physiology.* Ed. R. Jung. Berlin, Springer-Verlag, 7: 333–429.

Grüsser, O.-J. and U. Grüsser-Cornehls (1976). Neurophysiology of the anuran visual systems. In *Frog Neurobiology.* Ed. R. Llinas and W. Precht. Berlin, Springer-Verlag, 297–385.

Grüsser, O.-J. and T. Landis (1991). *Visual Agnosias and other Disturbances of Visual Pereception and Cognition.* Basingstoke-Hampshire, U.K., Macmillan.

Hammett, S. T., T. Ledgeway, et al. (1993). Transparent motion from feature- and luminance-based processes. *Vision Research* 33: 1119–1122.

Hammond, P., G. S. V. Mouat, et al. (1985). Motion after-effects in cat striate cortex elicited by moving gratings. *Experimental Brain Research* 60: 411–416.

Hammond, P., G. S. V. Mouat, et al. (1986). Motion aftereffects in cat striate cortex elicited by moving texture. *Vision Research* 26: 1055–1060.

Hammond, P. and G. S. V. Mouat (1988). Neural correlates of motion after-effects in cat striate cortical neurones: Interocular transfer. *Experimental Brain Research* 72: 21–28.

Hammond, P., G. S. V. Mouat, et al. (1988). Neural correlates of motion aftereffects in cat striate cortical neurones: monocular adaptation. *Experimental Brain Research* 72: 1–20.

Hammond, P. and C. J. D. Pomfrett (1989). Directional and orientational tuning of feline striate cortical neurons: Correlation with neuronal class. *Vision Research* 29: 653–662.

Hammond, P., C. J. D. Pomfrett, et al. (1989). Neural motion aftereffects in the cat's striate cortex: Orientation selectivity. *Vision Research* 29: 1671–1683.

Harris, J. (1994). The duration of the movement aftereffect as an index of psychiatric illness. *Perception* 23: 1146–1153.

Harris, J. P. and J. E. Calvert (1985). The tilt aftereffect: Changes with stimulus size and eccentricity. *Spatial Vision* 1: 113–129.

Harris, J. P. and J. E. Calvert (1989). Contrast, spatial frequency, and test duration effects on the tilt aftereffect: Implications for underlying mechanisms. *Vision Research* 29: 129–135.

Harris, J. P. and M. J. Potts (1980). Interocular transfer of the colour-contingent movement aftereffect: Doubts and difficulties. *Vision Research* 20: 277–280.

Harris, L. R., M. J. Morgan, et al. (1981). Moving and the motion after-effect. *Nature* 293: 139–141.

Harris, L. R. and A. T. Smith (1992). Motion defined exclusively by second-order characteristics does not evoke optokinetic nystagmus. *Visual Neuroscience* 9: 565–570.

Hartline, H. K. (1940). The receptive fields of optic nerve fibres. *American Journal of Physiology* 130: 690–699.

Hekler, A., Ed. (1912). *Greek and Roman Portraits*. London, Heinemann.

Heller, D. and M. Ziefle (1990). Zur Bedingungsanalyse von Bewegungsnacheffekten. *Schweizerische Zeitschrift für Psychologie* 49: 139–149.

Heller, D. and M. Ziefle (1991). *Zum interokularen Transfer beim Bewegungsnacheffekt. Experimentelle Beiträge zu einer Metrik des Psychischen: Festschrift für O. Heller*. Ed. H.-P. Krüger, Würzburg, Germany, 125–134.

Helmholtz, H. von (1867). Handbuch der physiologischen Optik. In *Algemeine Encycklopädie der Physik*, Vol. 9. Ed. G. Karsten. Leipzig, Voss.

Helmholtz, H. von (1925). *Treatise on Physiological Optics*, Vol. III. Trans. J. P. C. Southall. New York, Optical Society of America.

Helson, H. (1948). Adaptation-level as a basis for a quantitative theory of frames of reference. *Psychological Review* 55: 297–313.

Helson, H. (1964). *Adaptation-Level Theory: An Experimental and Systematic Approach to Behavior*. New York, Harper & Row.

Hepler, N. (1968). A motion contingent aftereffect. *Science* 162: 376–377.

Hershenson, M. (1989). Duration, time constant, and decay of the linear motion aftereffect as a function of inspection duration. *Perception and Psychophysics* 45: 251–257.

Hershenson, M. (1993). Linear and rotation aftereffects as a function of inspection duration. *Vision Research* 33: 1913–1919.

Hiris, E. and R. Blake (1992). Another perspective on the visual motion aftereffect. *Proceedings of the National Academy of Sciences U S A* 89: 9025–9028.

Hoffmann, M., M. Bach, et al. (1996). Is the adaptation of motion onset visually evoked potentials direction-specific? In *Proceedings of the 24th Gottingen Neurobiology Conference*, Vol 11. Eds. N. Elsner and H. Schnitzler. Stuttgart, Thieme Verlag.

Holland, H. C. (1965). *The Spiral After-Effect*. Oxford, U.K., Pergamon.

Holliday, I. E. and S. J. Anderson (1994). Different processes underlie the detection of second-order motion at low and high temporal frequencies. *Proceedings of the Royal Society of London. Series B. Biological Sciences* 257: 165–173.

Howard, I. P., and N. J. Wade (1996). Ptolemy's contributions to the geometry of binocular vision. *Perception* 25: 1189–1202.

Hubel, D. H. (1988). *Eye, Brain, and Vision*. New York, Scientific American Library.

Hubel, D. H., and T. N. Wiesel (1959). Receptive fields of single neurones in the cat's striate cortex. *Journal of Physiology (London)* 148: 574–579.

Hubel, D. H., and T. N. Wiesel (1962). Receptive fields, binocular interaction and functional architecture in cat visual cortex. *Journal of Physiology (London)* 160: 106–154.

Hubel, D. H., and T. N. Wiesel (1968). Receptive fields and functional architecture of monkey striate cortex. *Journal of Physiology (London)* 195: 215–243.

Hunter, W. S. (1914). The after-effect of visual motion. *Psychological Review* 21: 245–277.

Iordanova, M., L. Riscaldino, et al. (1996). Attentional modulation of motion aftereffect to first- and second-order motion. *Investigative Ophthalmology and Visual Science* 37 (Suppl.): 529.

Johansson, G. (1956). The velocity of the motion aftereffect. *Acta Psychologica (Amsterdam)* 12: 19–24.

Johnston, A., P. W. McOwan, et al. (1992). A computational model of the analysis of some first-order and second-order motion patterns by simple and complex cells. *Proceedings of the Royal Society of London. Series B. Biological Sciences* 250: 297–306.

Jones, P. D. and D. H. Holding (1976). Extremely long persistence of the McCollough effect. *Journal of Experimental Psychology: Human Perception and Performance* 1: 323–327.

Julesz, B. (1960). Binocular depth perception of computer-generated patterns. *Bell System Technical Journal* 30: 1125–1162.

Julesz, B. (1971). *Foundations of Cyclopean Perception*. Chicago, University of Chicago Press.

Kaiser, P. and Boynton, R. (1996) *Human Colour Vision*. Optical Society of America, Washington DC.

Keck, M. J., F. W. Montague, et al. (1980). Influence of the spatial periodicity of moving gratings on motion response. *Investigative Ophthalmology and Visual Science* 19: 1364–1370.

Keck, M. J., T. D. Palella, et al. (1976). Motion aftereffect as a function of the contrast of sinusoidal gratings. *Vision Research* 16: 187–191.

Keck, M. J. and B. Pentz (1977). Recovery from adaptation to moving gratings. *Perception* 6: 719–725.

Keck, M. J. and R. L. Price (1982). Interocular transfer of the motion aftereffect in strabismics. *Vision Research* 22: 55–60.

Kim, J. and H. R. Wilson (1993). Dependence of plaid motion coherence on component grating directions. *Vision Research* 33: 2479–2489.

Kinoshita, T. (1909). Zur Kentniss der negativen Bewegungsnachbilder. *Zeitschrift für Sinnesphysiologie* 43: 420–433.

Kleiner, A. (1878). Physiologisch-optische Beobachtungen. *Archiv für die gesammte Physiologie des Menschen und der Thiere* 18: 542–573.

Kohler, W., and H. Wallach (1944). Figural aftereffects: An investigation of visual processes. *Proceedings of the American Philosophical Society* 88: 269–357.

Krauskopf, J., and B. Farell (1990). Influence of colour on the perception of coherent motion. *Nature* 348: 328–331.

Kuba, M., and Z. Kubova (1992). Visual evoked potentials specific for motion onset. *Documenta Ophthalmologica* 80: 83–89.

Kubova, Z., M. Kuba, et al. (1995). Contrast dependence of motion-onset and pattern-reversal evoked potentials. *Vision Research* 35: 197–205.

Kuffler, S. W. (1952). Neurons in the retina: organization, inhibition and excitation problems. *Cold Spring Harbor Symposia on Quantitative Biology* 17: 281–292.

Kwas, M., M. von Grünau, et al. (1995). The effects of motion adaptation and disparity in motion integration. *Canadian Journal of Psychology* 49: 80–92.

Kwas, M., M. von Grünau, et al. (submitted). Multiple depth attributes merge in motion signal intergration.

Lagae, L., B. Gulyas, et al. (1989). Corticofugal feedback influences the responses of geniculate neurons to moving stimuli. *Brain Research* 496: 361–367.

Landy, M. S., B. A. Dosher, et al. (1991). Kinetic depth effect and optic flow—II. First- and second-order motion. *Vision Research* 31: 859–876.

Lankheet, M. J. M. and F. A. J. Verstraten (1995). Attentional modulation of adaptation to two-component transparent motion. *Vision Research* 35: 1401–1412.

Ledgeway, T. (1994). Adaptation to second-order motion results in a motion aftereffect for directionally-ambiguous test stimuli. *Vision Research* 34: 2879–2889.

Ledgeway, T. and A. T. Smith (1992). Adaptation to second-order motion: Direction-specific threshold elevation for direction identification. *Perception* 21 (Suppl.): 44.

Ledgeway, T. and A. T. Smith (1993). Adaptation to second-order motion results in a motion aftereffect for directionally-ambiguous test patterns. *Perception* 22 (Suppl.): 89.

Ledgeway, T. and A. T. Smith (1994a). The duration of the motion aftereffect following adaptation to first-order and second-order motion. *Perception* 23: 1211–1219.

Ledgeway, T. and A. T. Smith (1994b). Evidence for separate motion-detecting mechanisms for first- and second-order motion in human vision. *Vision Research* 34: 2727–2740.

Ledgeway, T. and A. T. Smith (1997). Changes in perceived speed following adaptation to first-order and second-order motion. *Vision Research* 37: 215–224.

Lehmkuhle, S. and R. Fox (1977). Stereoscopic motion aftereffects. Presented to Midwestern Psychological Association, Chicago, 1977.

Levinson, E. and R. Sekuler (1975). The independence of channels in human vision selective for direction of movement. *Journal of Physiology (London)* 250: 347–366.

Levinson, E. and R. Sekuler (1976). Adaptation alters perceived direction of motion. *Vision Research* 16: 779–781.

Lu, Z. and G. Sperling (1995a). Attention-generated apparent motion. *Nature* 377: 237–239.

Lu, Z.-L. and G. Sperling (1995b). The functional architecture of human visual motion perception. *Vision Research* 35: 2697–2722.

Lucretius (1975). *De Rerum Natura*: Trans. W. H. D. Rouse. Cambridge. Mass., Harvard University Press.

Mach, E. (1875). *Grundlinien der Lehre von den Bewegungsempfindungen*. Leipzig, Engelmann.

Mack, A., J. Goodwin, et al. (1987). Motion aftereffects associated with pursuit eye movements. *Vision Research* 27: 529–536.

Mack, A., J. Hill, et al. (1989). Motion aftereffects and retinal motion. *Perception* 18: 649–655.

Maffei, L., N. Berardi, et al. (1986). Interocular transfer of adaptation effect in neurons of area 17 and 18 of split chiasm cats. *Journal of Neurophysiology* 55: 966–976.

Maffei, L., A. Fiorentini, et al. (1973). Neural correlate of perceptual adaptation to gratings. *Science* 182: 1036–1038.

Maier, J., G. Dagnelie, et al. (1987). Principal components analysis for source localization of VEPs in man. *Vision Research* 27: 165–177.

Mareschal, I., H. Ashida, et al. (1997). Linking lower and higher stages of motion processing? *Vision Research* 37: 1755–1759.

Marlin, S. G., S. J. Hasan, et al. (1988). Direction-selective adaptation in simple and complex cells in cat striate cortex. *Journal of Neurophysiology* 59: 1314–1330.

Masland, R. (1969). Visual motion perception: Experimental modification. *Science* 165: 819–821.

Mather, G. (1980). The movement aftereffect and a distribution-shift model for coding the direction of visual movement. *Perception* 9: 379–392.

Mather, G. (1991). First-order and second-order visual processes in the perception of motion and tilt. *Vision Research* 31: 161–167.

Mather, G., P. Cavanagh, et al. (1985). A moving display which opposes short-range and long-range signals. *Perception* 14: 163–166.

Mather, G., and B. Moulden (1980). A simultaneous shift in apparent directions: Further evidence for a "distribution-shift" model of direction coding. *Quarterly Journal of Experimental Psychology* 32: 325–333.

Mather, G., and S. West (1993). Evidence for second-order motion detectors. *Vision Research* 33: 1109–1112.

Maunsell, J. H. R. and W. T. Newsome (1987). Visual processing in monkey extrastriate cortex. *Annual Review of Neuroscience* 10: 363–401.

Maunsell, J. H. R., and D. C. Van Essen (1983a). Functional properties of neurons in middle temporal area of the Macaque monkey. I. Selectivity for stimulus direction, speed and orientation. *Journal of Neurophysiology* 49: 1127–1147.

Maunsell, J. H. R., and D. C. Van Essen (1983b). Functional properties of neurons in middle temporal area of the Macaque monkey. II. Binocular interactions and sensitivity to binocular disparity. *Journal of Neurophysiology* 49: 1148–1167.

Mayhew, J. E. W. and S. M. Anstis (1972). Movement after-effects contingent on color, intensity and pattern. *Perception and Psychophysics* 12: 77–85.

McCarthy, J. E. (1993). Directional adaptation effects with contrast modulated stimuli. *Vision Research* 33: 2653–2662.

McCollough, C. (1965). Color adaptation of edge detectors in the human visual system. *Science* 149: 1115–1116.

Mitchell, D. E., J. Reardon, et al. (1975). Interocular transfer of the motion after-effect in normal and stereoblind observers. *Experimental Brain Research* 22: 163–173.

Mitchell, D. E. and C. Ware (1974). Interocular transfer of a visual aftereffect in normal and stereoblind humans. *Journal of Physiology (London)* 236: 707–723.

Mohn, G. and J. van Hof-van Duin (1983). On the relation of stereoacuity to interocular transfer of the motion and the tilt aftereffect. *Vision Research* 23: 1087–1096.

Mollon, J. (1974). After-effects and the brain. *New Scientist*, February, 479–482.

Morant, R. B. and J. R. Harris (1965). Two different aftereffects of exposure to visual tilts. *American Journal of Psychology* 78: 218–226.

Morgan, M. J., R. M. Ward, et al. (1976). The aftereffect of tracking eye movements. *Perception* 5: 309–317.

Moulden, B. (1980). After-effects and the integration of patterns of neural activity within a channel. *Philosophical Transactions of the Royal Society London. Series B. Biological Sciences* 290: 39–55.

Moulden, B. and G. Mather (1978). In defense of a ratio model for movement detection at threshold. *Quarterly Journal of Experimental Psychology* 30: 505–520.

Moulden, B. P. (1974). *Aftereffects, or a Treatise of the Consequences of Adaptation to Movement and Tilt*. PhD thesis, Reading, U.K., University of Reading.

Movshon, J. A., E. H. Adelson, et al. (1985). *The Analysis of Moving Visual Patterns. Pattern Recognition Mechanisms*. Ed. C. Chagass, R. Gattass, et al. Rome, Vatican Press. Available as Supplement to Experimental Brain Research vol 11. Springer, Berlin, pp. 117–151.

Movshon, J. A., B. E. I. Chambers, et al. (1972). Interocular transfer in normal humans and those who lack stereopsis. *Perception* 1: 483–491.

Mullen, K. T. and C. L. Baker (1985). A motion aftereffect from an isoluminant stimulus. *Vision Research* 25: 685–688.

Müller, J. (1838). *Handbuch der Physiologie des Menschen*, Vol. 2. Coblenz, Hölscher.

Murakami, I. and S. Shimojo (1995). Modulation of motion aftereffect by surround motion and its dependence on stimulus size and eccentricity. *Vision Research* 35: 1835–1844.

Newsome, W. T., K. H. Britten, et al. (1989a). Neuronal correlates of a perceptual decision. *Nature* 341: 52–54.

Newsome, W. T., K. H. Britten, et al. (1989b). Neuronal mechanism of motion perception. *Cold Spring Harbor Symposia on Quantitative Biology* 55: 697–706.

Newsome, W. T. and E. B. Paré (1988). A selective impairment of motion perception following lesions of the middle temporal visual area (MT). *Journal of Neuroscience* 8: 2201–2211.

Newsome, W. T., M. N. Shadlen, et al. (1995). Visual motion: Linking neuronal activity to psychophysical performance. In *The Cognitive Neurosciences*. Ed. M. S. Gazzaniga. Cambridge, Mass., MIT Press, 401–414.

Newsome, W. T., R. H. Wurtz, et al. (1988). Relation of cortical areas MT and MST to pursuit eye movements: II. Differentiation of retinal from extraretinal inputs. *Journal of Neurophysiology* 5: 825–840.

Newton, I. (1691/1961). Letter to Locke. In *The Correspondence of Isaac Newton*, Vol. 3. Ed. H. W. Turnbull. Cambridge, U.K., Royal Society, Cambridge University Press, 152–154.

Niedeggen, M., S. Müller, et al. (1992). Motion aftereffects in radial and circular patterns: Visual evoked potentials. *Journal of Psychophysiology* 7: 164.

Niedeggen, M. and E. R. Wist (1995). Relationship between N2–on and off amplitudes in evoked potentials and motion after-effects after adaptation to rotating spiral patterns. Unpublished manuscript.

Nilsson, T. H., C. F. Richmond, et al. (1975). Flicker adaptation shows evidence of many visual channels selectively sensitive to temporal frequency. *Vision Research* 15: 621–624.

Nishida, S. (1993). Spatiotemporal properties of motion perception for random-check contrast modulations. *Vision Research* 33: 633–645.

Nishida, S., H. Ashida, et al. (1994). Complete interocular transfer of motion aftereffect with flickering test. *Vision Research* 34: 2707–2716.

Nishida, S. and H. Ashida (1997). The role of relative motion in two types of motion aftereffect. *Vision: The Journal of the Vision Society of Japan* 9: 100.

Nishida, S., H. Ashida, et al. (1997a). Contrast dependencies of two types of motion aftereffect. *Vision Research* 37: 553–563.

Nishida, S., M. Edwards, et al. (1997b). Simultaneous motion contrast across space: Involvement of second-order motion? *Vision Research* 37: 199–214.

Nishida, S., T. Ledgeway, et al. (1997c). Dual multiple-scale processing for motion in the human visual system. *Vision Research* 37: 2685–2698.

Nishida, S. and T. Sato (1992). Positive motion after-effect induced by bandpass-filtered random-dot kinematograms. *Vision Research* 32: 1635–1646.

Nishida, S. and T. Sato (1995). Motion aftereffect with flickering test patterns reveals higher stages of motion processing. *Vision Research* 35: 477–490.

O'Craven, K. M., B. R. Rosen, et al. (1997). Voluntary attention modulates fMRI actvity in human MT-MST. *Neuron* 18: 591–598.

Ohzawa, I., G. Sclar, et al. (1985). Contrast gain control in the cat's visual system. *Journal of Neurophysiology* 54: 651–667.

Ono, H. and T. Comerford (1977). Stereoscopic depth constancy. In *Stability and Constancy in Visual Perception: Mechanisms and Processes*. Ed. W. Epstein. New York, Wiley.: 91–128.

Oppel, J. J. (1856). Neue Beobachtungen und Versuche über eine eigentümliche, noch wenig bekannte Reaktionsthätigkeit des menschlichen Auges. *Annalen der Physik und Chemie* 99: 540–561.

Osgood, C. E. (1953). *Method and Theory in Experimental Psychology*. New York: Oxford University Press.

Ossenblok, P. and H. Spekreijse (1991). The extrastriate generators of the EP to checkerboard onset. A source localization approach. *Electroencephalography and Clinical Neurophysiology* 80: 181–193.

Over, R., J. Broerse, et al. (1973). Spatial determinants of the aftereffect of seen motion. *Vision Research* 13: 1681–1690.

Pantle, A. (1971). Flicker adaptation—I. Effect on visual sensitivity to temporal fluctuations of light intensity. *Vision Research* 11: 943–952.

Pantle, A. (1974). Motion aftereffect magnitude as a measure of the spatio-temporal response properties of direction-selective analyzers. *Vision Research* 14: 1229–1236.

Pantle, A. (1978). Temporal frequency response characteristics of motion channels measured with three different psychophysical techniques. *Perception and Psychophysics* 24: 285–294.

Pantle, A., S. Lehmkuhle, et al. (1978). On the capacity of directionally selective mechanisms to encode different dimensions of moving stimuli. *Perception* 7: 261–267.

Pantle, A., A. Pinkus, et al. (1991). The puzzling influence of high spatial frequencies on motion perception. *Investigative Ophthalmology and Visual Science* 32 (Suppl.): 892.

Pantle, A. J. and R. W. Sekuler (1969). Contrast response of human visual mechanisms sensitive to orientation and direction of motion. *Vision Research* 9: 397–406.

Pantle, A. and K. Turano (1992). Visual resolution of motion ambiguity with periodic luminance- and contrast-domain stimuli. *Vision Research* 32: 2093–2106.

Papert, S. (1964). Stereoscopic synthesis as a technique for localizing visual mechanisms. *MIT Quarterly Progress Report* 73: 239–243.

Parker, D. M. (1972). Contrast and size variables and the tilt aftereffect. *Quarterly Journal of Experimental Psychology* 24: 1–7.

Patterson, R. and S. Becker (1996). Direction-selective adaptation and simultaneous contrast induced by stereoscopic (cyclopean) motion. *Vision Research* 36: 1773–1781.

Patterson, R., C. Bowd, et al. (1994). Properties of stereoscopic (cyclopean) motion aftereffects. *Vision Research* 34: 1139–1147.

Patterson, R., C. Bowd, et al. (1996). Disparity tuning of the stereoscopic (cyclopean) motion aftereffect. *Vision Research* 36: 975–983.

Patterson, R., P. Hart, et al. (1991). The cyclopean Ternus display and the perception of element versus group movement. *Vision Research* 31: 2085–2092.

Patterson, R. and W. L. Martin (1992). Human stereopsis. *Human Factors* 34: 669–692.

Patterson, R., C. Ricker, et al. (1992). Properties of cyclopean motion perception. *Vision Research* 32: 149–156.

Patzwahl, D. R., J. M. Zanker, et al. (1994). Cortical potentials reflecting motion processing in humans. *Visual Neuroscience* 11: 1135–1147.

Pelah, A. and H. B. Barlow (1996). Visual illusion from running. *Nature* 381: 283.

Petersen, S. E., J. F. Baker, et al. (1985). Direction-specific adaptation in area MT of the owl monkey. *Brain Research* 346: 146–150.

Petersik, J. T. (1984). A three-dimensional motion aftereffect produced by prolonged adaptation to a rotation simulation. *Perception* 13: 489–497.

Petersik, J. T. (1995). A comparison of varieties of "second-order" motion. *Vision Research* 35: 507–517.

Phinney, R., C. Bowd, et al. (1997). Direction-selective coding of stereoscopic (cyclopean) motion. *Vision Research* 37: 865–869.

Plateau, J. (1849). Quatrième note sur de nouvelles applications curieuses de la persistance des impressions de la rétine. *Bulletin de l'Académie Royale des Sciences, des Lettres et des Beaux-Arts de Belgique* 16: 254–260.

Plateau, J. (1850). Vierte Notiz über neue, sonderbare Anwendungen des Verweilens der Eindrücke auf die Netzhaut. *Annalen der Physik und Chemie* 80: 287–292.

Probst, T., H. Plendl, et al. (1993). Identification of the visual motion area (area V5) in the human brain by dipole analysis. *Experimental Brain Research* 93: 345–351.

Purkinje, J. (1820). Beiträge zur näheren Kenntniss des Schwindels aus heautognostischen Daten. *Medicinische Jahrbücher des kaiserlich-königlichen öesterreichischen Staates* 6: 79–125.

Purkinje, J. E. (1825). *Beobachtungen und Versuche zur Physiologie der Sinne. Neue Beiträge zur Kenntniss des Sehens in subjektiver Hinsicht.* Berlin, Reimer.

Ramachandran, V. S. and R. L. Gregory (1978). Does colour provide an input to human motion perception? *Nature* 275: 55–56.

Ramón y Cajal, S. (1892/1972). *The Structure of the Retina.* Trans. S. A. Thorpe and M. Glickstein. Springfield, Ill., Thomas.

Rapoport, J. (1964). Adaptation in the perception of rotary motion. *Journal of Experimental Psychology* 67: 263–267.

Raymond, J. E. (1993a). Complete interocular transfer of motion adaptation effects on motion coherence thresholds. *Vision Research* 33: 1865–1870.

Raymond, J. E. (1993b). Movement direction analyzers: Independence and bandwidth. *Vision Research* 33: 767–775.

Raymond, J. E. (1994). The effects of displacement size and frame duration on the motion incoherence aftereffect. *Perception* 23: 1203–1209.

Raymond, J. E. and O. J. Braddick (1996). Responses to opposed directions of motion: Continuum or independent mechanisms? *Vision Research* 36: 1931–1937.

Raymond, J. E. and S. M. Darcangelo (1990). The effect of local luminance contrast on induced motion. *Vision Research* 30: 751–756.

Raymond, J. E., and H. L. O'Donnell (1996). Motion capture vs. contrast by prior events. *Investigative Ophthalmology and Visual Science* 37 (Suppl.): 744.

Raymond, J. E., H. L. O'Donnell, et al. (1997). Attention modulates global motion sensitivity. *Investigative Ophthalmology and Visual Science* 38 (Suppl.): 369.

Raymond , J. E. and M. Isaak (1998). Successive episodes produce direction contrast effects in motion perception. *Vision Research* 38: 579–590.

Regan, D. (1989). *Human Brain Electrophysiology: Evoked Potentials and Evoked Magnetic Fields in Science and Medicine.* Amsterdam, Elsevier.

Reichardt, W. (1957). Autokorrelationsauswertung als Funktionsprinzip des Zentralnervensystems. *Zeitschrift für Naturforschung* 12: 447–457.

Reinhardt-Rutland, A. H. (1981). Peripheral movement, induced movement, and aftereffects of induced movement. *Perception* 10: 173–182.

Reinhardt-Rutland, A. H. (1983a). Aftereffect of induced rotation: Number of radial lines in inducing stimulus. *Perceptual and Motor Skills* 57: 39–42.

Reinhardt-Rutland, A. H. (1983b). Aftereffect of induced movement: Separation of inducing and static areas, and monocular component. *Perceptual and Motor Skills* 56: 239–242.

Reinhardt-Rutland, A. H. (1984). Negative aftereffect arising from prolonged viewing of induced movement-in-depth. *Perceptual and Motor Skills* 58: 359–362.

Reinhardt-Rutland, A. H. (1987a). Aftereffect of visual movement—the role of relative movement: a review. *Current Psychological Research and Reviews* 6: 275–288.

Reinhardt-Rutland, A. H. (1987b). Motion aftereffect can be elicited from large spiral. *Perceptual and Motor Skills* 64: 994.

Riggs, L. A. and R. H. Day (1980). Visual aftereffects derived from inspection of orthogonally moving patterns. *Science* 208: 416–418.

Ross, W. D., Ed. (1931). *The Works of Aristotle.* Vol. 3, *Parva Naturalia De Somniis.* Transl. J. I. Beare. Oxford, U.K., Clarendon Press.

Roy, J. P., H. Komatsu, et al. (1992). Disparity sensitivity of neurons in monkey extrastriate area MST. *Journal of Neuroscience* 12: 2478–2492.

Roy, J. P. and R. H. Wurtz (1990). The role of disparity-sensitive cortical neurons in signal-ling the direction of self-motion. *Nature* 348: 160–162.

Sabra, A. I. (1989). *The Optics of Ibn Al-Haytham*. Books I–III. *On Direct Vision*. London, Warburg Institute.

Sachtler, W., and Q. Zaidi (1993). Effect of spatial configuration on motion aftereffects. *Journal of the Optical Society of America* A10: 1433–1449.

Salzman, C., Britten, K., et al. (1990). Cortical microstimulation influences perceptional judge-ments of motion direction. *Nature* 346: 174–177.

Schiller, P., H., B. L. Finlay, et al. (1976). Quantitative studies of single-cell properties in monkey striate cortex. II Orientation specificity and ocular dominance. *Journal of Neurophysiology* 39: 1320–1333.

Sclar, G., J. H. R. Maunsell, et al. (1990). Coding of image contrast in central visual pathways of the macaque monkey. *Vision Research* 30: 1–10.

Scott, T. R., A. D. Lavender, et al. (1966). Directional asymmetry of motion aftereffect. *Journal of Experimental Psychology* 71: 806–815.

Scott, T. R. and J. H. Noland (1965). Some stimulus dimensions of rotating spirals. *Psycho-logical Review* 72: 344–357.

Seidman, S. H., R. J. Leigh, et al. (1992). Eye movements during motion aftereffect. *Vision Research* 32: 67–171.

Sekuler, R. W. (1975). Visual motion perception. In *Handbook of Perception*. Vol. 5, *Seeing*. Ed. E. C. Carterette and M. P. Friedman. New York, Academic Press, 387–430.

Sekuler, R. and A. Pantle (1967). A model for after-effects of seen movement. *Vision Research* 7: 427–439.

Sekuler, R. W. and L. Ganz (1963). Aftereffect of seen motion with a stabilized retinal image. *Science* 139: 419–420.

Sherrington, C. S. (1906). *The Integrative Action of the Nervous System*. New Haven, Yale Uni-versity Press.

Shulman, G. L. (1991). Attentional modulation of mechanisms that analyze rotation in depth. *Journal of Experimental Psychology: Human Perception and Performance* 17: 726–737.

Shulman, G. L. (1993). Attentional effects on adaptation of rotary motion in the plane. *Perception* 22: 947–961.

Skowbo, D., T. A. Gentry, et al. (1974). The McCollough effect: Influence of several kinds of visual stimulation on decay rate. *Perception and Psychophysics* 16: 47–49.

Smith, A. M. (1996). *Ptolemy's Theory of Visual Perception: An English Translation of the Optics with Introduction and Commentary*. Philadelphia, American Philosophical Society.

Smith, A. T. (1983). Interocular transfer of colour-contingent threshold elevation. *Vision Research* 23: 729–734.

Smith, A. T. (1985). Velocity coding: Evidence from perceived velocity shifts. *Vision Research* 25: 1969–1976.

Smith, A. T. (1992). Coherence of plaids comprising components of disparate spatial fre-quencies. *Vision Research* 32: 393–397.

Smith, A. T. (1994a). Correspondence-based and energy-based detection of second-order motion in human vision. *Journal of the Optical Society of America* A 11: 1940–1948.

Smith, A. T. (1994b). The detection of second-order motion. In *Visual Detection of Motion*. Ed. A. T. Smith and R. J. Snowden. London, Academic Press, 145–176.

Smith, A. T. and P. Hammond (1985). The pattern specificity of velocity aftereffects. *Experi-mental Brain Research* 60: 71–78.

Smith, A. T., R. F. Hess, et al. (1994). Direction identification thresholds for second-order motion in central and peripheral vision. *Journal of the Optical Society of America* A 11: 506–514.

Smith, A. T. and T. Ledgeway (1994). Dissociation of second-order motion and "long-range" motion by adaptation. *Investigative Ophthalmology and Visual Science* 35 (Suppl.): 1268.

Smith, A. T. and T. Ledgeway (1997). Separate detection of moving luminance and contrast modulations: Fact or artifact. *Vision Research* 37: 45–62.

Smith, A. T., M. Musselwhite, et al. (1984). The influence of background motion on the motion aftereffect. *Vision Research* 24: 1075–1082.

Smith, R. A. (1970). Adaptation of visual contrast sensitivity to specific temporal frequencies. *Vision Research* 10: 275–279.

Smith, R. A. (1971). Studies of temporal frequency adaptation in visual contrast sensitivity. *Journal of Physiology (London)* 216: 531–552.

Smith, R. A. (1976). The motion/disparity aftereffect: A preliminary study. *Vision Research* 16: 1507–1509.

Spekreijse, H., G. Dagnelie, et al. (1985). Flicker and movement constituents of the pattern reversal response. *Vision Research* 25: 1297–1304.

Spigel, I. M. (1960). The effects of differential post-exposure illumination on the decay of the movement after-effect. *Journal of Psychology* 50: 209–210.

Spigel, I. M. (1962a). Contour absence as a critical factor in the inhibition of the decay of a movement aftereffect. *Journal of Psychology* 54: 221–228.

Spigel, I. M. (1962b). Relation of MAE duration to interpolated darkness intervals. *Life Sciences* 1: 239–242.

Spigel, I. M. (1964). The use of decay inhibition in an examination of central mediation in movement aftereffects. *Journal of General Psychology* 70: 241–247.

Spigel, I. M. (1965). Contour absence as a critical factor in the inhibition of the decay of a movement aftereffect. In *Readings in the Study of Visually Perceived Movement*. Ed. I. M. Spigel. New York, Harper & Row, 212–221.

Spitz, H. H. (1958). Neural satiation in the spiral aftereffect and similar movement aftereffects. *Perceptual and Motor Skills* 8: 207–213.

Stadler, M. and C. Kano (1970). Richtungsspezifische Bewegungsdetektion in der menschlichen Gesichtswahrnehmung. *Psychologische Beiträge* 12: 367–378.

Steinbach, M. and S. M. Anstis (1976). Paper presented to the Annual Conference of the Association for Research in Vision and Ophthalmology Sarasota, Florida, 1976.

Steiner, V., R. Blake, et al. (1994). Interocular transfer of expansion, rotation, and translation motion aftereffects. *Perception* 23: 1197–1202.

Stirling, W. (1902). *Some Apostles of Physiology*. London: Waterlow.

Stork, D. G., J. A. Crowell, et al. (1985). Cyclopean motion aftereffect in the presence of monocular motion. *Investigative Ophthalmology and Visual Science* 26 (Suppl.): 55.

Stromeyer, C. F. (1978). Form-color aftereffects in human vision. In *Handbook of Sensory Physiology*, Vol 8. Ed. R. Jung, H. W. Leibowitz, et al. Heidelberg, Springer-Verlag.

Stromeyer, C. F., S. Klein, et al. (1982). Low spatial-frequency channels in human vision: adaptation and masking. *Vision Research* 22: 225–234.

Stumpf, P. (1911). Über die Abhängigkeit der visuellen Bewegungsempfindung und ihres negativen Nachbildes von den Reizvorgängen auf der Netzhaut (Vorläufige Mitteilung). *Zeitschrift für Psychologie* 59: 321–330.

Sutherland, N. S. (1961). Figural aftereffects and apparent size. *Quarterly Journal of Experimental Psychology* 13: 222–228.

Swanston, M. T. (1994). Frames of reference and motion aftereffects. *Perception* 24: 1257–1264.

Swanston, M. T., N. J. Wade, et al. (1987). The representation of uniform motion in vision. *Perception* 16: 143–159.

Swanston, M. T., N. J. Wade, et al. (1990). The binocular representation of uniform motion. *Perception* 19: 29–34.

Swanston , M. T. and N. J. Wade (1992). Motion over the retina and the motion aftereffect. *Perception* 21: 569–582.

Swanston, M. T., and Wade, N. J. (1994). A peculiar optical phænomenon. *Perception* 23: 1107–1110.

Symons, L. A., P. M. Pearson, et al. (1996). The aftereffect to relative motion does not show interocular transfer. *Perception* 25: 651–660.

Taylor, M. M. (1963). Tracking the decay of the after-effect of seen rotary movement. *Perceptual and Motor Skills* 16: 119–129.

Thalman, W. A. (1921). The aftereffect of seen movement when the whole visual field is filled by a moving stimulus. *American Journal of Psychology* 32: 429–440.

Thompson, K. G., Y. Zhou, et al. (1994). Direction-sensitive X and Y cells within the A laminae of the cat's LGNd. *Visual Neuroscience* 11: 927–938.

Thompson, P. (1976). *Velocity Aftereffects and the Perception of Movement*, Ph.D thesis, Cambridge, U.K., University of Cambridge Press.

Thompson, P. (1981). Velocity aftereffects: The effects of adaptation to moving stimuli on the perception of subsequently seen moving stimuli. *Vision Research* 21: 337–380.

Thompson, P. (1993). Motion psychophysics. In *Visual Motion and Its Role in the Stabilization of Gaze*. Ed. J. Wallman and F. A. Miles. Amsterdam, Elsevier, pp. 29–52.

Thompson, P. and J. Wright (1994). The role of intervening patterns in the storage of the movement aftereffect. *Perception* 23: 1233–1240.

Thompson, S. P. (1877). Some new optical illusions. *Report of the British Association for the Advancement of Science. Transactions of the Sections* 32.

Thompson, S. P. (1880). Optical illusions of motion. *Brain* 3: 289–298.

Timney, B., L. M. Wilcox, et al. (1989). On the evidence for a "pure" binocular process in human vision. *Spatial Vision* 4: 1–15.

Tipper, S. and M. Cranston (1985). Selective attention and priming: Inhibitory and facilitatory effects of ignored primes. *Quarterly Journal of Experimental Psychology* 37: 591–611.

Todorovic, D. (1996). A gem from the past: Pleikart Stumpf's (1911) anticipation of the aperture problem, Reichardt detectors, and perceived motion loss at equiluminance. *Perception* 25: 1235–1242.

Tolhurst, D. J., and G. Hart (1972). A psychophysical investigation of the effects of controlled eye movements on the movement detectors of the human visual system. *Vision Research* 12: 1441–1446.

Tolhurst, D. J., and L. P. Barfield (1978). Interactions between spatial frequency channels. *Vision Research* 18: 951–958.

Tolhurst, D. J., and P. G. Thompson (1975). Orientation illusions and aftereffects: Inhibition between channels. *Vision Research* 15: 969–972.

Tootell, R. B. H., J. B. Reppas, et al. (1995). Visual motion aftereffect in human cortical area MT revealed by functional magnetic resonance imaging. *Nature* 375: 139–141.

Treisman, A. (1986). Features and objects in visual processing. *Scientific American* 255(5): 114–126.

Treue, S. and J. H. R. Maunsell (1996). Attentional modulation of visual motion processing in cortical areas MT and MST. *Nature* 382: 539–541.

Trotter, Y., S. Celebrini, et al. (1992). Modulation of neural stereoscopic processing in primate area V1 by the viewing distance. *Science* 257: 1279–1281.

Trueswell, J. C. and M. M. Hayhoe (1993). Surface segmentation mechanisms and motion perception. *Vision Research* 33: 313–328.

Tse, P., P. Cavanagh, et al. (in press). The importance of parsing in high-level motion processing. In *High Level Motion Processing*. Ed. T. Watanabe. Cambridge, Mass., MIT Press.

Turano, K. (1991). Evidence for a common motion mechanism of luminance-modulated and contrast-modulated patterns: Selective adaptation. *Perception* 20: 455–466.

Turano, K. and A. Pantle (1985). Apparent motion of an amplitude-modulated grating. *Investigative Ophthalmology and Visual Science* 26 (Suppl.): 188.

Turano, K. and A. Pantle (1989). On the mechanism that encodes the movement of contrast variations: Velocity discrimination. *Vision Research* 29: 207–221.

Ullman, S. and G. Schechtman (1982). Adaptation and gain normalisation. *Proceedings of the Royal Society of London. Series B. Biological Sciences* 216: 299–313.

Vaina, L. M., M. Le May et al. (1990). Intact "biological motion" and "structure from motion" perception in a patient with impaired motion mechanism: A case study. *Visual Neuroscience* 5: 353–369.

Vaina, L. M., M. Le May, et al. (1993). Deficits on non-Fourier motion perception in a patient with normal performance on short-range motion tasks. *Neuroscience Abstracts* 19: 1284.

Vallortigara, G. and P. Bressan (1991). Occlusion and the perception of coherent motion. *Vision Research* 31: 1967–1978.

Van de Grind, W. A., O.-J. Grüsser, et al. (1972). Temporal transfer properties of the afferent visual system. In *Handbook of Sensory Physiology*, Vol. 8/3A. Ed. R. Jung. Heidelberg, Springer-Verlag, 451–573.

Van Doorn, A. J. and J. J. Koenderink (1982). Temporal properties of the visual detectability of moving spatial white noise. *Experimental Brain Research* 45: 179–188.

Van Doorn, A. J., J. J. Koenderink, et al. (1985). Perception of movement and correlation in stroboscopically presented noise patterns. *Perception* 14: 209–224.

Van Kruysbergen, A. W. H. and C. M. M. de Weert (1993). Apparent motion perception: The contribution of the binocular and monnocular systems. An improved test based on motion aftereffects. *Perception* 22: 771–784.

Van Kruysbergen, A. W. H. and C. M. M. de Weert (1994). Aftereffects of apparent motion: The existence of an AND-type binocular system in human vision. *Perception* 23 1069–1083.

Van Wezel, R. J. A., M. J. M. Lankheet, et al. (1996). Responses of complex cells in area 17 of the cat to bi-vectorial transparent motion. *Vision Research* 36: 2805–2813.

Van Wezel, R. J. A., F. A. J. Verstraten, et al. (1994b). Spatial integration in coherent motion detection and in the movement aftereffect. *Perception* 23: 1189–1196.

Vautin, R. G., and M. A. Berkley (1977). Responses of single cells in cat visual cortex to prolonged stimulus movement: Neural correlates of visual aftereffects. *Journal of Neurophysiology* 40: 1051–1065.

Verriest, G. (1990). Life, eye disease and work of Joseph Plateau. *Documenta Ophthalmologica* 74: 9–20.

Verstraten, F. A. J. (1994). *Multi-Vectorial Motion and Its Aftereffect(s)*. Utrecht, Netherlands, Helmholtz Instituut, Universiteit Utrecht.

Verstraten, F. A. J. (1996). On the ancient history of the direction of the motion aftereffect. *Perception* 25: 1177–1187.

Verstraten, F. A. J., R. E. Fredericksen, et al. (1994a). The movement aftereffect of bi-vectorial transparent motion. *Vision Research* 34: 349–358.

Verstraten, F. A. J., R. E. Fredericksen, et al. (1994b). Recovery from motion adaptation is delayed by successively presented orthogonal motion. *Vision Research* 34: 1149–1155.

Verstraten, F. A. J., R. E. Fredericksen, et al. (1996). Recovery from adaptation for dynamic and static motion aftereffects: Evidence for two mechanisms. *Vision Research* 36: 421–424.

Verstraten, F. A. J., R. J. A. van Wezel, et al. (1994c). Movement aftereffects of transparent motion: The art of "test" noise. *Investigative Ophthalmology and Visual Science* 35 (Suppl.): 1838.

Verstraten, F. A. J., R. Verlinde, et al. (1994d). A transparent motion aftereffect contingent on binocular disparity. *Perception* 23: 1181–1188.

Von der Heydt, R., P. Hänny, et al. (1978). Movement aftereffects in the visual cortex. *Archives Italienne de Biologie* 116: 248–254.

Von der Malsburg, C. and W. Schneider (1986). A neural cocktail party processor. *Biological Cybernetics* 54: 29–40.

Von Grünau, M. W. (1986). A motion aftereffect for long-range stroboscopic apparent motion. *Perception and Psychophysics* 40: 31–38.

Von Grünau, M. and S. Dubé (1992). Comparing local and remote aftereffects. *Spatial Vision* 6: 303–314.

Von Szily, A. (1905). Bewegungsnachbild und Bewegungskontrast. *Zeitschrift für Psychologie und Physiologie der Sinnesorgane* 38: 81–154.

Von Szily, A. (1907). Zum Studium des Bewegungsnachbildes. *Zeitschrift für Sinnesphysiologie* 42: 109–114.

Wade, N. J. (1976). On the interocular transfer of the movement aftereffect in individuals with and without normal binocular vision. *Perception* 5: 113–118.

Wade, N. J. (1977). Distortions and disappearances of geometrical patterns. *Perception* 6: 407–433.

Wade, N. J. (1994). A selective history of the study of visual motion aftereffects. *Perception* 23: 1111–1134.

Wade, N. J. (1996). Descriptions of visual phenomena from Aristotle to Wheatstone. *Perception* 25: 1137–1175.

Wade, N. J. (1998). *A Natural History of Vision.* Cambridge, Mass., MIT Press.

Wade, N. J., L. Spillman, et al. (1996). Visual motion aftereffects: Critical adaptation conditions. *Vision Research* 36: 2167–2175.

Wade, N. J. and M. T. Swanston (1987). The representation of non-uniform motion: Induced movement. *Perception* 16: 555–571.

Wade, N. J. and M. T. Swanston (1991). *Visual Perception: An Introduction.* London, Routledge.

Wade, N. J., M. T. Swanston, et al. (1993). On interocular transfer of motion aftereffects. *Perception* 22: 1365–1380.

Wainwright, M. and P. Cavanagh (1997). Suppression of motion after-effects by overlaid lines. *Investigative Ophthalmology and Visual Science* 38 (Suppl.): 374.

Wallach, H. and C. Zuckerman (1963). The constancy of stereoscopic depth. *American Journal of Psychology* 76: 404–412.

Walls, G. L. (1953). Interocular transfer of after-images. *American Journal of Optometry* 30: 57–64.

Watanabe, T. (1995). Motion aftereffects show that attention may selectively activate local motion units located in V1. *Investigative Ophthalmology and Visual Science* 36 (Suppl.): 857.

Watanabe, T. and S. Miyauchi (in press). Effects of attention and form on visual motion processing: Psychophysical and brain imaging studies. In *High Level Motion Processing.* Ed. T. Watanabe. Cambridge, Mass., MIT Press.

Weisstein, N., W. Maguire, et al. (1977). A phantom-motion aftereffect. *Science* 198: 955–958.

Wenderoth, P., D. Alais, et al. (1994). The role of blobs in determining the perception of drifting plaids and their motion aftereffects. *Perception* 23: 1163–1169.

Wenderoth, P., R. Bray, et al. (1988). Psychophysical evidence for an extrastriate contribution to a pattern-selective motion aftereffect. *Perception* 17: 81–91.

Wenderoth, P. and S. Johnstone (1987). Possible neural substrates for orientation analysis and perception. *Perception* 16: 693–709.

208   References

Werkhoven, P., G. Sperling, et al. (1993). The dimensionality of texture-defined motion: A single channel theory. *Vision Research* 33: 463–485.

Wertheimer, M. (1912). Experimentelle Studien über das Sehen von Bewegung. *Zeitschrift für Psychologie* 61: 161–265.

Wertheimer, M. (1912/1961). Experimentelle Studien über das Sehen von Bewegung. In *Classics in Psychology*. Ed. T. Shipley. New York, Philosophical Library, 1032–1089.

Wiesenfelder, H. and R. Blake (1992). Binocular rivalry suppression disrupts recovery from motion adaptation. *Visual Neuroscience* 9: 143–148.

Wilcox, L. M., B. Timney, et al. (1990). Measurement of visual aftereffects and inferences about binocular mechanisms on human vision. *Perception* 19: 43–55.

Wilkes, A. L. and N. J. Wade (1997). Bain on neural networks. *Brain and Cognition* 33: 295–305.

Wilson, H. R. (1994) Models of two-dimensional motion perception. In *Visual Detector of Motion*. Eds. A. T. Smith and R. J. Snowden. London, Academic Press.

Wilson, H. R., V. P. Ferrera, et al. (1992). A psychophysically motivated model for two-dimensional motion perception. *Visual Neuroscience* 9: 79–97.

Wilson, H. R. and R. Humanski (1993). Spatial frequency adaptation and contrast gain control. *Vision Research* 33: 1133–1149.

Wilson, H. R., and J. Kim (1994). A model for motions coherence and transparency. *Visual Neuroscience* 11: 1205–1220.

Wist, E. R., J. D. Gross, et al. (1994). Motion aftereffects with random-dot checkerboard kinematograms: Relation between psychophysical and VEP measures. *Perception* 23: 1155–1162.

Wohlgemuth, A. (1911). On the after-effect of seen movement. *British Journal of Psychology* (Supp.) 1: 1–117.

Wolfe, J. and R. Held (1983). Shared characteristics of stereopsis and the purely binocular process. *Vision Research* 23: 217.

Wolfe, J. M. (1984). Short test flashes produce large tilt aftereffects. *Vision Research* 24: 1959–1964.

Wolfe, J. M. and R. Held (1981). A purely binocular mechanism in human vision. *Vision Research* 21: 1755–1759.

Wolfe, J. M. and R. Held (1982). Binocular adaptation that cannot be measured monocularly. *Perception* 11: 287–295.

Wolfe, J. M. and K. M. O'Connell (1986). Fatigue and structural change: Two consequences of visual pattern adaptation. *Investigative Ophthalmology and Visual Science* 4: 538–543.

Wood, W., Ed. (1885). *Portraits of the One Hundred Greatest Men in History*. London, Sampson Low, Marston, Searle, & Rivington.

Wright, M. J. and A. Johnston (1985). Invariant tuning of motion aftereffect. *Vision Research* 25: 1947–1955.

Wundt, W. (1874). *Grundzüge der physiologischen Psychologie*. Leipzig, Engelmann.

Wurtz, R. H., B. J. Richmond, et al. (1984). Modulation of cortical visual processing by attention, perception, and movement. In *Dynamic Aspects of Neocortical Functions*. Ed. G. M. Edelman, W. E. Gall, et al. New York, Wiley, 195–217.

Yo, C. and H. R. Wilson (1992). Perceived direction of moving two-dimensional patterns depends on duration, contrast and eccentricity. *Vision Research* 32: 135–147.

Zanker, J. M. (1993). Theta motion: A paradoxical stimulus to explore higher order motion extraction. *Vision Research* 33: 553–569.

Zeevi, Y. Y. and G. A. Geri (1985). A purely central movement aftereffect induced by binocular viewing of dynamic visual noise. *Perception and Psychophysics* 38: 433.

Zeki, S. M. (1974). Functional organization of a visual area in the posterior bank of the superior temporal sulcus of the rhesus monkey. *Journal of Physiology (London)* 236: 549–573.

Zeki, S. M. (1978). Uniformity and diversity of structure and function in rhesus monkey prestriate visual cortex. *Journal of Physiology (London)* 277: 273–290.

Zeki, S. M. (1993). *A Vision of the Brain.* Oxford, Blackwell.

Zhou, Y. and C. L. J. Baker (1993). A processing stream in mammalian visual cortex neurons for non-Fourier responses. *Science* 261: 98–101.

Zhou, Y. and C. L. J. Baker (1994). Envelope-responsive neurons in areas 17 and 18 of cat. *Journal of Neurophysiology* 72: 2134–2150.

Zhou, Y. and C. L. J. Baker (1996). Spatial properties of envelope-responsive cells in area 17 and 18 neurons of the cat. *Journal of Neurophysiology* 75: 1038–1050.

Zhou, W. and L. Chen (1994). Modulation of motion aftereffects (MAE) by engagement of attention in an auditory task. *Investigative Ophthalmology and Visual Science* 35 (Suppl.): 1838.

Ziefle, M. (1992). Zum Einsatz des Bewegungsnacheffekts als Diagnoseinstrument des visuellen Systems. *Zeitschrift für Neuropsychologie* 1: 68–78.

Zihl, D., D. von Cramon, et al. (1983). Selective disturbance of movement vision after bilateral brain damage. *Brain* 106: 311–340.

Zöllner, F. (1860). Über eine neue Art von Pseudoskopie und ihre Beziehungen zu den von Plateau und Oppel beschriebenen Bewegungsphänomenen. *Annalen der Physik und Chemie* 110: 500–523.

Contributors

David Alais
Vanderbilt Vision Research Center
Vanderbilt University
Nashville, Tennessee

Stuart Anstis
Department of Psychology
University of California at San
Diego
La Jolla, California

Patrick Cavanagh
Department of Psychology
Harvard University
Cambridge, Massachusetts

Jody Culham
Department of Psychology
University of Western Ontario
London, Ontario, Canada

John Harris
Department of Psychology
University of Reading
Reading, UK

Michelle Kwas
Department of Psychology
Concordia University
Montreal, Quebec, Canada

Timothy Ledgeway
Department of Experimental
Psychology
University of Oxford
Oxford, UK

George Mather
Experimental Psychology
Biology School
University of Sussex
Brighton, UK

Bernard Moulden
Vice Chancellor
James Cook University
Townsville, Queensland, Australia

Michael Niedeggen
Department of Psychology
Philipps University Marburg
Marburg/Lahn, Germany

Shin'ya Nishida
Information Research Laboratory
NTT Basic Research Laboratories
Atsugi-Shi, Japan

Allan Pantle
Department of Psychology
Miami University
Oxford, Ohio

Robert Patterson
Department of Psychology
Washington State University
Pullman, Washington

Jane E. Raymond
School of Psychology
University of Wales-Bangor
Bangor, UK

Michael Swanston
School of Social and Health
Sciences
University of Abertay Dundee
Dundee, UK

Peter Thompson
Department of Psychology
University of York
York, UK

Frans Verstraten
Helmholtz Research Institute
Utrecht University
Utrecht, The Netherlands

Michael von Grünau
Department of Psychology
Concordia University
Montreal, Quebec, Canada

Nicholas Wade
Department of Psychology
University of Dundee
Dundee, UK

Eugene Wist
Department of Experimental and
Clinical Neuropsychology
Institute of Physiological
Psychology
Heinrich Heine University
Düsseldorf
Düsseldorf, Germany

Sources

Permission to use copyrighted material has been sought for the following:

Figure 6.1: From *Visual Agnosias and Other Disturbances of Visual Perception and Cognition* edited by Grusser and Landis (1991). Copyright Macmillan Press Ltd.

Figure 6.2: Reprinted with permission from *Nature* (Barlow and Hill, *Nature* 200: 1345–1347, 1963). Copyright (1991) Macmillan Magazines Limited.

Figure 6.3: Reprinted with permission from Maffei et al. (1973) *Science* 182: 1036–1038. Copyright (1973) American Association for the Advancement of Science.

Figure 6.4: From von der Heydt et al. (1978) *Archives Italiennes de Biologie*.

Figure 6.5: From Vautin and Berkley (1977) *Journal of Neurophysiology* 40: 1051–1065. Copyright The American Physiological Society.

Figure 6.6: From Marlin et al. (1988) *Journal of Neurophysiology* 59: 1314–1330. Copyright The American Physiological Society.

Figure 6.7: From Giaschi et al. (1993) *Journal of Neurophysiology* 70: 2024–2034. Copyright The American Physiological Society.

Figure 6.8: Reprinted from *Brain Research*, 346, Petersen et al., "Direction-specific adaptation in area MT of the owl monkey," 146–150. Copyright (1985), with permission from Elsevier Science.

Figure 6.9: Reprinted from *Vision Research*, 35, Kubova et al., "Contrast dependence of motion-onset and pattern-reversal evoked potentials," 197–205. Copyright (1995), with permission from Elsevier Science.

Figure 6.10: From Hoffmann et al. (1996) in Elsner and Schnitzler (eds) *Proceedings of the 24th Gottingen Neurobiology Conference, Vol. II*, p. 425. Copyright Georg Thieme Verlag.

Figure 6.11: From *Perception*, 1994, 23: 1155–1162, fig. 2. Copyright Pion Limited, London.

Figure 6.12: From Niedeggen et al. (1992) *Journal of Psychophysiology*, 7: 164.

Figure 6.14: Reprinted with permission from *Nature* (Tootell et al., *Nature* 375: 139–141, 1995). Copyright (1995) Macmillan Magazines Limited.

Figure 7.7: Reprinted from Barlow (1990) in *Vision: Coding and Efficiency* edited by C. Blakemore with permission of the publishers, Cambridge University Press.

Index